Staring Memory in the Face

a memoir (sort of)

Michael Rice

Copyright © Michael Rice 2021

Set in 11 point Baskerville

All rights reserved. Except for the quotation of short passages for the purpose of criticism or review, no part of this book may be reprinted or reproduced or utilised in any form or by any electronic, mechanical or other means, including photocopying or recording, or in any information storage or retrieval system.

fischer
press

ISBN: 978-0-620-92928-8 (HB); 978-0-620-93674-3 (PB)

Cover picture: Ruth Rice, Pondoland cattle

∽ Contents ∽

Prologue 1

PART ONE

"The Universe is change, our lives are what our thoughts make it" ... 9
"Niver firgit me boy, yu're British." 16
Even this Eden had its serpents 24
Mosquito weight champion 33
"You might as well live" 40
Newcastle-on-Tyne 53
All the fun of the fair 67
The Rendezvous 78
"She phoned *The Star* with her last tickey" 85
School days, those Golden Rule days 91
Miss Fairfax 103
On His Majesty's Service ??? 111
Longwood House 120
"*Hambakahle*" 138
A long weekend 147
L'Albergo di Luigi 154
A life sentence 163

PART TWO

In the deep end 175
The Crucible 186
A certain smile 194
"Yes, that's him." 204
Becoming a teacher 210
"She's pretty!" 218
Breaking eggs 226

Hottentots Holland 239
"Free, white and over twenty-one".. 245
The best laid plans … 252
"That's something special" 260
Free the children 266
"Guess who's coming to dinner?" 278

～ Acknowledgements ～

I wish to express my appreciation for the advice and support I have had from the following friends: Claire and Rory Wilson who had the idea in the first place, Nadine Gordimer, Adam Hochschild, Mary Reynolds, Diana Simons, Sholto Cross and Guiliana Ashford for their comments and advice; Christine Woods for her interest and the information about 27 Riverleigh Avenue; my cousins Duncan Rice, Alison Johnson, Kathy Trevelyan in Britain, and Karolyne Quinn in Australia who cleared up some of the details regarding my grandparents with my Aunt Winnie; my teachers, Monty Sholund, Jacque van Oortmeersten, Malcolm Armstrong and Joyce Rapson; and, of course, my wife Ruth without whose encouragement it would never have happened. I must not forget those friends who stood by me at various times when friendship was the only thing between hope and despair, Jocelyn Cloete, Gilles and Daphne Botbijl, Ernie and Hilary Saks, Mike Muller, Laurence and Heather Bam, Graham Hall, Iris Terblanche, Sheila du Plessis, Alan and Elizabeth Schwarer, Jan and Cindy Esterhuisen, Greg and Ann Kerr, Digby and Penny Hoets, Anton and Margaret Gouverneur, Leon Hugo, Bitty and Shake Seigel, Jean and Hennie Muller and their children Mary and Jimmy, Coleen Taylor, Paul Verryn and Chris Niland. And finally thanks to Alison Johnson (née Rice) and her husband Andrew for their help with copyediting and typesetting, which has made my story into a finished book.

I have been blessed in my friends.

*I sometimes hold it half a sin
To put in words the grief I feel;
For words, like Nature, half reveal
And half conceal the Soul within.*

(Tennyson: In Memoriam)

"I remember even what I do not want to remember, and I can't forget what I wish to forget"

(Cicero, quoting Themistocles)

Prologue

From his lookout in the loft he can see a line of cattle coming down the lane, a dark current of moving shapes between banks of brambles and briar. Stopping. Complaining. Bunching at the gate, surging forward as it opens, udders bulging. The winter sun gleams faintly through broken cloud. A wet wind begins to stir.

"There'll be a raid tonight."

The two young women below move about the yard busy mixing warm mash and cleaning buckets, companionable and comfortable.

In the loft above the byre a boy tosses bundles of hay into the mangers below. Clumsy, as though moving in a dream, he stumbles in the dark trying to move the bales near to the trapdoor. Anxious. He must fill the mangers before the herd arrives.

A mighty responsibility for a four-year-old.

His arms and legs are heavy, uncoordinated. The air is thick with dust, the floor underfoot slippery and uneven. Tugging with all his childish strength, he slips trying to free a bale from a stack against the back wall. Awkward and heavy, it resists. His arms feeble, an infant Sisyphus. Raw and sore. Baling twine cuts his hands. The bale suddenly comes free and bursts on the floor knocking him over. Getting to his feet he shovels the scattered hay to the trap door with his hands into the space below, hoping it will fall where it should.

In a few minutes, he must climb down the rickety ladder, the treads too far apart for his short legs, into a world of monstrous shadows, restless haunches and flicking tails, and find his way to the double doors at the end of the barn. The light is fading fast. He can hear the animals approaching. There isn't enough unbundled hay. He looks down through the trap door. The cattle are already gathering in the yard outside. He has lost his moment but is determined not to call for help. The paraffin lamps flicker as the barn doors open to admit a thicket of jostling, tossing black tipped horns.

He slips awkwardly down the ladder, the treads uneven and too far apart. The stalls on either side of the barn a gauntlet. The only way through is the wet and slippery gutter between them. At any moment one of the animals might back out of its stall, lashing out with a hind hoof, or turn sweeping the air with its horns. The sounds of banging buckets, slipping hooves and bovine protest fill the evening.

2

Staring Memory in the Face

And, tonight, because they are short-handed he must tie each animal's halter to the ring above its manger; climb up on the rails that separate the stalls, catch hold of the halter while they are rummaging in their mangers and slip the rope through the iron ring attached to the wall.

Eight cows and a bull. Each has a different temperament. The bull turns a baleful eye on him as he tries to tie its halter rope to the ring above its manger. Short horned and wet nosed, its dark eyes are ringed by half circles of blood-tinged white. It looks at him, breathing hard. The air is thick with the smell of cattle and hay and warm mash. Just as he is about to thread the rope through the ring the bull jerks its head. The rope is torn from his grasp. It hangs between the animal's forelegs. Steam from wide flared nostrils fills the air. Baleful eyes and heavy breathing.

"Just climb down and pick it up. You'll be alright. He won't hurt you".

This is not the first time this has happened. The boy tries to reach the halter from the rail. Sensing his fear, the bull tosses its head and steps back a pace or two, well out of reach. They regard each other. The boy doesn't have the courage to climb down from his perch and pick up the rope. He's trapped and the bull knows it. Just as he is about to capitulate, Dorothy emerges from the gloom, slaps the bull on the rump, picks up the rope and passes it to him. He slips it through the ring and scrambles past. Somehow, he manages to get to the door without slipping or being kicked, and bursts into the icy air.

An early flash back and an early lesson. A prologue to the drama. A metaphor? I search for an image. A passage in a labyrinth? A voyage? There will be a voyage. A river? There was a river. A black English river, swollen and deceptively quiet. Or, was it just a bad dream?

"That cow what's in calf didn't come in. We'll have to go out and fetch her. We'll lose her if she stays out on a night like this."

Dorothy and Mum hose down the yard, clean out the milk pails unaware of my pounding heart. Life goes on. And, now we will have to go out in the wet and dark to make sure that it does.

We put on our raincoats and balaclavas and set off before the dark settles. I'm too small to keep up. Dorothy hoists me onto her shoulders where I ride well above the slush in the lane. Clinging to her forehead I can see over the hedgerows. A flock of crows flies low over an adjoining

Prologue

field, cawing to each other. The last light is fading as low clouds scud across the darkening sky. Snow lies in patches on the ground. We turn off the lane and follow a muddy track across a field down to the river. Thin sheets of ice crackle underfoot. An air-raid siren wails in the distance.

The heifer is wedged fast between a tree trunk and the riverbank. She must have been grazing next to the river and slipped as part of the bank collapsed and is now trapped. Whether panic has sent her into labour, or her time has come anyway, she is struggling to give birth. The calf has started to emerge. Head and forelegs reach out blindly into the gathering gloom. The earth is opening. There is nothing she can do to help it come away. The tree moves.

Mum clambers down the bank. She takes the halter and holds the heifer's head while Dorothy rolls up her sleeves, grasps the calf's protruding legs and pulls for all she is worth. The sound of rushing water, the cow's bellowing, Dorothy's heaving and grunting fill the air. Knee deep in blood and mud and cow shit, her faced streaked with sweat and blood, she holds on, trying to calm and encourage the animal. "Come on old girl. Just one more push." Suddenly the calf comes loose with a rush of blood and afterbirth. There is no time to draw breath. The river is rising fast.

Somehow Dorothy and Mum scramble the calf up the bank between them and lay it in a wheelbarrow. The heifer frees herself and climbs the bank where she stands licking her calf. As we try to collect ourselves the tree lurches. With a sudden sucking sound its roots come free, and it crashes into the river, and is swept away.

On the journey back to the barn I sit in the wheelbarrow, the calf half in my lap, holding a lantern to light our way. The searchlights from the artillery emplacements around Coventry are beginning to sweep the sky. The drone of aircraft is in the air.

I know I have seen something amazing. I say nothing of my terror earlier. I am hurried off to my bath and bed where I dream of wild rivers, the earth splitting open and horns, hooves and twitching tails.

4

Staring Memory in the Face

There was a heavy raid on the city that night. The following morning a thousand-year-old cathedral lay in ruins.

The Blitz. The Battle of Britain. Search lights stretching across the sky, the drone of bombers, the rumble of anti-aircraft fire. I did not understand. Nor could I. I was three going on four, perhaps a little older. *"The memories of childhood have no order and no end."*[1] There would be another war on another continent, a lifetime between.

Whether these are my earliest memories or simply those that have become mythologised is beside the point. There is the story and there is the writer. Can they be separated? Birth and death. The images are buried deep, and have disturbed my dreams for eighty years. This story is an imperfect exploration of those dreams, memories, and the feelings and fantasies they engendered. Past imperfect. Death comes in many guises; *"fate, chance and desperate men"*[2]: war, suicides, sickness and murder. This tale has them all.

I begin, then, without the usual diaries, letters or family documents that most writers rely on. I have little but my memory and imagination: *"Imagination and Memory are but one thing"*[3] says Hobbes. The past is never quite the past. Things catch up. Memory is tricky. We all know it is selective; that it embellishes and changes with the passage of time. It is not trapped in an amber bubble. Forgotten memories surface unexpectedly, continually reshaping the present, filtering past events making them almost unrecognisable, making for dangerous byways. Things you said or did forty or fifty years ago of which you are deeply ashamed; things you had long hoped you had forgotten. The imagination can give them a relevance they never had, make links, draw parallels. Woven together,

---

1. Dylan Thomas: *Reminiscences of Childhood*.
2. John Donne: 'Death, Be Not Proud'.
3. Thomas Hobbes: *Leviathan*.

Prologue

they create the myths we make of our lives: the way we understand who we were and who we've become.

Fact and fiction, myth and history; a case history. Sometime in the early 2000s, the newly elected post-liberation Johannesburg City Council Parks & Gardens Department decided, as part of its 'Keep Johannesburg Neat and Tidy' campaign, to cut down a Lombardy poplar tree opposite our house, by then Die Boekehuis, but they didn't count on the opposition or determination of the bookshop manager to preserve it. She contacted us wanting to know if it could in any way be associated with the struggle against Apartheid. It was a long shot. Her motives were, I suspect, arboreal rather than political. Could we help?

During the Eighties our house had often been used for clandestine meetings, and as a safe house for those on the run from the Special Branch and Winnie Mandela. Over the course of some months' email correspondence a narrative gradually emerged that the tree had been an important landmark for people on the run needing sanctuary. Once they saw the tree they knew they were safe. It was nonsense of course, but this is the way myths are made.

So, the tree was duly preserved and stands to this day undermining the municipal sewerage system. An ironic monument to the unsung heroes of the Struggle; preserved by municipal fiat. More than that, it has entered the portals of literature and has been commemorated as one of the *Great Trees of the World*, a glossy coffee table book. It now has historical as well as mythological status as part of our official heritage.

Anyone who embarks on this sort of exploration is faced with the same issues. For exploration it is. But why? Why begin at all? Why dredge it all up? What does it all mean? Is there any meaning? Perhaps a clue of some sort will emerge in the telling. Books have a way of taking on their own lives. We create and console ourselves with memory; and it is through narrative that memory is created.

One does not write what one wants to write, but what one is capable of writing. I have lived a turbulent life in turbulent times. Unpredictable memories pop up and distract and lead in unexpected directions. The

Staring Memory in the Face

amazing thing is how much one remembers, or thinks one remembers; and how memories are as much of a glimpse into the past as they are of things one has been told which are so woven into the fabric it is impossible to disentangle the bare facts from the reconstruction. Nothing is as it seems.

I make no claims for what follows.

Part One

∼ 1 ∼

"The Universe is change, our lives are what our thoughts make it" [4]

Seventy-odd years on, a lifetime later, wars have been fought, dictators have come and gone, empires have disappeared, revolutions have been betrayed. The millennium celebrations are well past, and I need a model. Who better than Marcus Aurelius, politician, soldier, philosopher?

He begins his *Meditations*: *"Courtesy and serenity of temper I first learnt to know from my grandfather, Verus. Manliness without ostentation I learnt from what I have heard and remember of my father. My mother set me an example of piety and generosity, avoidance of all uncharitableness."*[5]

---

4. Marcus Aurelius: *Meditations*.
5. Op cit.

10

Staring Memory in the Face

Grandfather, father, mother. My grandfather died in 1930, well before I was born. My feelings about my parents are at best ambivalent. There are too many unresolved questions regarding my parents.: a tale still to be told. I do not recall inheriting wisdom from them, only a tangle of disjointed and unsubstantiated anecdotes, claims and counter claims. And yet, their presence is there.

So, taking my cue from Marcus Aurelius …

'Courtesy', I learned from Agatha Christie and Richmal Crompton the creator of *Just William*. An odd combination I must admit for a ten-year-old. I have no doubt those two worthy women would be mildly surprised to learn they had shaped the understanding of one of their young readers as much as they did mine. Sunday school and religious instruction, Bible study and Christian Fellowship did not bring out the best in me. Though, ironically there is a Calvinist streak, which I attribute to my Scots forbears. The English middle classes, as portrayed by these two writers of popular detective and children's fiction, were my first conscious role models. I am alive to the irony. Having rejected institutional coercion, I accepted the conservative social conformity portrayed in their novels.

I discovered their writing at the impressionable age of ten or thereabouts, when I realised (I was not the first child to realise this) I could use books as a screen behind which I could cut myself off and find refuge from reality. They were the only way I could get a window into a world I knew must exist somewhere; a world of stability and propriety. They were also the only books to which I had access. My mother, Flora, was an avid whodunit reader. I read everything she read. From an early age, I learned to forage among the stacks of public libraries. Whodunits were our fare, Ngaio Marsh, Leslie Charteris, Raymond Chandler, Dornford Yates, Nicholas Blake, Ellery Queen, Michael Innes, and of course, Agatha Christie. I also discovered a pile of moth-eaten *Boys' Own Paper* annuals from the 1930s containing tales of intrepid school boy heroes saving the Empire from hordes of savages, or worse, the machinations of mysterious German spies, which provided the inspiration for my own fantasies. My reading was indiscriminate, uncritical and uncensored. The

"The Universe is change, our lives are what our thoughts make it"

result was I developed a wide general knowledge beyond my years, the foundation for interests to come.

Agatha Christie's country houses, their owners, weekend guests, the village inhabitants and even the butlers and chamber maids represented (notwithstanding the murders) ordered social relations, where people ate meals at predictable times, went to bed and rose again in the morning, spent their lives in useful and fulfilling ways and could look forward to the future with confidence. Their lives had structure. They were leisured and moneyed. They played Bridge (which I learned to loathe) and sometimes fell dead at the table (with which I could sympathise). There was intrigue, but it was intrigue according to specific rules, and I knew that good would triumph in the end. That justice would prevail. It was simply a question of finding the thread and following it. There was a pattern. There was meaning.

William Brown too, lived in a well-ordered household, with parents who did the sorts of things I knew parents were meant to do, and had a brother and sister. He also had his gang, and so, in my imagination, I had mine. He had his dog Jumble and I had Ranger. He did appallingly at school (so did I) and was an outlaw, which certainly fitted with my own view of myself, though in reality I was too timid to challenge anything. Above all, William had a profound sense of justice, which often got him into trouble. My sense of justice, too, has often led me into troubled waters, not the least of which was to be in conflict with the custodians of the Apartheid régime and for a short while into some real danger; it also, on one occasion, was to cost me my job. The values that Christie and Crompton represented were conservative; rooted in the rural English middle classes. It is a world now long gone in which social conventions provided a significant degree of security. Adults and children knew their place and what was expected of them

Both Christie and Crompton stood for a moral order that is largely in retreat these days, if it existed at all. But what attracted me most, I think, was their depiction of stability, of a rooted society, and the importance they gave to individual responsibility, effort and initiative, to loyalty and steadfastness. They provided not a bad base from which to graduate to other things later.

'Serenity of temper' has for the most part eluded me. I have lived a turbulent life, moving between hemispheres, always caught in a no man's land. More often than not, my emotions have triumphed over my intellect. In this, I have come to realise, I'm no different from most of humanity. I have struggled to hold my head above the quick sands of self-doubt. As I grew up it was increasingly clear to me that there are no easy explanations, no easy answers. I have learned, to distrust instant solutions to anything. This has gone hard against my personality, which is impulsive and impatient.

As for *'manliness'*, it is a concept almost without meaning today, though I suspect all the more important and misunderstood for what it represents of a world long lost. Much could be said about manliness. As a youngster, I was no less sports-mad than any of my contemporaries and played most games with, it must be admitted, more enthusiasm than skill well into adulthood. I grew up in an era when physical prowess was not, at least in theory, sufficient of itself. Sportsmanship was taken seriously. My generation must have been the last in which the invocation to *"play up and play the game"*[6] was taken seriously. It was a point of honour not to wait for the umpire's finger.

'Piety': ah, another concept in disrepute. Times change and with them so do many of the values held sacred by each generation. While it may be expected that what are conceived of as traditional Western middle-class values mean little or nothing to the vast majority of mankind, they are certainly in decline in the cultures which gave them birth.

Talking of piety, what of vows and oaths, both so much a part of ancient concepts of honour? What does it mean to give your word? What meaning do vows and oaths hold in a secular world where the gods have been overthrown by ideology? *"This is the truth, the whole truth and nothing but the truth, so help me God"* is not even demanded in court these days, lest it offend the beliefs of those who take the stand. And marriage vows have

---

6.   Sir Henry Newbolt: 'Vitai Lampada'.

"The Universe is change, our lives are what our thoughts make it"

been so adapted to accommodate fashionable changes in that institution they have become little more than ritualised platitudes. My grandson, Jack, then all of eight years old, brought this home to me. The discussion around the dinner table was about what it meant to take a vow; but more pertinently, what it meant to renew one's vows. Jack pointed out that renewing one's vows implies that they would have had to have been broken to need renewing. A vow, he asserted, was forever. It could only be renewed if it had been broken. His insight suggests we are hard-wired for morality, like language. How it expresses itself, is determined by the family and culture we are born into; by our life experience.

'Generosity'. I was once asked at a job interview what I thought were the essential characteristics of a successful teacher. "Generosity of spirit, intellectual curiosity and an enthusiasm for life", I replied. I still think so.

I make no claims to emulate Marcus Aurelius. I am no Stoic. Nonetheless, his example is useful. In everything he did and thought he remained aware, self-reflective, self-critical. His musings on the mysteries of life and death, on the great questions that perplex us all are as good a place as any from which to take a lead. I encountered Marcus Aurelius early on in my mid-teens about the time I read Victor Frankel's *Man's Search for Meaning*, and he has remained with me. What was it about him that attracted me then, and has continued to influence me? It was, I think, his insistence on self-reliance, on enduring and winning through; of taking everything that life flung at one and getting on with it; of having modest ambitions, and learning to live with them. But there was more to it than that. It was also the realisation that endurance alone was not enough. There are choices. The choices we make are who we are. There must be being with a purpose. But that purpose, I was convinced, had to be generated from within my own experience, memories and feelings whatever they were; not imposed from without. Somewhere along the line I must have inherited something of my forebears' Calvinism. For I have always been driven by the notion that I have to justify my existence. This has not been, nor does it continue to be easy.

14

Staring Memory in the Face

There must be a purpose. I clung to that belief to the point where I was able to deny reality. Where, in fact, reality gave way to fantasy. Fortunately, time and experience whittle away at fantasy. One of life's most salutary lessons is learning to accept one's own ordinariness. For the rest, it is largely a muddle in which we try to do the best we can. Mistakes there have been many, and I have made a fool of myself more often than I care to think; but we are what we are. The trick is not to succumb to fatalism, to become a victim and feel powerless, or to anesthetise one's sensitivity to others and the possibility of change. Easier said than done. Existential doubt always lurks in the shadows, flicking its tail.

So, to the great existential questions. *"Who in the world am I? Ah, that's the great puzzle!"* How do we know who we are? Where do we come from? What were the forces that shaped us and gave us the understanding we have of the world we find ourselves in? There is much evidence to show that the bedrock of personality is laid down well before birth. How it develops thereafter depends on Fate, chance, luck. A tangled web.

I am reminded of the Venerable Bede who wrote that the life of man on earth is like the flight of a sparrow though the mead hall where the king and his nobles sit at supper in winter while the fire blazes and the hall is warmed but the wintry storms of rain and snow rage outside. A sparrow flies in one door and out the other, for a brief moment safe from the tempest, and then vanishes from sight, passing from winter into winter. So is the life of man, but of what is to follow or what went before we know nothing. I'm not sure about the safety of the 'brief moment'. It has its terrors no less.

The human heart is ever in conflict with itself. Our links with the past provide at best a tenuous sense of identity, especially in an uprooted world, dislocated by war, tyranny and modernity. *"I had not thought death had undone so many."*[7] Millions of people who survived the Second World War found themselves struggling to survive in a world that was only vaguely recognisable. Huge swathes of the population had been annihilated. Cities all but erased. Familial and social bonds broken. There could be

---

7. T.S. Eliot: 'The Waste Land'.

"The Universe is change, our lives are what our thoughts make it"

no going back to life as it had been before. Vestiges of the old world remained, of course, but they were soon to vanish under the onslaught of the new. My envy of those who have the stability of being rooted in a culture, a place, a family is not unique.

Throughout my life I have wrestled with the uncertainties of not belonging to a culture, a country or a family. As a youngster, I grew up thinking of myself as English not South African, though by the time I came to think about such things I had spent most of my life in South Africa. What I knew of England was picked up from William books and the *Boys' Own Paper*, both relics of a bygone age. South Africa was the world I knew most intimately, though I felt alienated from it. By the time I left school I knew next to nothing of its history. I could barely speak Afrikaans, and none of the black indigenous languages. My experience of its geography was limited to a few years in my early childhood when my family lived in Cape Town, a small part of Johannesburg and the adjacent countryside. As for my parentage, and even my name, nothing can be taken for granted.

What I know of my family I had largely from my father, and as I learned many years later, much that he had to say fell short of the truth. He, like I, was never able to resist a good story. One way or another, I've had to stare memory in the face and make of it an admittedly imperfect tale.

~ 2 ~

"Niver firgit me boy, yu're British."

In the winter of 1942, one of the worst of the War, we lived, Flora and I, on a farm just outside Coventry in the English midlands, having been evacuated from London shortly after the Blitz started. My father was in the Royal Artillery and as fortune would have it, was stationed for a short time just outside Coventry, where according to him, he was in charge of the defences around the only factory in Britain making aircraft propellers. It was a prime German target and he delighted in telling how he held the Luftwaffe at bay with twenty-five men, two machine guns and a World War One 25 pounder. At that time Coventry was bombed almost every night. I can still see the searchlights sweeping across the sky and hear the drone of aeroplanes and the sound of gunfire.

After he left university my father got a job at ICI and, according to him, he worked with Lord Rutherford on the splitting of the atom. I say, "according to him" because, as I later discovered, he had a slender grasp of the truth, and as I have no way of checking the facts have to rely on his word. And his word, as I came to find out, was often embroidered. I don't know why he left ICI but he had ambitions to be a writer and tried to crack journalism. His timing was not good.

The Depression was in full swing and journalists were two a penny in Fleet Street. He and a friend, Bill Harte, took it in turns to attend Edgar Wallace's "at homes" once a week to get a square meal and a free drink. The only requirement for admission was membership of Fleet Street and a dress suit. The first was no problem, but the second meant they had to hire a dress suit every week. They didn't have enough money for two suits so they took turns. He also used to cadge drinks and the occasional meal off Eric Linklater the novelist, whom he had known at university.

From his stories, life was very like Orwell's descriptions of being down and out in Paris and London. Grinding poverty, living from one scrounged meal to the next, one drink to the next and always hoping for

"Niver firgit me boy, yu're British."

a lucky break. This was the time of the Great Depression and the rise of fascism in Europe. It was also the height of pacifism when university unions the length and breadth of Britain were proposing motions and passing them never to fight for king and country. Although not a communist, my father was not immune to the general feeling in the country.

He was very friendly at this time with Krishna Menon, the controversial Indian politician, who may have influenced his political thinking. For he was no imperialist, even though he was proud to be British, not English. His Scots heritage was very important to him, and he claimed, probably falsely but with immense pride, to have learned Gaelic as a child before English. I remember going to see him shortly before I went overseas, just after I left school. He went with me to the front door, shook me by the hand; his parting words were, (rolling his rs): "Niver firgit me boy, yu're British."

Not for the first time I wondered, who am I? Why should I care? I was teenager after all. Since then I have a better idea of what he meant. What it meant for me then was something along the lines of fair play and support for the underdog. It certainly did not imply blind patriotism, my country right or wrong. Patriotism, I had been taught, was the last refuge of a scoundrel. It meant for him, I think, something rooted in the common (especially literary) culture of the British Isles that reflected an ironic scepticism about, but sympathetic view of the human condition. He often spoke of Menon as a man he had admired and liked. I don't remember the details but it is worth recalling that Menon was a convinced socialist who dedicated his life to Indian independence and the Ghandian notion of self-reliance. Like so many of his generation my father was a theoretical pacifist, but when it came to the war he joined up.

His contribution to literature was (again according to him) three short stories published in *The Saturday Evening Post*. He eventually got a job on *The Daily Mirror*. It must have been about this time, in 1936 or 1937 that he met Flora McDonald Bland. As he told it, and as she confirmed, he picked her up in a Lyons Corner House by asking her to cut the nails on his right hand!

18

Staring Memory in the Face

Flora was working as a window dresser in a departmental store painting the faces on the mannequins. Not five feet tall, she was petite, very pale with high cheek bones, a rather severe expression on her face most of the time, and blue eyes. She came from the North Country, Newcastle-on-Tyne. Border Country. She was very proud of her double barrel: McDonald Bland. Flora McDonald, of course, was the Scots heroine who disguised Bonnie Prince Charlie as her maid when he was trying to escape to France after his defeat at the Battle of Culloden:

> *There is Flora, my honey,*
> *sae dear and sae bonnie,*
> *And ane that's sae tall,*
> *and handsome withal.*
> *Put the ane for my king*
> *and the other for my queen*
> *And they're dearly welcome*
> *to Skye again....*

It's always useful to have a romantic figure in one's heritage, no matter how tenuous the connection.

I know little of her background but it seems to have been lower-middle-class. I remember her telling me how as a child she had to walk through the snow in clogs to piano lessons. So, her family was poor, but not so poor as not to be able to afford piano lessons, and feel the disgrace of her brother John marrying "a common waitress". The class war was far from over.

Her brother Bill's wife, Joyce, was a member of the Communist Party and introduced Flora to the Party. But, apart from a vague resentment of the rich, I don't think she absorbed too much of the ideology. She cried the day George VI died. She played endless games of Monopoly with me during my adolescence after which we would fantasise about what we would do if we had "all that money". I don't recall the poor and unemployed being beneficiaries. Her life was played out as a string of contradictions. Strange, that I should know so little about her early life and the forces that shaped it: after all, I spent nearly all my youth and

"Niver firgit me boy, yu're British."

adolescence with her, living very often in one room and until quite late in life sharing the same bed. I have lost touch with her family, having briefly met them in the early Sixties. Lives spiral out in different directions, into different hemispheres, different universes.

We had been evacuated from London, and to begin with we lived in a caravan in a farmer's orchard with a vicious border collie that hated men. The owner, Dorothy (strange that I should remember her name seventy odd years on) and Flora became firm friends. Two young women forced to fend for themselves in a manless world, they fell into a natural alliance.

It was decided that the caravan was too isolated and we moved into the farmhouse. One night while I was sitting in my high chair being fed a German plane must have flown off course and dropped its bombs near to the farmhouse. In the ensuing explosion, I was flung from my high chair and cracked my skull against the fireguard.

I was an only child. I do not recall having any companions. Too young for school, I was left for the most part to amuse myself. This I did by exploring the farmyard and talking to Dorothy who encouraged me to help her with the chickens and milking. The reward was a fresh egg for breakfast and warm milk straight from the udder. In wartime Britain this was luxury indeed. The farm had run down since Dorothy's husband had been killed at Dunkirk. She was hanging on, and anyway had nowhere else to go. So, except for a few milking cows, some poultry, a pig or two, and an old orchard there was little to do. But even that was more than enough for a single woman.

The farm, especially the enclosed yard with its barn, implement shed full of rusting broken and useless machinery, abandoned piggery and house defined my world. It always seemed gloomy, rain or mist, wet, damp and mud. Tall rank nettles invaded the kitchen garden. There was plenty to do what with milking, feeding, collecting eggs and firewood and blackberries in the neighbouring wood. I had the run of the yard, barn and outbuildings. During the day, I played on broken-down tractors and wagons, my Mickey Mouse gas mask hung around my neck, and fought the Battle of Britain, training my ack-acks at the vapour trails in the sky.

Beyond the gate lies the world and war. The Germans are at the gates of Stalingrad. Within, all is rich and strange, the manure of incident, birth and death: without, the roar of aircraft, searchlights and the distant rumble of guns and ghostly figures in the dusk. Geese stand sentinel near a dim loft full of hay and hidden possibilities from which a young soldier and girl from the village emerge one winter's evening. She, brushing hay from her dress and smoothing her hair: he, tightening his belt. He winks as they pass me standing at the wellhead. Foxes lurk in the bracken. Frost crackles. Trees shift their shadows. An owl hoots, and the pond reflects a frozen moon.

I remained solitary. There were no children of my own age near at hand. Living on the farm ensured we were remote from the village; my only companions, Flora and Dorothy. In this, I have no doubt I was no different from most children of my age in wartime Britain. My father was, understandably, a remote figure, someone who hardly existed. I spent most of my time in the company of women.

Role models for growing children have been a source of much debate since the virtual collapse of the family through the onslaught of divorce and the emergence of the single parent, by which is usually meant abandoned motherhood. The War, of course, hastened the process. War and abandoned motherhood, two permanent features of human existence. The one dedicated to its destruction, the other bearing the burden of its survival.

The world outside holds its own terrors. The searchlights, the drone of aircraft, the sound of gunfire and above all the fear of invasion. One winter's afternoon in 1943, when the allies were preparing for the Normandy landings, I look out of the window of the farmhouse and see through the rain the first German troops entering the yard coming to kill us. Flora discovers me trying to hide, squeezing between an ancient Victorian sofa and the wall. It's like a recurrent nightmare. Every effort slow, heavy and exhausting. Co-ordination of my limbs abandons me.

"Niver firgit me boy, yu're British."

I am overtaken by waves of panic. Chest heaving. My eyes blinded by tears. The world is determined to resist every effort I make to put it between me and certain death. The limitations of my infant strength are all too apparent. I have a vision of being ripped from behind the sofa and impaled on a bayonet and cast into a vortex of darkness and chaos. The War entered my imagination and memory, dominating my dreams and fantasies.

The terror of that moment lived with me for many years, well into adulthood, when I would be involved in a different kind of war with much more chance of being killed. It also set the pattern for a recurrent nightmare. Everything is peaceful, delicate, in complete harmony with itself like the notes on the piano daintily descending the scales in the adagio movement of Grieg's piano concerto, but at any moment can slip out of control and spiral into chaos. As soon as the thought occurs an infinitesimal discord begins which I try to deny and hold back but which irresistibly swallows me into its vortex, and I know I am going to die. Somehow, I emerge, terrified it will repeat itself. And it does, again and again. My only escape is to wake. But waking means re-entering the world. There is no escaping the terror.

I am sure that for millions of children growing up during the War, the fears they absorbed shaped their understanding and responses to life in subtle ways forever after. My memories of war remain vividly embedded, and no doubt enhanced by my imagination. I can't untangle them.

At about this time Flora and I travelled up to Newcastle-on-Tyne by train. It was one of those interminable wartime train journeys that always seemed to pass through endless tunnels, punctuated by sudden loud noises and bright lights, the hiss of steam and grime everywhere. Scenes from *Anna Karenina*? Or, embellished by another midnight journey nearly 35 years later? The trains are always full, with standing room only.

A soldier going home on leave is standing in the corridor next to us. He can see Flora is exhausted and offers to hold me to give her a break. It also helps that she is young and attractive. They share cigarettes. I fall asleep but wake as he passes me back to her just as the train pulls into a station. He jumps onto the platform to see if he can find a cup of tea and a sandwich, which he shares as the train pulls out of the station. The rumble of wheels is drowned by sirens as dive bombers strafe the carriages. You can hear bullets and shrapnel hitting the railway lines and carriage wheels, like gravel thrown against metal. Suddenly, he slumps forward, collapsing in the corridor, his skull split open, half a sandwich between his fingers. That image of death has haunted me all my life.

Towards the end of the war my father was invalided out of the army. He had a bad dose of cerebral malaria in India and was sent back to England where he joined his old newspaper *The Daily Mirror* in Fleet Street. My most enduring memories of him are of his bald head, pale blue eyes and his deep voice and faint Scots accent. We moved up to London and he bought the only house he ever owned, in Kennington near the Oval. It was one of those tall 19th century houses with one room on every floor.

Early one summer morning I look out of a window and see him make a bonfire in the backyard of all his army equipment, uniform, badges, boots and papers; everything he owns that can remind him of the past four years. It is quite a pile. He douses the lot with petrol and sets it alight, stepping back hastily as the flames leap at him. He was an emotional man, my father. But the war was not finished with him yet.

His newspaper sent him to Germany to follow up what were then rumours of the death camps. He never told me what he saw, but he did tell me that it was as a consequence of that trip he decided to emigrate and get as far away from Europe as he could. The irony was he chose to bring his family to South Africa.

I learned much later that he had spent a long while in a mental hospital on being released from the army in 1944, suffering from what was then called shell shock. He had several courses of shock treatment, which given the state of the science then, probably did more damage than good. Certainly, the rest of his life was a catalogue of disasters: alcoholism, broken marriages, the inability to hold down a job for any length of time, ending in a pitiful and pointless death. None of the promise of his

"Niver firgit me boy, yu're British."

youth was ever realised. Perhaps it was a result of his disturbed mental state that he decided to cut all contact with his family, even sending Flora north to Glasgow shortly before we left for South Africa to inform the family that he wanted to have nothing more to do with them. However, as I was later to learn, the truth was very much more complicated and opaque. But I'm getting ahead of myself.

My grandparents with four of their seven children. From left: Johnny, Duncan, Tommy, Nancy in front.

~ 3 ~

Even this Eden had its serpents

I wasn't consulted about the decision to come to South Africa. The *Carnarvon Castle*, still clad in her wartime camouflage grey, sailed from Southampton in August 1946 with well over a thousand steerage passengers on board, mostly demobbed service men and their families fleeing post-war Britain, lured by the promise of a new life in the colonies. Britain was mired in unemployment. There seemed no end to rationing. There had to be more to life than the dole. The colonies, especially those in warmer climates, beckoned.

The *Carnarvon Castle* was still fitted out as a troop carrier. Luxury was at a minimum. We, that is Flora, Auntie (Flora's maiden aunt, only known as Auntie) and I, found ourselves along with several hundred other women and children, in one of the segregated holds (women and children in one, men in the other), bunks arranged in tiers three high. In one corner a group of nuns on their way to Rhodesia managed to preserve a semblance of privacy by hanging sheets around their corner of the hold. One of those *en route* for Rhodesia was a little girl I would meet again as a grandmother some 50 years later, Anne Field. The tangle of time.

For the rest of us the voyage is suffered in that spirit of cheerful endurance Britain had been so famous for during the Blitz. The children run wild and their mothers are content to let them do so. Two weeks of enforced idleness lie ahead. As England disappears and we sail towards the tropics, the anguish of the last six years seems to evaporate. A new world, a new life lies just over the horizon.

Cape Town: Tavern of the Seas; the Cape of Good Hope; according to Sir Francis Drake 'the fairest Cape in all the World'; for Bartholomew Diaz, the 'Cape of Storms'.

The waters of Table Bay are black, whipped white with foam. A South-Easter, the Cape Doctor. Table Mountain, described by the Por-

Even this Eden had its serpents

tuguese poet Camoens as the exiled Titan god Adamastor, is swathed in cloud, menacing and inimical.

We disembark and board a train to Johannesburg almost immediately, where we are to join my father who had come out to South Africa a month or so earlier.

The train pulls out of the station and heads across the Cape Flats, through the wine lands towards the Boland mountains and the Karoo. Each carriage has an observation platform open to the elements at either end where passengers can stand and get some relief from the heat. Air conditioning has not been invented. They are also ideal places from which to watch the passing countryside. After Paarl, the railway line rises sharply following the pass through the mountains to Worcester, Touwsrivier and De Doorns. Blue grey mountains overgrown with purple erica and protea slashed by mysterious kloofs and tumbling rivers accompany us on either side for miles and miles through the Elandskloofberge, Witsenberge and the Hex River Valley. Not the Congo, but into the heart of darkness nonetheless. It is spring and the veld is covered in new green, and purple, red, white and blue. Namaqualand Daisies are a golden carpet. Beyond the Hex River mountains, the Karoo, the Outeniekwaberge and Swartberge, "*Blazing, amazing – aglow .... Opal and ash-of-roses, Cinnamon, umber, and dun.*"[8] To my seven-year-old eyes though, the Karoo is boring, brown and featureless, especially after the dramatic mountain passes.

Our first night in Johannesburg was spent in the Chelsea Hotel in Hillbrow with my parents up most of the night catching and killing bed bugs that emerged in phalanxes the moment the light was switched off. Not quite lions in Eloff Street, but a bloody beginning to Africa "*red in tooth and claw*"[9]. The following morning, my father presented the management with a matchbox in which he had collected all the corpses. We left without paying.

I was enrolled at the Twist Street Primary School, where I spent about six months before we moved back to Cape Town when my father

---

8. Rudyard Kipling: 'Bridge-guard in the Karoo'.
9. Tennyson: 'In Memoriam'.

Staring Memory in the Face

moved from the *Rand Daily Mail* to *The Argus* as chief sub-editor. This was the beginning of a pattern that was to emerge later. Sudden unexplained moves from one city to another, from one school to another. All in all, I attended nine schools in twelve years.

We moved into a flat in Milnerton, then on the outskirts of Cape Town, where we had a wonderful picture postcard view across the bay of Table Mountain flanked on either side by Lion's Head and Devil's Peak. Robben Island, destined to become infamous as a high security prison under the Nationalist government, where Nelson Mandela, Walter Sisulu and Govan Mbeki were incarcerated for many years, lay low in the water five miles off shore. But that was still to come. The Nationalists were not yet in power and the country was entering a post-war boom.

Today, as I write, South Africa is barely recognisable from what it was then. The population has grown at least fivefold. There has been a peaceful transition of power from white minority rule to a black democratically elected majority, much to the world's amazement. South Africa has seen six successful democratic elections since 1994 when the ANC first won power, a moment in history in which I am proud to say I played a minor role. Some things, of course, have not changed. The racial disparities in wealth still exist with the vast majority of black people still living in poverty. And, most predictably, human nature remains the same: those who have, want more; and those who don't have much or anything to speak of, feel the bitter resentments of disappointment and betrayal. This is, of course, fertile ground for corruption and populist politics. The miracle of '94 has turned decidedly rancid. The fate of all revolutions is to be betrayed. Ours is no different. Corruption and crime are rampant. The social fabric is in tatters. Truth and Reconciliation. Little truth and less reconciliation: populism is on the rise fertilised by crude racial rhetoric.

Milnerton in 1947 was on the very edge of the city. I quickly discovered the stables that served the racecourse and spend as much of my free time as possible hanging around, learning to ride. During the holidays and on Saturday mornings I rode horses from Syd Garrett's racing stables

Even this Eden had its serpents

on the beach, and what was known as "the sand track" where I galloped them for a mile or so. The sand was deep and the horses could not reach full speed. I was small for my age and had ambitions to become a jockey.

Life was idyllic. I was eight years old. I could ride. I had a dog and I could swim. The sun shone all day. I can still smell the flowering gums and feel the fierce South-Easter buffeting my bicycle as I struggled up Knysna Road from the beach.

I divided my time between the beach and the stables. In those days, you reached the Milnerton beach over a wooden bridge across the lagoon, past the golf club opposite the lighthouse. When the South-Easter was not blowing in summer, the beach was spectacular. It stretched almost uninterrupted from the harbour to Blaauwbergstrand, easily twenty miles; the icy waves, gigantic rollers crashing onto the sand and rushing up the beach and withdrawing into a treacherous backwash. Completely unpolluted and unspoiled, all but deserted, except for an occasional fishing boat drawn up above the high-water mark. On Saturday mornings, I sometimes went down to the beach and waited for the boats to bring in their catch.

Each boat was owned by a family syndicate of local coloured[10] fishermen who lived in thatched cottages just beyond the dunes. The men rowed the boats out through the breakers and generally did the dangerous hard work. Women gutted the fish once they were landed. The boats could only be launched at low tide or when the sea was calm. Waves rolled in from the Southern Ocean, thunderous mountains of water.

The boats are rowed out in a wide semi-circle trailing a net behind them, a team of men holding one end at the water's edge. The fishermen are very skilled, manoeuvring their clumsy craft in the breakers, catching the waves at just the right moment and slipping over the crest, or plunging bow first into the foam. The most dangerous moment comes when they turn parallel to the breakers before returning inshore. If the sea is too high a boat could be rolled onto the beach and the crew flung overboard into the backwash. It is not unusual to hear of men being

---

10. The accepted term in South Africa for people of mixed race.

Staring Memory in the Face

drowned. Strangely, few of the fishermen are good swimmers and none of them wears a life jacket.

When the boats return to shore some of the crowd dash into the water and help draw them up onto the sand, eager to be part of the collective effort of harvesting the sea. The air is full of laughter and shouting. This is the best part for me, to be part of the serious world of adults for a few minutes, making a physical contribution, testing my strength, straining against the sea, and no doubt getting in the way. Though I never meet with anything but encouragement and thanks for my efforts. The world was simpler then and racial attitudes had not hardened as they would in the coming years.

Indulge me.

On Milnerton beach with Ranger (1947)

The nets are pulled in, the water thrashing with silver as the fish try to escape. At last the catch is hauled into ankle deep water and the women and children dash in tossing red roman, galjoen, steenbras, stump nose and kabbeljou to gasp on the dry sand.

Even this Eden had its serpents

Sometimes, a shark is caught in the net. The crowd gathers round, curious and tentative, confronting one of the terrors of the ocean, beached and gasping but still capable of inflicting terrible wounds on the unwary or foolhardy. Fifteen or eighteen-foot sharks are not unusual. Even in those days it was recognised that what could not be used should be returned to the sea. The sharks are always dragged back into the shallows by the tail and let escape. This can involve quite a struggle, and the men have to look sharp, not to be knocked off their feet or come within range of the gaping jaws as the fish thrashes about. Once subdued by a lack of oxygen it is passive, but there is always the possibility of a sudden and violent convulsion. When it has been manoeuvred into deeper water and released, it turns slowly towards the open sea as if bewildered, and makes its way, its dorsal fin visible for a while between the breakers. And suddenly, it is gone: there is nothing to show where it has been. The crowd is stilled for a few moments, reminded of the danger lurking unseen beneath the waves.

Then the bidding and bargaining begins. The fish shops, housewives and people simply looking for a good fish to braai on the beach argue with the fishermen's wives, all looking to get the best price they can. All the transactions are handled by the coloured women who know that their only hope of feeding their children and limiting the cheap sweet wine their men folk drink is to control the money. The bulk of the catch goes to the fish shops and it is they who set the prices. We count ourselves lucky, to get fish fresh from the sea and at a third of the price in the shops. A tickey extra ensures it is gutted and scaled on the boat's gunwales. Sometimes we make a small fire on the beach and braai our fish there, forgetting to go home. This is a tradition that still exists today, though changed by inflation and technology. I have Mrs (Fish) Sylvia's number on my cell phone for when the fishing boats return to Kalk Bay harbour with their catch.

During the War, a road had been built parallel to the Milnerton beach but spring tides and shifting dunes eroded it beyond repair. As a result, few people went much beyond the car park between the lighthouse and the golf course. For the most part, the beach was deserted for nearly ten miles. The sea was also dangerous and freezing cold. Parents forbade their children to swim without an adult nearby, but to little avail. Raymond Swanepoel, Bobby Ermer, Kevin Butler and I formed a gang that roamed the dunes all summer long. We lived in our swimming costumes and were nut brown, our noses in a constant state of disrepair. The ozone layer hadn't been heard of, much less the UV factor. Our feet were so hard from going barefoot the soles cracked. But even this Eden had its serpent.

One Saturday afternoon the four of us were lying sunbathing on the dunes, having spent the morning surfing in the icy water and helping the fisher folk beach their boats and untangle their nets. We were suddenly aware an adult had joined us. This memory has not been supressed. There would be another episode with a more dramatic conclusion.

"You look as if you have been enjoying yourselves", he says as he sits down next to us. We recognise him as someone we have often seen around the golf course and who we have often greeted as we pass by on our way to the beach. He has the reputation of being a local character and something of a drinker. But today he is perfectly sober. Even so, he still looks down at heel. His shorts are stained with oil and his shirt has obviously been slept in. He has brought a picnic lunch with him and offers to share it with us. The morning in the sea and the sun has made us ravenous. We answer his questions though mouths full of bread, peanut butter and jam about school and rugby and life on the beach.

"And, do you have any girl friends?" he asks.

"Michael does," Kevin blurts. "Yvonne. He goes riding with her every day."

They all giggle. I blush furiously. Yvonne is Syd Garrett's daughter. Yvonne taught me to ride and we spend hours in the bush galloping ponies bareback at breakneck speed along the narrow paths in the dense Port Jackson Willow bush surrounding the stables. Yvonne and riding

Even this Eden had its serpents

are aspects of my life I do not share with the gang. If anything, they are slightly resentful, if not jealous, of my access to the stables.

The questions quickly accelerate. Have I ever kissed her? Do I ever get stiff? Have we ever seen the milky stuff that comes out when you are stiff? Would we like to see? And then follows a demonstration. I am too young or too naive or too ignorant to understand what is going on, much less feel shocked or guilty. I have seen dogs and horses mate, the latter a particularly brutal performance, but have not connected their behaviour in any way with human beings. Certainly not with what I am witnessing now. It's just weird. Here is this man, whom we know vaguely by sight, behaving in a very odd way. What is it all about? When it is all over he looks embarrassed, gets up and leaves hurriedly. We jump up once he is out of sight and run down to the breakers and plunge into the icy foam where we swim until we turn blue with cold.

Most of my time is spent hanging around the Garrett's racing stables. I ride nearly every day as soon as I get home from school and all weekend when I'm not on the beach. Yvonne teaches me to ride one of her ponies, Socks, a stocky, bad tempered little beast with four white socks and a full white blaze down the front of his face. We spend hours riding; chasing each other along the sand tracks that wove through the bush. No one is ever hurt. The sand is thick and the undergrowth so dense that it's difficult to get up a real turn of speed. We ride bareback most of the time, sometimes even scorning to use a bridle, with just a halter. It is an ideal way to learn to move with, respond to and to control a horse. We have a wonderful time playing Cowboys and Indians, riding helter-skelter through the bush, tracking each other and swimming the horses in the farm dam. Yvonne is my age but infinitely more self-assured. Her blonde hair drawn tightly back from her forehead and tied in a single plait falls down her back, not a strand out of place, giving her a severe look even as a child.

Sometimes we stage our own gymkhanas, Yvonne insisting (she is quite an organiser, and I am willing to be organised as long as I have unrestricted access to Socks), that horses and riders have to be perfectly turned out with clean jodhpurs and shining tackle. Obstacle courses are organised, jumps assembled. All the children in the neighbourhood gather with their ponies determined to win the rosettes she has made. Socks is no jumper so I never shine there, but we usually do well in the obstacle race. All of which fires my desire to be a jockey when I am old enough to be apprenticed.

Sometimes we sit on the top rung of the paddock fence and watch the yearlings being broken in and trained for their first race. Yvonne's father, a grey felt hat on his head and a cigarette dangling from his mouth, stands in the middle of the paddock: a small man with a huge stock whip which he flails and cracks overhead as the yearlings circle him. Individual horses are haltered and attached to a long rope which he holds. With a crack of the whip they charge off, bucking and prancing, galloping around the perimeter of the paddock until exhausted, the whip cracking like a gun all the while. Occasionally, because I am so small and light I am put up on a newly broken horse's back to get it used to being ridden. This is always an occasion of great excitement as the horses are highly strung and very nervous. You can feel them shiver between your legs as they are led around the paddock, a groom on either side to control them and to make sure I am not tossed off.

Long sultry afternoons in summer are spent in the feed loft lounging on bales of teff, the South-Easter howling outside, eating endlessly from sacks of carrots, fantasising about riding champion jumpers or Durban July winners. This last I actually achieved. *Melesia's Pride*, winner in 1949 and 1950, was boarded at the stables and I was allowed on one occasion to ride her around the paddock.

For the present, the beach and the stables are my world. The South-Easter: sunlight at low tide on wet sand; the frantic surf crashing on the beach; the smell of eucalyptus and horses. Everything else, a blur.

~ 4 ~

Mosquito weight champion

I was not a success at school. In fact, school had me completely baffled and bewildered. Everyone else seemed to know what was going on and what was expected of them. The South African College School (SACS), the oldest school in the country, had a reputation for attracting bright, athletic and ambitious youngsters destined for the University of Cape Town, the professions and the Western Province rugby team. I was an outsider. I knew nothing of the mystique of being a Capetonian: the mountain, the university and its tradition-laden rivalry with Stellenbosch, Ikkies vs. Marties.

None of the school subjects meant anything to me. Arithmetic completely frustrated me. We were expected to model the sums we had been given in plasticine instead of writing them down. I found it next to impossible to manipulate the plasticine. By the time I had twisted it into what bears some resemblance to the numbers, I had forgotten what I was supposed to be doing.

My teacher was obviously using the latest in hand/eye co-ordination pedagogy combining it with her arithmetic classes. It probably works for the quick and dexterous, but I am soon left behind. I feel as if I'm on a treadmill going ever faster and faster and I'll never catch up. It's a feeling that remains with me for my entire school career. Reading is a stumbling nightmare. Afrikaans makes no sense at all. My response is to lapse into frustrated rage and refuse to co-operate. The teacher simply ignores me and so I spend a great deal of time sitting in a corner gazing out of the window waiting for the morning to pass. This is well before the days of child-centred education. Children are expected to do what they are told.

I have one friend: Colin Dreyer, who not only can make the most elegant plasticine numbers but who also speaks Afrikaans. He sits next to me in class, patiently doing my sums with me when I am kept in at break. He also teaches me a few words of Afrikaans. He too is an outsider, but not because of a lack of brains. He is a Roman Catholic. In a country dominated by Calvinism, Catholics are regarded as the next thing to the Anti-Christ. The Nationalist Party has just come to power and Afrikaner nationalism in an alliance with the Dutch Reform Church is about to impose its vision of social order on the nation.

Every afternoon on my way from school, down through the Company Gardens to the Parade Ground where I catch the bus, Colin and I stop off at the Catholic cathedral near the Houses of Parliament. Colin genuflects and disappears into the confessional leaving me alone in the gloom to contemplate the crucified Christ above the altar, the mysteries of atonement and redemption, my fingers wet with holy water, the South-Easter howling outside. A presage of things to come.

History, geography and nature study made little impact, though the history classes were responsible for awakening my scepticism. Miss la Cock was in her first year as a teacher. She was one of those Afrikaners who had seen teaching as much as an escape from poverty, and achieving status, as about advancing the Afrikaner Nationalist cause. Although Christian National Education was still some twenty years in the future, she was ahead of her time. God and civic responsibility united in nationalism. Her eyes lit up with a fierce and intense emotion whenever she extolled the virtues of the Afrikaners as a chosen people: their courage and sacrifices in the face of imperial tyranny and their creativity. The same historical and moral arguments were presented to me by an earnest and well-intentioned colleague at the University of the North some thirty odd years later to justify Apartheid, or as he called it Separate Development. By then I was better able to see through the shades of grey that cloud our convictions. Miss la Cock, though, gave me my first conscious object lesson in the use of propaganda, and awakened my innate cynicism.

The first song I remember learning at school was Brahms' Lullaby, which she told us was a traditional Afrikaans folk song. We learnt to sing it in Afrikaans: "*Slaap my kindjie, slaap sag, onder rose van nag. /Eers die armpies om my nek en dan warmpies toe gedek. /Môre vroeg as God wil, word my kindjie*

Mosquito weight champion

gewek....".[11] It was the most beautiful piece of music I had ever heard. Not that I had heard much. We had a small radio at home that I was not allowed to touch, except to listen to *Just William* dramatised at *Children's Hour* in the afternoon. I thought Afrikaners must be wonderful people and was prepared to believe everything she said about them. I went home and enthusiastically sang the Lullaby to my parents who quickly disabused me of my idealism. My first lesson in scepticism. My first lesson in politics. A pattern had been put in place. But the melody remains.

A few years later, while still a schoolboy, I was taken on a tour of a sugar mill in Triangle in Rhodesia. It was there that I learned that ordinary brown sugar was simply dyed white sugar. I was shocked. Ever since, I have distrusted politicians, advertisers, PR and marketing specialists and their assorted acolytes intent on defrauding the world. Vance Packard's *The Hidden Persuaders* caught me at the right age and contributed in no small measure to my growing scepticism by introducing me to the world of subterfuge aided and abetted by the then latest developments in mind manipulation used in advertising.

Miss la Cock, as I remember her, was of that generation of Afrikaners who believed that they had finally been vindicated by the Nationalist Party victory in 1948. A new dawn was breaking and they would shape South Africa to their own design. There were still many alive who had fought in the Boer War less than 50 years earlier. Their children now assumed the mantles of power. They understood right from the start that education was vital to their survival. It not only provided an escape from poverty to salaried security, but it would become the major means of promoting Afrikaner Nationalism. So deeply were myths of the Boer Republics entrenched that as recently as 1984, after completing my doctoral thesis on the Boer War (*From Dolly Gray to Sarie Marais*), the chairman of the Rand Afrikaans University council, a prominent member of the Broeder Bond and a Nationalist theoretician, congratulated me, saying it was now time to "start talking about these things".

Miss la Cock's history classes were largely a recapitulation of the

---
11. FAK – sangbundel: *Wiegelied van Brahms.*

sufferings of the Afrikaners at the hands of the English from the time of Slagtersnek and the botched execution of the Boer rebels. She dwelt at length on the suffering of the women and children in the concentration camps during the Second Anglo-Boer War. I never heard her mention the more recent atrocities in Europe and the bravery of the British as they faced Hitler's Germany alone after the fall of Dunkirk. These were events with which I had some passing knowledge, though I must admit that I was less critical of my father's propaganda than I was of hers. As far as I was concerned we English (I was still to discover my Scots heritage) had saved the world from the forces of darkness. Anyway, she had lied about Brahms' Lullaby.

I did have one small triumph at school. In 1949, the year before Vic Toweel became the first South African world boxing champion, he gave me my first and last taste of glory. Such was the prestige of SACS that the school could invite him to judge and hand out the prizes for the junior school boxing championships. After three rounds of sheer terror, Toweel stepped into the ring and much to my amazement, held my hand aloft as the new mosquito weight champion of SACS, all of 63 pounds. I didn't feel like a champion. I knew I had been absolutely terrified of Adrian Futron and had spent most of the three rounds in the ring warding him off with my only defence, a straight left. But it was enough to convince Toweel, if not me, that I had won the fight.

I never fought in a competition again. About ten years later I was involved in a fight in my final year of school in circumstances that did me no honour, and discovered the hard way that whatever skill I possessed when I was eight had deserted me. I was thoroughly beaten by a boy who had real skill and I carry the injury to this day. The point was, of course, I was scared of physical pain, of violence, and to put not too fine a point on it was a coward. I managed to bluff my way through the fight with Adrian and thereafter avoided any physical conflict, until my over confidence and inability to distinguish between fantasy and reality found me out and I had to stand and take my punishment.

Mosquito weight champion

We moved into No. 2 *van Riebekhof*, Knysna Road, Milnerton sometime in the middle of 1947. Ours was a one bedroomed flat with a living room and an entrance that could be used as a dining area. Flora's maiden aunt, Auntie (to this day I have no idea if she had any other name), and I occupied the bedroom, while my parents slept on divans at opposite ends of the living room.

Van Riebekhof was put up in the post war building boom, and in fact the final finishing touches were being done as we moved in. It was inhabited mostly by young married couples who, having survived the war, were now intent on living their lives and starting families; on surviving the peace. The owner would arrive on horseback at mid-morning to check how things were progressing and spent most of his time chatting up the young women whose husbands were conveniently absent at work. Flora was outraged that he should take advantage of vulnerable young women in this way and once he had gone she and the others gathered together in a flurry of righteous indignation, though I never did see them be anything but pleasant to him when he appeared on his horse the next day. It was an early object lesson in the inconsistency of female sexual behaviour.

The Forties and early Fifties were not good times for sex. The Pill was not available and Elvis Presley had yet to rock the age into sexual liberation. Most of the men had returned from the war suffering from what is recognised today as post-traumatic stress syndrome, but was unacknowledged then. Sexual dysfunction is a common symptom of post-traumatic stress. And, in a society that understood little or nothing about psychology, except that they had heard about this chap Freud who said everything had to do with sex, which was patent nonsense, young couples were under extreme pressure. Marriages during the war had often been hasty affairs followed by long periods of separation during which the partners had little opportunity to get to know one another. Brought together by a world at war they were destined to be torn apart by the terrors of peace. It is no small wonder that after the war when normality returned and they were expected to get on with their lives, they found themselves having to live with virtual strangers with whom they had little in common, least of all sex. This is not an original observation, but it certainly fits my parents.

Flora too, had her own burdens. I was always aware that she never touched me, never kissed me. I was never cuddled. To be fair, there was much less kissing and cuddling of children in those days. Whether my parents' vulnerability was inherited (there was a history of mental instability in both their backgrounds), the result of the shocks of war which smashed a generation's psyche, the trauma of emigration or some other profound fear hidden from consciousness, I don't know. Their only defence was to build a barrier between themselves and reality, behind which they could lapse into unconsciousness. Even then, I was aware they slept in separate beds at opposite ends of the room.

Within a short time, I began to pick up unguarded talk between Flora and Auntie about my father's drinking. Often, he disappeared for days on end. Occasionally, I would encounter him on a Sunday morning looking haggard and hunched. In subtle ways, I became aware of the sexual tension between them. Whether the drinking caused the tension, or the tension the drinking I do not to know, but I did know all was not well and it had to do with more than just alcohol.

Children have extraordinarily sensitive intuitions about what is happening in their families. The disappearances become more frequent and prolonged. When he was at home the tension was palpable, frequently bursting out in shouting matches. One morning Flora appeared with a black eye. There was no doubt where my loyalties lay. I listened sceptically to my father as he tried to explain how she bumped into a door during the night.

Some days later he said: "if there's one thing you must never do, m'boy, it's hit a woman."

It was the only bit of advice he ever gave me. Nor was it the last time Flora showed signs of being on the wrong end of his fists. She spent the next few days moving about in bruised silence. I stayed out of the flat as much as I could. These episodes were followed by embarrassing

Mosquito weight champion

displays of remorse, inevitably drowned in brandy. And, what becomes a cycle starts over again.

Nor am I the only one to pick up the tension. Ranger, my Alsatian, began to adopt a peculiar hangdog expression as though expecting to be beaten at any moment. One afternoon while we were having tea in the sitting room I put my arms around his neck as children are wont to do. He growled at me, but I took no notice, having often hugged him in the past. Suddenly, he turned on me and savaged me in the face, just missing my right eye and tearing my upper lip.

Ranger fled from the room out into the garden and disappeared. He did not come back for two days. So much for dogs not suffering guilt. When he returned, he crawled in the door on his stomach. It took him days to recover his *joie de vivre*, even though he was never punished.

There was blood everywhere. My parents were stunned. I was too confused to understand what had happened. It had all been so sudden and so quick. Fortunately, our doctor lived just down the road. I was bundled off, amid admonitions not to cry, to be stitched up and given an anti-tetanus injection. Even to this day, I am anxious when confronted by large dogs, especially when there are small children around.

Auntie went to see her relatives in Adelaide, probably to give my parents the space to sort out their lives. She was away a year. Things did not improve. If anything, they got worse without her mediating presence. When she returned my father suddenly vanished. Flora decided it was time to return to England. For the first time, I become conscious of the importance of money. My father had left, lost his job and disappeared. Suddenly we were poor and I was aware we were poor; an awareness that was to haunt me for the rest of my childhood and adolescence. So, we packed up and together with Auntie and Ranger boarded the *Dunottar Castle* (black and red funnel, white superstructure and lilac hull) one rain swept afternoon in September 1949.

～ 5 ～

"You might as well live"

We left Cape Town in a wild South Atlantic storm in the spring of 1949. Within hours of leaving port most of the passengers were groaning on their bunks. Mountainous seas washed over the bows, the spray stinging our eyes. For hours we were hurled between waves that rose higher than the smokestack, or were poised, momentarily immobile, on the crest gazing down into black canyons of water. The ship lurched and groaned. Everything that could move was lashed down, but still boxes skidded like missiles across the deck. A tray of shattered cups and saucers slid haphazardly across the stateroom floor. Ranger lay in his kennel in the stern confused and frightened. Every now and then with a tremendous roar the propellers rose above the water where they thrashed the air, as the ship plunged headlong into another watery trough. Below decks, pale wide-eyed individuals staggered along gangways awash with vomit. It was terrifying but exhilarating. The drill for abandoning ship was well attended. Only a few hardy souls turned up for supper that night.

Flora and Auntie were assigned an inner cabin with four other women. I was lucky. I was in an outer cabin with a porthole. I shared it with two men one of whom would to play a central role in my life for several months. Eric and his friend Tony, a twenty-one-year old youngster with piercing blue eyes, were returning to England after spending a year trying unsuccessfully to farm near Port Elizabeth. They were an odd pair. An unremarkable fair skinned middle-aged man with a receding hairline who looked as if he had spent too much time in the sun without a hat, incipient skin cancer beginning on his forehead; and a dark and brooding youngster reminiscent of Heathcliff. Something about them made me uneasy. I couldn't say what, nor did I express my feelings to Flora.

Eric offered to keep an eye on me for Flora and see that I didn't run wild. As the voyage progressed it became clear that he and Flora had struck up a good friendship, though hardly a shipboard romance.

"You might as well live"

Eric took a keen interest in me, encouraging me to read, finding me interesting books in the ship's library: *Kidnapped* and *Lorna Doone*. Tales of youthful struggle against injustice and the abuse of power, of endurance and loyalty. They struck a chord. Until now I had not read, spending most of my time riding or at the beach. Now I had two weeks of enforced idleness. It was an ideal opportunity to get into the habit. It was also an ideal opportunity to explore ways of escaping from what was going on around me.

When we reached St Helena, Eric organised a visit to Napoleon's house. Longwood House made a powerful impression on me. It looked so modest, so small, much too small to contain a colossus: whitewashed clapboard nestling in a dell on the side of a hill in an untended garden. The house was boarded up and neglected. Dark green shadows surrounded and overhung the house. The grass was rank and overgrown. Could this be where a man who had made the world tremble had lived? There should be evidence of his presence everywhere. Surely, the hillside, the trees, even the grass should show he had been here. There must be clues of Austerlitz, Jena, the retreat from Moscow, Waterloo. I almost expected to catch a glimpse of his shadow through the trees. The echoes of greatness faded the more I strained to catch them. Through a window we could see a print on the wall showing him on a white horse surveying a battlefield surrounded by his marshals Murat, Bernadotte and MacDonald. Was it Austerlitz or Borodino?

Longwood House was destined to loom large. Within a few years my life, my attitudes and values were destined to be shaped by a charismatic teacher who regarded Napoleon as next to God. By then, fortunately, I was able to counter his francophone propaganda with my own no less bigoted British brand. The reading bug had taken hold, and if nothing else, my visit to St Helena started me on a career of voracious and indiscriminate reading.

I could not wait to get back to the ship where I struggled through a 1928 edition of the *Encyclopaedia Britannica*, van Loon's *Lives* and Arthur Mee. Here was the sort of man I could look up to and follow. I was sorely in need of a male figure whom I could admire and who would provide me with a moral touchstone. Life had so far proved disappointing. Perhaps history or literature would make up the deficit. I devoured everything I could find in the ship's library, which was not a lot, though enough to whet my appetite. My mind was consumed with thrilling cavalry charges, brilliant battles and glorious triumphs. I had never encountered real history before. To be in the very place where a great man had lived, and not so long ago, thrilled me. And yet, at the same time, the image that remains in my mind is of the neglected little house on the side of a windswept hill surrounded by dark overhanging trees. Lonely, lost and forgotten, the shadows gathering. *"Look on my works, ye Mighty, and despair … ."*[12] I was destined to learn when I became an adult that there is nothing romantic about dictatorships, and even less about opposing them.

Eric was so attentive that by the end of the voyage when we reached Southampton we were invited to stay with him in his mother's house in Canterbury.

"Eric wants to marry me", Flora said.

"Why?"

"Because he thinks you are special, and that you need a proper home to grow up in."

Even to my ten-year-old understanding that seemed a strange reason for wanting to marry anyone. It did not occur to me that my father had any claims on our lives. Flora had so filled my mind with loathing for him I could not conceive that we would ever have anything to do with him again. He was a wife beater, a drunk. He had abandoned us. He had destroyed our life in Cape Town. The lessons were drummed in every day. I was never to drink, never to hit a woman, accept life's responsibilities, never abandon my children, always provide for them. Never drink. Never drink. I had cut him out of my life with all the moral certitude a ten-year-old can muster. He was of no consequence. He had always been remote. In fact, I knew virtually nothing of him as a father except for a

---

12. Shelley: 'Ozymandias'.

"You might as well live"

brief period after the war when he had made me model boats we sailed together on the Serpentine.

Still, I found Eric's offer of marriage odd. There seemed to be no love as I understood it between the two of them. I never saw them exchange any gesture of affection or intimacy. The arrangement, for that is how it was presented to me, was purely practical and for my benefit, and I was not sure I want to be a beneficiary.

On the other hand, it did not strike me as odd when Flora occupied the spare bedroom and I had to share a double bed with Eric. Presumably, as they were not married they could not share a bed. Someone has decided that it is not right for me to sleep in her bed. Somehow, a ten-year-old boy in a forty-year-old man's bed is more acceptable.

Today, of course, it is not possible to regard these sleeping arrangements innocently. Given the limitations on the number of beds available some sort of rationale could have been offered to anyone interested enough. Eric's invalid mother had the only other bed in the house, downstairs in the front room which she occupied with two African Grey parrots. I have no idea what she made of these arrangements, or if she even knew. She was no more than a vague presence around which I was expected to tiptoe.

Flora offered no explanation. I had no standard by which to judge the situation. The only clue I had, and it was not recognisable as a clue at the time, was that I was frightened of Tony and avoided being alone with him. This was not always possible. We saw him virtually every weekend and often during the week. He made it clear he loathed me. Whenever we were alone he told me I was a little shit.

"What you need is a bloody good hiding and I'll give it to you one of these days."

I asked Eric, "Why doesn't Tony like me?"

"He's jealous of you."

No explanation was offered, and I did not think to ask for one, or if I did, decided it was not wise to.

Staring Memory in the Face

Tony's malice was never more than petty. I had just discovered conkers and as luck would have it had acquired a champion conker which brought me a small measure of status in the school playground. It is famous for its twelve victories. Shades of Stephen Dedalus. I polished it every day to keep up its resilience. It was my only possession. One Saturday afternoon the four of us were on our way to Dover in Eric's decrepit Austin when we stopped at a roadside pub. Flora and Eric left Tony and me in the car while they went in search of tea. Tony suddenly reached across and yanked the conker from my grasp, and before I realised it flung it through the open window into the river next to the road.

"And don't you start snivelling or I'll belt you," he muttered through clenched teeth as the adults came back to the car.

I said nothing, told no one. There was no one to tell. This was a battle I would have to fight on my own. My only defence was to keep out of his way as much as possible.

Everything about England was dismal and grey. Rationing was still the order of the day. And it was cold: like living in an endless cemetery of disintegrating buildings separated by fields of overgrown nettles and brambles tangled over the rotting hulks of abandoned vehicles. The whole surrounded by dark and menacing trees. Everything dank and smelling of rust.

I discovered a field near where we lived and longed to play in the decaying remains of old tractors and lorries, but the brambles and nettles made it impossible. It was emblematic of most of my experience of England. The wreckage and detritus of war littering the landscape. And silence. And the ghostly remains of bombed houses down the way. For some reason I can never fathom, Flora refused to buy me long trousers and my legs between the tops of my socks and the bottoms of my shorts were perpetually pink and chapped. I began to chew the quicks of my fingers till they bled: a habit a lifetime has not cured. Imagine my feelings when I discovered that Mr Jaggers in *Great Expectations* suffered from the same affliction.

"You might as well live"

Eric's bedroom looked out over the backyard. A small rectangle of overgrown grass and nettles surrounded a ragged army tent in which he had stored his things while he had been in South Africa. The remains of a motorbike stood on its pedestal at the back of the tent behind rotting boxes of books, old clothes, a few chairs, kitchen utensils and crockery. Behind the tent a dilapidated split pole fence looked over the service lane. The tent was an ideal place to escape to on rainy afternoons, especially when Tony came to visit. I spent a lot of solitary time there amusing myself on the motorbike and reading water stained novels, dreading the call to supper and bed when Eric read the adventures of Bulldog Drummond to me.

I made no friends. School was no more than a place at which to spend a certain number of hours each day between getting out of bed in the morning and going to bed at night. It had no impact on my life. I made no sense of the lessons. The other children with their pale skins and strange accents spoke an incomprehensible language made all the more frustrating because I could understand individual words but could make no sense of what they are saying. They reminded me of the boiled potatoes we had every lunchtime. Their colour, if they ever had colour, had been bleached out. The teachers were vague authoritarian shapes moving in a landscape smelling perpetually of boiled cabbage.

I cannot imagine what we are doing in Canterbury; what we are doing in England. There is no more talk of marriage and I can feel things are strained between Flora and Eric. The house always dark. Voices never raised. No spontaneous outbursts of laughter. No music, no sunshine. Everything heavy, bleak. The only colour, the crimson tails of the parrots in the invalid's room. Their startled shrieks the only sound. Everything smells slightly mouldy. I am in limbo. Waiting, but for what I cannot imagine. Will it never end? I am not always sure I am awake or asleep, for my nightmares do not appear in any way different from what I experience during the day. Dark rooms with silent silhouetted figures. The world outside drizzling from dawn to dusk. Flora, remote. She says nothing and asks nothing of me. She has never been overtly affectionate.

Staring Memory in the Face

She never kisses or hugs me; or even touches me. I trust and love her because that is what children do, but beyond that I have no expectations. I am trapped, waiting for the overriding event of the day, bedtime. A damp gloom of autumn settles over everything. Something has to happen.

∼

I often sat on the top of the fence in the backyard chewing my fingers, looking down the hill over a glass sea of greenhouse roofs, streaked with soot, gleaming dully in the wet sunlight. In the distance, a row of oaks had already lost their leaves, their bare branches black against the grey sky. And rows and rows of grey plastered council houses, blind windows staring onto cobbled streets. All the same, like a child's drawing. The occasional abandoned bombsite, overgrown with nettles.

A rotten piece of rope has been left tied to the top of the fence where I balance six or so feet above the ground. The fence trembles and I wobble between heaven and earth. Without thinking, I tie the loose end around my neck, and jump. The sun breaks through the clouds and I see the blue arch overhead turning and turning. Midway through my fall I feel my head jerked back and a burning sensation across my throat, my descent arrested. Red brick and grey slate and blind windows wheel about me. The rope snaps. I plunge to the ground.

I lie on my back for a few minutes trying to make up my mind. Am I dead or alive? The sky turns overhead. Clouds pass. A flock of pigeons swings across the sky. Endless peace. Everything is resolved. Gradually, I become aware of the damp on which I'm lying. The burning sensation around my neck convinces me I'm still alive. There's no escape, no easy solution. I pick myself up, swallow awkwardly and rub the back of my head. I'm in the lane. The fence on one side, a bland brick wall on the other. There are no witnesses. My throat is tender; swallowing an effort. Feeling vaguely disappointed, I wonder what to do next. A mantle of fatalism enfolds me. It had all seemed so simple: I had forced the moment to a crisis and all I have achieved is a sore throat and bruised knees. Not

"You might as well live"

for me the grand exit. Life has to go on. There is no avoiding it. Nor is there any question of repeating the exercise. I get up, dust myself off, smooth my hair and notice there's mud on my jersey I am going to have to explain, and I make my way out of the lane and knock on the front door.

The memory of that wobbly moment poised between the absence of thought and the act recurs unbidden, without warning, over the next seventy odd years. I see a pale-faced small boy with pink knees, absent-mindedly chewing the quicks of his fingers till they bleed, on top of a rickety fence balanced between earth and sky, etched against the glare from the greenhouse roofs.

When I discovered it, many years later, Dorothy Parker's ruminations on suicide struck a personal and permanent cord.

> *Razors pain you;*
> *Rivers are damp;*
> *Acids stain you;*
> *And drugs cause cramp.*
> *Guns aren't lawful;*
> *Nooses give;*
> *Gas smells awful;*
> *You might as well live.*[13]

Nooses give. I might as well live.

I didn't tell Flora what I had done. Not because I felt guilty, but simply because I knew she would not understand, and anyway, it was none of her business. I also felt pretty foolish. How could I possibly explain? Adults have such a way of asking impossible questions with no answers. If nothing else I knew I was on my own.

Suicide was to haunt me. I had survived my own botched attempt, but that did not protect me. Mine was a dress rehearsal for the next twelve years. When I attended a Catholic school a few years later, it was impressed upon me during the course of religious instruction that suicide was the only unforgivable act. The suicide, we were told, despairs of God's

---

13. Dorothy Parker: *Résumé*.

mercy and therefore will be condemned to everlasting damnation. I had not yet heard of Faust. The sin of pride was at the root. The suicide, we were told, is so consumed by pride that he conceives of himself as being beyond God's help or mercy. Heady stuff for a twelve-year-old. More was to come.

～

A day or two later, Flora suddenly announced without explanation that she was not going to marry Eric and that we were going to London. We arrived at Waterloo Station on a bleak winter's afternoon.

"Where are we going to live, mum?"

"I don't know. I'm going to phone a friend. Wait here."

And she disappeared into the crowd. I sat on a suitcase watching the milling crowds for half an hour wondering when she would come back, bored and hungry. She suddenly appeared out of the crowd.

"Come on. Let's get a cup of tea and something to eat. I've sorted it out."

Over a cup of tea and baked beans on toast in a Lyons Corner House I asked: "Where are we going?"

"To a friend."

She was never very forthcoming and I learned to wait for events to unfold. The friend turned out to be an old lover (I now suppose) who was living in a bombed house that was being renovated. Here, I was destined to have my first introduction to public baths and lavatories, as none of the plumbing was connected; an experience that resulted in me developing severe constipation. The friend expected Flora to share his bed (this was a change) and I was put on a sofa. This arrangement lasted about two days whereupon he disappeared and Flora and I shared the bed for the remainder of the week. Where he had gone and why he left I did not ask. The ways of the adult world I decided are unpredictable and incomprehensible.

"You might as well live"

We moved into her sister-in-law's flat in Primrose Hill. Joyce had been married to Flora's brother Bill, who had either died or disappeared. Flora and I occupied an attic room that looked out over an endless sea of grey shingle roofs. The room had no electricity or gas, and it was here that I had another brush with death, albeit accidentally. I was given an erratic oil lamp by which to read. One night I fell asleep reading *Thunderhead* before turning it off. The next thing I knew I was being shaken awake and dragged from my bed out of suffocating smoke into the flat below. Everything was caked with soot and Flora and Joyce spent much of the following day washing bedding and curtains.

In the winter of 1949 I was sent to Marylebone Grammar School. This was shortly before the end of the legendary headmaster P.A. Wayne's reign, a period regarded as the school's golden age. That was not how I experienced it. While I had not shone at school in South Africa, I had managed to survive and had been beginning to outgrow my feelings of bewilderment. At Marylebone, I soon experienced the terror of inadequacy, and, quite understandably, began to hate school. I was eleven years old and required to do algebra, chemistry, Latin and French, none of which I had encountered before. I quickly established myself at the bottom of the class, a position I was to maintain steadfastly for most of the rest of my school career. Even my dismal experience at Canterbury had not prepared me for this. Marylebone Grammar had been founded in 1792 as the Philological School to provide *"free education for the sons of reduced persons."* I qualified by any standard.

The master sat in deep shadow behind a desk raised on a platform above the class, a dim gothic presence wrapped in his academic gown, hovering beyond the utmost bound of pre-adolescence understanding, from whence his cavernous voice demanded the conjugation of French verbs, the recitation of Pythagorean theorems and the Periodic Table.

The winter sun struggles to penetrate the soot-grimed gothic windows, dimly illuminating four rows of penknife-scarred desks, ten deep, at which sat 40 bowed and pale faced forms; the silence broken only by perpetual sniffing, the scratch of nibs on paper and the occasional measured tread of the master's footsteps as he descends from on high and patrols the rows. The high vaulted ceiling looks as if it houses all kinds of bats and creatures of the night roosting there, waiting to swoop down on the miserable ignoramuses below. I occupy a desk in an obscure corner of the room where, once it is discovered how backward I am, I am left to my own devices. No one, neither teachers nor pupils, shows any interest in me. I have no identity. No one seems to know my name or is interested in finding it out. No one is interested in tales I might have to tell about living in the wilds of Africa, of a land of perpetual sunshine, golden beaches, and no rationing.

In order not to slip completely into oblivion I start trying to write stories in Afrikaans, but of course my vocabulary is non-existent, and my despair increases. Anything, just to give me a sense that I am not about to disappear. When Afrikaans fails me I try devising codes, but to no avail. It is at this time that my island begins to form in my imagination, no doubt the result of reading *Robinson Crusoe*, *Treasure Island*, *Coral Island* and *The Swiss Family Robinson* in rapid succession. Like Crusoe I am the sole inhabitant. Like Jim, I find an apple barrel. A dagger poised above me in the dark. I retreated.

The storm raged for three nights. Mountainous waves broke the masts and swept sails and rigging over board. The boat lurched from foaming trough to foaming trough, helpless, buffeted by wind and waves. The crew had long abandoned ship and I, a stowaway, emerge from hiding only to see their lifeboat disappear with all hands beneath a monstrous tumble of water. Clinging to what remains of the foremast I lash myself to a spar. Drenched by rain and salt spray, catching my breath I am dimly aware of another sound, the thunderous roar of surf beating on rocks. Through the rain the black shapes of cliffs rear out of the dark, overhanging the surf and the little boat that is being driven relentlessly towards the rocks at its base. The boat lurches and comes to a shuddering stop, listing violently to starboard. The surf surges across the main deck sweeping spars and barrels over the side into the foaming tumult. A hundred yards of tempestuous white water separate us from the shore and safety. The mainmast splits and falls over the side where it smashes against the hull. The storm continues to rage all night, but the boat remains stuck fast. Gradually, with the first

"You might as well live"

gleams of dawn the wind begins to drop. By mid-morning all is still and I can see, as the tide recedes, that the boat is fast on a sand bar near the entrance to a lagoon. Just beyond the breakers, placid blue water edged by yellow sand is overhung by gently swaying palms. I lash some spars and barrels together to make a raft onto which I put everything I can find I will need ashore, tools, food, the ship's dog and push off through the breakers for the beach.

Admittedly derivative and heavily indebted to Robert Louis Stevenson and R M Ballantyne, my island was to become more elaborate and detailed over the next ten years; a thinly disguised metaphor for my state of mind. It was also one of my earliest attempts at composition. I wish I could, but I can't claim to have shown any promise of becoming a worthy successor to the school's genuine literary lights: Jerome K Jerome, Patrick O'Brian and Len Deighton. Eric Hobsbawm was there in 1935.

There was not a stone, plant, tree, hill I did not know. I mapped it, explored it, fled to it every night and often during the day. It provided me with sustenance, hills to roam, caves to explore, streams and sea to swim in. The forest was full of exotic parrots and birds of paradise. Fruit and nuts hung from the trees all year round. I was its only human inhabitant. There were no footprints in the sand but my own. When an occasional storm blew up I was able to retreat to a shelter built in a cave on a hillside high above the sea, safe and snug.

Meanwhile, in the Third Remove the windows are above head height. Gargoyles clinging to gutters and flying buttresses peer in, vomiting water onto the stone pavement below. The playground is a death trap. Ice and filthy puddles lie everywhere. One wrong step and you could end up drenched or with a broken limb. The boys' lavatory can only be reached by skating the full length of the playground. It is surrounded by piles of soot-stained snow which provide the bigger boys with ample ammunition to rain down rock-hard snowballs on any youngster foolish enough to have a full bladder. You enter the lavatory only as a last desperate resort. Urinals occupy one side and cubicles the other; between, a passage, reminiscent of an earlier world, runs the whole length with doors at either end. It stinks alternately of stale urine or disinfectant.

Staring Memory in the Face

This area is bespoke by a group of older boys who congregate there to smoke and terrorise anyone who dares to violate their territory. It truly is a chamber of horrors. The irony does not escape me that it could easily be used as an exhibition at Madam Tussaud's.

Madam Tussaud's Wax Works is just down the road. I passed it twice a day on my way to and from the Baker Street tube station. On one occasion, I managed to save enough for the entrance fee and spent an hour there on my way home from school. The Chamber of Horrors held no terrors for me. I had experienced much worse in the lavatories and classrooms of Marylebone Grammar.

Baker Street was also home to Sherlock Holmes. I spent a lot of time on my slippery way to and from the tube station that winter looking for 221B Baker Street, imagining myself as Billy the page boy a hundred years ago, helping untangle the mysteries discussed in Holmes's study.

~ 6 ~

Newcastle-on-Tyne

Winter gives way to spring, and with it comes news of Auntie's death. Auntie had gone up to Newcastle-on-Tyne as soon as we had arrived in England the previous autumn to stay with her nephew, Flora's other brother, John. Flora, Ranger and I duly went north, and ended staying for a year, sharing a tiny two bed-roomed house with John, his wife Joy and daughter Pamela. Flora and I occupied a bed in the front bedroom, John and Joy the back bedroom, and Pamela was displaced onto a sofa in the sitting room. Ranger slept in the kitchen, the warmest room in the house. He had been released from quarantine and there was no doubt in Flora's mind that he belonged with us no matter how cramped our circumstances.

I was intrigued to meet my aunt Joy, the woman who had occasioned so much scorn from Flora for simply being a waitress, and therefore common. Far from being especially marked in any way she is simply another adult; neither tall nor short, pretty nor plain, blonde nor brunette. John, on the other hand, is quite eccentric, with hair that seems to grow out of the side of his head in two brown bushes divided by a bald pate. He has false teeth that he clacks together in an absentminded way while reading the newspaper. A soggy dead cigarette dangles permanently from his lower lip. He rolls his own. Pamela, their daughter, is about my age. She is a pale neat little girl who seldom speaks. She shows no interest in me and the feeling is reciprocated. What does she know of riding racehorses on the beach, of a world where the sun shines every day? She and her mother must have resented our invasion of their house which is now full to bursting.

The house is typical of 19th century North Country mass accommodation for the working-class in which millions continued to live well into the 20th century. It is only five years after the War, and there is still a massive housing shortage in Britain. Uninterrupted rows of slowly dissolving red brick houses face each other across cobbled streets, rank upon rank. Front doors arranged in pairs serve upstairs and downstairs dwellings, looking directly onto the pavement. At the end of the street stands a soot-encrusted church, opposite a dingy news agency. A phone box on the corner provides the only phone in the street. Not a hint of green to be seen anywhere. The sky is perpetually grey.

The accommodation upstairs and down is identical. Two bedrooms front and back, a living room next to the front bedroom and a kitchen, effectively the main living space, behind it. No bathroom or lavatory. Baths are conducted on Friday evenings in a galvanised iron tub in the kitchen with hot water from the hob, Pamela and I being forced to share the same tub, to our acute embarrassment. For the rest, we wash and John shaves in the kitchen sink. Each pair of houses shares a backyard which also contains in the farthest corner an outdoor privy. Indoor lavatories and bathrooms are a luxury few can afford in working-class Britain. A service lane, which separates a mirror image row of red brick walls and black slate roofs in reverse, provides access for the buckets and dustbins emptied once a week. We occupy an upstairs house, which means access to the yard and privy is via a rickety, soot-begrimed wooden balcony off the kitchen. In winter, when the balcony is covered in ice, it requires skill and courage to descend into the yard. The steps are frozen, as is the banister. Descending into the yard is perilous. There is nothing to hold on to. At any moment you might lose your grip and slip. Below, frozen washing hangs on a line in the yard. Shirts hang like so many crucifixes, pegs impale their sleeves, constant reminders of the fate that awaits me if I miss my step.

The washline is a constant source of dispute between us and the Woods who live below. The privy is an even greater source of conflict. Complaints are flung back and forth about the state of the bog, usually reaching a pitch a day or so before the bucket is emptied. The children in either house bear the brunt of most of the criticism for our "filthy habits". A low-level feud is maintained by the womenfolk, for the most part in an atmosphere of stony silence with occasional outbreaks of shouting. We

Newcastle-on-Tyne

are all officially on "no speaks". The women sniff elaborately whenever they chance upon one another hanging out the washing. Vigilance has to be maintained to ensure they do not meet coming out of or going into the bog. The children are, of course, forbidden to play with each other. This we get around simply by arranging to play with friends down the street whose working parents let them have the run of their house during the day. This arrangement, as might be imagined, leads to much early preadolescent experimentation during which I have my first glimpses of the female anatomy: "you show me yours and I'll show you mine."

The husbands, my uncle John and Fred Woods, simply avoid the war zone for most of the time by being at work. Weekends though, are tricky. They both work at the same factory where they apparently get on quite well, often stopping off together at the local together for a pint on a Friday night. At home under the tyranny of their womenfolk they keep a discreet distance. Flora is soon part of this imbroglio. She seems to thrive in an atmosphere of intrigue and backbiting tittle-tattle. She and Joy are in an alliance against Mrs Woods, 'that hussy', though that does not stop her from criticising Joy behind her back to me.

Matters come to a head one wet and miserable February morning. Mrs Woods' voice can be heard rising to a crescendo as she accuses Pamela of using some of her pegs she has forgotten on the line, to hang up our washing. The pegs are merely the pretext. Crime after crime is heaped on her head, and the fact that I had neglected to clean up Ranger's turds. The frozen evidence is indisputable. Flora and Joy rush out onto the balcony and enter the fray. Throughout this whole fracas I pretend to be absorbed in the adventures of Biggles, Algy and Ginger, ignorant of what is going on. However, the row reaches such a pitch that I feel impelled to go outside and see what is going on. From the balcony, I can see the three women in violent confrontation, Pamela standing awkwardly to one side; Mrs Woods, red hair adrift, hanging tangled and loose about her shoulders, her more than ample bosom heaving with passion; Joy, arms akimbo, not retreating an inch as she defends Pamela. It is a cold morning and they look like two dragons squaring up at each other, their breath condensing in the air with every outburst. Flora notices I have appeared and calls me to come down into the yard to explain the frozen turds. They are the only indisputable concrete facts in a welter of accusation and counter accusation. As I come down the steps I slip and catch hold of the banister, cutting the palm of my hand on a rusty nail. The sight of blood gives the women the respite they need to retrieve their dignity, and they withdraw to their respective houses in high dudgeon, nursing their grievances for future recriminations. I am told to go upstairs and get a plaster.

Three days later my hand was badly swollen and enflamed, an angry red line reaching up the inside of my arm. Flora's solution was a hot poultice to draw the poison. Preparations were made and I submitted my hand to have the poultice applied. The pain was excruciating and I howled.

"Shut up, and stop blubbering".

Pain is something you put up with. It does not last forever so there is no point in whining. My hand was bound and I was left to get on with it.

The following evening the bandages were removed to reveal my hand in an even worse state. The pain and stench nearly made me faint as the skin cames away with the bandage and the raw flesh was revealed. I knew better than to complain. The poultice was much too hot and my whole palm was blistered and suppurating. The next three weeks saw my hand gradually heal. I think Flora was a little chastened by the experience. She never referred to it again. One of the advantages for me was that I couldn't hold a pen and was exempt from writing anything at school. I also had to carry my hand in a sling, which gave me a certain status in the playground.

School, as before, was not a success. But worse was to come. I had been enrolled at the local primary school as an interim measure until Flora could find a school which satisfied her social pretensions. Flora believed that private schools (in England perversely called Public Schools) or grammar schools were better than ordinary government comprehensive schools. She may well have been right, but her motivation was social

Newcastle-on-Tyne

rather than educational. We had to show, she and I, that we were not common, not lower class. I had begun to pick up from her that we were a cut above our relations in Newcastle, and that I need never forget it. This was a bit rich from someone with supposed Marxist sympathies: hers was essentially the politics of envy. How she was going to pay the fees I never enquired. She had no money other than what she had managed to acquire when she sold all our household possessions before we left South Africa, which could not have been much, and a small inheritance from Auntie. We stayed with her brother rent-free. I am not sure if or how she contributed to the household expenses. I received sixpence a week from my uncle for pocket money. My ambition was to save enough to buy a sword I had seen in a pawnshop window. But the enormous cost and a Mars Bar and the *Beano* once a week defeated my efforts to save the necessary 30 shillings. I dreamt of that sword, but like Excalibur it remained beyond my grasp.

I was duly taken to one of the grammar schools one Monday morning to write an entrance exam. I had been washed and brushed and provided with a clean jersey to disguise my grubby shirt. My shoes shone, though one sock kept falling about my ankle. As we walked up the long tree lined drive to the imposing Victorian gothic structure (why were so many of my experiences of school associated with buildings that looked as if they could have provided a setting for *Dombey and Son*?) I had a feeling of impending disaster. After the usual introductions in which my presence was hardly acknowledged, I was led away, as if to execution, and left by myself in a vast room that seemed a combination of a laboratory and a library. I was required to answer questions on arithmetic and English. I could do none of the sums and made up answers, hoping I would get something right. A spelling test completely defeated me. This was followed by dictation, which was equally disastrous. Finally, I was asked to write a composition. The options were "Spring", "A walk in the park", "A visit to the circus". None of them bore any relation to my life or experience except, perhaps, the walk in the park.

Staring Memory in the Face

Some days previously, Pamela and I had been playing on the swings in the local park when we had been approached by a middle-aged man in a brown raincoat who had asked Pamela to show him her knickers. There was something about him that made us both very uncomfortable. He said he had to buy a pair for his daughter and wanted to see what he should get. As he fumbled with his spectacles we ran off.

Wisely, I decided the incident would not be an appropriate topic. I was given a dictionary and started looking up how to spell "once". There was nothing under W. I sat for an hour almost paralysed with fear without an idea in my head. In the end, I managed to produce ten lines or so of incoherent gibberish. After three hours I was released, exhausted by the ordeal.

Flora was summoned to the headmaster's study to receive the school's verdict. Later at home that afternoon she told me that she had never been more humiliated in her entire life. I had produced the worst results the headmaster had ever encountered. I had scored less than 5% for the arithmetic test and had got only one word correct out of 20 in the spelling test.

The headmaster, a tubby red-faced little man, showed her my pathetic attempts at dictation and composition to underline what a hopeless case I am: there is no way the school could or would accept me. I am doomed according to her. I will never rise out of the gutter. It's appalling. There is no doubt I will never improve. God only knows what sort of life I can look forward to. I am incapable of doing anything to improve my lot. I am stupid beyond redemption. She has never been more humiliated. She bursts into tears while I sit in stony silence. It's my fault. There is no getting away from it. The results speak for themselves. I have nothing to say.

Worse was to come. I was entered for the Eleven Plus exam at my school to see which of the three schooling streams that then existed would suit me best when I went into the secondary phase the following year. There was no doubt that I wasn't academically inclined. I was certainly not scholarship material. Flora's final humiliation came when the Eleven

Newcastle-on-Tyne

Plus results reveal I do not possess enough ability to be admitted to a technical school where I could be prepared for a trade. Tradesmen represent the lowest but one of the rungs on the social ladder. The evidence is incontrovertible: I have no brains and no talents. I am good for nothing.

Confirmation of all of this comes for me not so much from my manifest failure to pass any tests, but one afternoon when my teacher, who knows I have lived in South Africa, asks me during a geography lesson to tell the class about the South African climate and its effect on the Karoo. Not only am I stupid and without talent, I discover that I am ignorant as well. I can't remember ever having heard of the Karoo. I am in front of the class expected to point out on a map where the Karoo is. The class savours my humiliation. The one thing I had clung to was that I had lived in Africa. This had set me apart and given me, in my eyes if no one else's, a certain romantic status. I had lived in the land of big game hunting and naked black savages. Now, I've been found out about that too. I know nothing. South Africa, Cape Town, the beach and riding horses on the sand track seem as insubstantial as a dream that fades the more I try to remember it. I'm drenched with shame.

My only recourse is to withdraw more and more into myself. I lose myself in a world of books. I read anything and everything I can lay my hands on, just to keep the world at bay. At night: *the sound of the surf lulls my fears. A brilliant blue and yellow parrot flies over head while I sit at the entrance to my cave eating a mango. A long golden beach, edged with white foam and overhung with swaying palms stretches away to the end of a headland. Not a cloud. Not a sound, save the waves on the shore and a light breeze in the trees … .*

During the day when I was not at school I would take Ranger for long walks and explore the river that wound its way through the wooded hills that made up the common. One day I came upon a couple making love next to the river, the black water tumbling into a frothy pool beside them. They were unaware of me as I sat and watched with interest as they fumbled with each other. Occasionally, a naked female leg appeared as the girl's dress rode up to her hips, but not much else as they wrestled to exhaustion in the damp grass.

Staring Memory in the Face

I stayed away from home as much as possible, only returning when I could no longer resist the pangs of hunger. I can't share anything with Pamela, and Flora has made her opinion of me all too clear. Truly, I am alone with the timid beating of my heart, and am destined to remain so.

I find the local children and those I meet at school terrifying and violent. Radio was then coming into its own. Every afternoon at five Pamela and I listened to *Dick Barton, Special Agent* on the BBC; a radio serial for children that tells the story of a detective battling the criminal world, a sort of sanitised forerunner of James Bond. Full of action and suspense, it suited my need for a forceful male fantasy figure who takes on and triumphs over the forces of evil. The local Odeon had a special children's show on a Saturday morning that included a Dick Barton serial. One Saturday I resisted buying a Mars Bar, and Pamela and I set off for the Odeon. It was like entering one of the circles of the damned in Dante's Inferno. Six or seven hundred screaming, rioting boys and girls were crammed into the auditorium waiting for the show to start. I thought the noise would abate when the lights went down, but if anything, it increased. At least three fights broke out in various parts of the hall. Paper water bombs flew from one side to another as gangs of youths squared up against one another. Someone in the circle above us poured water onto the audience below. In one of the side aisles near our seats a couple of girls were wanking some boys who jostled around them waiting their turn, feeling their budding breasts.

As the credits for *Dick Barton* came up I strain to hear the familiar signature tune. With the first appearance of our hero on the screen all hell breaks loose. Hardly anyone sits in their seat for more than a few seconds. Everyone is jumping up and rushing from one side of the cinema to the other in a kind of random lunatic frenzy. There is so much noise that it is impossible to hear what is happening on the screen. After about five minutes the house lights go up and the film is stopped. The manager comes onto the stage and tells the audience they have to calm down and keep quiet, or the film will be cancelled. There is a momentary lull, but

Newcastle-on-Tyne

as soon as the lights go down and the film starts again the noise reaches its previous pitch.

I am becoming increasingly frustrated but I know there is nothing I can do. Pamela said we should just ignore the noise but it was impossible. The mob appear to be suffering from convulsions. After another fifteen minutes or so during which the seething, screaming, demented mass around us howls incessantly, the lights come on again. This time the manager was accompanied by a policeman who issued a stern warning: trouble makers will be removed if they do not behave themselves. This seems to calm the crowd down for a bit and *Dick Barton* finally gets under way. Within fifteen minutes though, things are as wild as they have ever been and the show is cancelled. There is no talk of refunding our money and so I go home doubly the poorer.

My hand had now healed and I was taking a more active part in the rough and tumble of the playground. The school was housed in an old building with many long corridors and flights of potentially lethal stairs, down which a torrent of children poured at the beginning and end of every break. We were continually forbidden to run up and down the stairs, especially in wet weather. I and a classmate, Currie (on the basis of our names it is assumed we must have much in common – in fact we loathe one another), were sent to deliver a message from our class teacher to the headmaster.

"And be quick about it."

We raced down the corridor to the stairs leading down to the head's study. Suddenly, my feet slipped from under me and I knew, as the world spun around, I am about to die. I hit the concrete. Lights flashed and I was overcome with nausea and pain with a wild ringing and throbbing pain in my head. I lay on the landing in a pool of blood, not daring to move. I must have been unconscious for some minutes, because by the time I summoned up the courage to open my eyes there was a crowd of faces peering down at me. I couldn't stand and was carried into the infirmary. An ambulance was called. On the way to the hospital it stopped off at our house and picked up Flora. She later told me that when she saw the ambulance man at the door, her first thought was of my father. I have often wondered about the significance of that remark.

At the hospital, I was duly stitched up and bandaged, and Flora and I made our way home by bus. I must have looked a sight as we sat at the back of the bus near the exit, all bloody bandaged and chalk faced. I had been drilled in certain codes of behaviour, which were meant to mark me apart as being one of more than lowly birth. Among my many social refinements was giving up my seat on a bus to an adult. The bus was full when a middle-aged woman got on and stood near us in the aisle. Head throbbing and feeling faint I got to my feet and offered her my seat. She took one look at me and insisted that I stay where I was. Flora, though, insisted I stand and give up my seat. A debate ensued in which Flora assured the woman that I was fine; that I had had a slight bump on the head.

"And you know how head wounds always look worse than they really are. There's really nothing wrong with him."

By this time any interest in me was purely academic. Flora's well-modulated educated accent, which identified her as someone from a different class, swayed the debate. I stood between the two rows of seats trying not to vomit. When we got home, I went to bed and did not wake for two days. When I reappeared at school the following Monday morning the headmaster made a point of pointing me out to the rest of the school at assembly as an example of what happens to unruly children who run in the corridors. The blood was left unwashed on the stairs for the rest of that term to remind anyone foolish enough to ignore school rules about what happens to the disobedient. The children were interested, but their interest is limited to the ghoulish not the moral aspects of my case.

It was around this time, no doubt as a result of having been confronted with her mostly suppressed thoughts about Tommy, that Flora started talking about returning to South Africa. I am not sure what her motivation was. Perhaps she really did love him and wanted to try for reconciliation. Perhaps she realised that life in South Africa provided more opportunities and a better environment than post-war Britain.

Newcastle-on-Tyne

One of the first moves she made was to insist that I phone him from the callbox (how she had got his phone number I never thought to ask) on the corner of the street and tell him how much I missed him and wanted to come back. I recoiled from the idea for two reasons. Firstly, I recognised it was dishonest and manipulative, though I would have been hard pressed to explain exactly why. In any event, I had no idea what I should say to him. My mind had been so thoroughly poisoned I could only think of him as the cause of all our troubles. And, secondly, I felt absolutely intimidated by the mechanics of dialling the correct number, putting money into the box, waiting for the voice on the other end and then pressing the button marked A or B.

I had never used a public phone, and phoning South Africa in those days involved what was called a trunk call which meant speaking to the exchange and waiting for them to make the connection. Phoning the exchange meant looking up the directions in the directory and doing everything according to the instructions. A further complication was, I was very short for my age and could barely reach the instrument. I went into a complete panic. The sense of responsibility of finding, then following the instructions in the phone directory, doing everything in the correct sequence, while at the same time rehearsing what I would have to say overwhelmed me. The first time I tried a queue formed at the door as I wrestled with the directory, the money and the phone. I gave up, covered in shame.

I resisted doing what she wanted for days. Every afternoon when I got home from school she asked me to go and phone. I either made excuses or came back half an hour later saying I had been unable to get through. After about a week of this, she insisted on coming with me to the callbox to make sure I did what I was told. When we got to the phone I had to confess that I couldn't remember the correct procedure. She wrenched the instrument from my hand and phoned the exchange. Then followed a long wait during which she told me again and again what I was to say.

Staring Memory in the Face

"Tell him how much you miss him. Tell him how much you want to go back to South Africa. Tell him .... Tell him ...."

I am in agonies that someone will want to use the phone while we are waiting. Eventually the connection is made.

The call was not a success. Apart from getting out a few banalities about being well and wanting to go back to South Africa, all of which sounded patently hypocritical to my ears, I had nothing to add and quickly dried up. My father sounded equally inadequate. We said goodbye with nothing resolved. I knew I had failed yet again. The lecture I got from Flora confirmed it.

"Why hadn't I said...."

The refrain went on and on.

⁓

1951 was famous for its pea soup fog. The whole of the north of England was shrouded in a yellow-grey blanket. The winter evenings settled down shortly after lunch when we were released from the boiled potatoes, dumplings, cabbage and gravy provided by the Ministry of Education. At home, I had the prospect of dripping on bread. I had a short walk from the bus stop to the top of our road where I usually dawdled at the news agency on the corner to have a quick and surreptitious read of the latest *Hotspur*, *Dandy* or *Beano* before going home. One afternoon, shortly after my accident, we were released earlier than usual from school. There had been a warning that the fog was going to be especially thick that day and people might get lost if they were caught out of doors. By the time I emerged from the news agency the winter evening had settled in, and with it the fog.

Visibility was down to a few yards. I crossed the road and was suddenly enveloped in a dense unmoving yellow-grey blanket. Within a few yards I lost all sense of direction. What should have been a straightforward half-mile walk turned into a nightmare. I couldn't recognise anything.

Newcastle-on-Tyne

There were no landmarks, virtually no light, no sound. Streetlights provided hardly any illumination.

Cautiously edging along, I could by this stage see no more than a foot in front of me. I felt my way along the edge of the pavement with my foot and was brought up short against a cold black stone wall. My outstretched hand encountered a wooden door. I felt for the handle and to my relief it swung open and I found myself inside a dimly lit church. I sat down in a pew, my head still swathed in bandages, shivering from the cold, cut off from the rest of the world. There was nothing for it. I would have to stay there until the fog lifted.

A single light flickered on the altar. Above, a ghostly cross cast a dim shadow. The silence sang in my ears. I was cold and bored. I tried reading pew leaflets, the Book of Common Prayer, the Hymnal. Anything to help the time pass, but it was too dark and my eyes were sore. I curled up and tried to sleep, a prayer cushion for a pillow. My head throbs. I am cold. I begin to pray.

"Dear God, keep me warm and help me to get home. Help me to be clever and do well at school and not disappoint Mum. Make her happy. Stop her fighting with everyone. Don't let us be poor. Let me have my own bed. Heal my head. Don't let us be poor. Don't let us be poor. Let someone find me here before I freeze to death. I promise to work hard and be good and not forget to clean up Ranger's turds every day."

If ever there was a time for Divine intervention, for some sort of revelation, it is now, but nothing happens. The darkness deepens. It gets colder. I get up and move about to keep warm. Then lie down again, hoping to help the passing of time.

"Hey, boy. What are you doing here?" A hand shakes me out of the dark. I sit up rubbing my eyes. "I was lost in the fog, sir, and couldn't find my way home."

A man in a long black dress looks down at me. "Aren't we all?" he mutters. "What's your name boy? Where do you live?"

Staring Memory in the Face

"Well, you can't go home now in this pea-souper. You had better stay with me until it clears. Come into the vestry and have a cup of tea and something to eat. What happened to your head?"

He sat me down next to the gas fire with a cup of tea and a thick jam sandwich and began to question me about my family and school. I don't have a Geordie accent and he's intrigued. And it all comes out. South Africa, my father, Flora, Eric, Ranger and the crack on my head. My first confession.

It would be tempting to imagine I received some spiritual solace. Perhaps I did. Whatever it was I don't remember. I felt no less muddled than before and I retreated more and more into a world of fantasy, to my island, where the world could not intrude.

For Sartre hell was other people, for others an absence, an inner emptiness.

> *Faust: How comes it then that thou art out of hell?*
>
> *Mephistophilis: Why this is hell, nor am I out of it;*
> *Think'st thou that I who saw the face of God,*
> *And tasted the eternal joys of heaven,*
> *Am not tormented with ten thousand hells,*
> *In being deprived of everlasting bliss?*[14]

Eventually, the fog lifted enough for me to find my way home. I left the church and the black cassocked figure standing beneath the arched doorway and disappeared into the choking mist. It was obvious when I got home I had hardly been missed. A cup of tea and a slice of bread and dripping were waiting for me.

---

14. Christopher Marlowe: *Doctor Faustus*.

~ 7 ~
All the fun of the fair

Somehow Flora managed to get the money together for our return tickets to South Africa, and so in the autumn of 1951 the two of us and Ranger boarded the *Lanstephan Castle* bound for Cape Town. I remember little of the trip except that this time there was no Eric; and less of the train journey to Johannesburg after we landed. Our first base in Johannesburg was the Elgin Hotel opposite the Union Grounds and the Drill Hall where the Treason Trial would be held within a few years. The hotel occupied the site that would become Shell House and the headquarters of the ANC forty years later, scene of a bloody clash between Mandela's supporters and the Inkata Freedom Party. Times were much more peaceful when we lived there. The country was still to go through its second election since the Nationalist Party came to power in 1948, and the screws of Apartheid were yet to be tightened.

I spent my time making friends with the black waiters and hall porters, helping them carry bags and wash up glasses. They were always kind and gentle, speaking in English whenever I was around so that I did not feel excluded. They were my only companions. They must have found it strange to have a small white boy underfoot listening to their gossip, hungry for companionship. Much later in life, when '*uBuntu*' became a popular watchword, I understood how important it is to recognise and affirm other people. Desmond Tutu described such inclusiveness as: *"our humanness, caring, hospitality, our sense of connectedness, our sense that my humanity is bound up with your humanity."* [15] Albeit unconsciously, but through lived demonstration, I think important seeds were sown which were destined to sustain me and give me a sense of purpose as I began to mature and become aware of other lives. They were destined to bear fruit when,

---

15. Desmond Tutu.

many years later, I became a teacher. *"My humanity is bound up with your humanity."[16]* I was never an ideologue.

Survival is about more than just surviving if it is to have any meaning. It is also about affirming life, which must necessarily mean affirming the lives of others. One cannot do that if one does not have an enthusiasm for living.

The beginnings of a new pattern were established while we lived at the Elgin. Flora spent much of her time in bed living on endless cups of tea. I lived downstairs with the black staff, and ate in the dining room.

Ranger joined us from the kennels where he had been quarantined and the three of us moved into a room in a Hillbrow boarding house, where Flora and I shared a double bed. It was all we could afford. Flora had not managed to get a job. The fear of having no money was never absent. We ate in the boarding house dining room, or at least I did, where I had to endure the shame of knowing that we were not paying our way. We cadged leftovers from the kitchen for Ranger. We fell behind on the rent. At about this time Flora admitted to me that she had made contact with Tommy, and that she had been able to get a few pounds from him.

One evening she went out without saying, as usual, where she was going. Ranger and I waited until late and then fell asleep. At about three in the morning there was a banging on our door. I heard a female voice calling, "Michael. Michael. Open the door. Open the door."

Ranger growled and I buried myself deeper in the bedclothes. The voice didn't stop. I lay in the dark terrified. My only protection, Ranger. Finally, when it became obvious that whoever it was wouldn't go away, I plucked up courage and opened the door on the chain. It was a dark night and the lights on the landing had long ceased to function. I could barely make out the figure of a woman in the passage.

"Michael, you must let me in. Your mother and father have been in a terrible accident. My name is Barbara and I've come to take you and Ranger to stay with me until they come out of hospital."

---

16. Ibid.

All the fun of the fair

The fact that she knew Ranger's name and he had ceased to growl encouraged me. I opened the door. She fumbled for the light as she entered the room. In the naked glare of the electric globe the scene that confronted her was an unmade double bed, a couple of suitcases, one small boy and one large Alsatian dog. She sat down on the edge of the bed and repeated what she had said through the door. It was three o'clock in the morning.

"Are these all your things?" she asked glancing round at our few possessions. A dumb nod from me and she rose to her feet and began packing everything into the suitcases. By this time, the owner of the boarding house had been alerted, and he and a few of the other guests arrived at the door to find out what was going on. More explanations and the promise of money to pay outstanding bills in the morning, and I found myself in a car being driven through the silent wintry streets of Johannesburg. During all this time, I had said hardly a word, simply accepting events as they unfolded. I regarded Barbara silently. She was then in her mid-thirties with shoulder length brown hair and would have been considered attractive, but to my twelve-year-old eyes was just another inexplicable adult; beings whose actions I had long ceased to wonder at.

In the morning, she told me that her husband, my parents, and another couple, Jimmy and Molly Westerby, had all been involved in an accident while driving out to a smallholding my father owned south of Johannesburg. What I later pieced together, when I began to understand the ways of the adult world a little better, was that the five of them had met in a hotel downtown where they had had quite a lot to drink. Whoever was driving lost control of the car on a sharp bend south of the city. It skidded and rolled into a donga. They were lucky to get out alive.

Barbara's home, as luck would have it, contained extensive kennels for about 30 or 40 dogs. I stayed with her for a couple of months until Flora came out of hospital. In desperation Flora flung herself onto the tender mercies of the South African Red Cross and was employed as a clerical worker. This was followed by a chaotic period when she was in and out of Tara Mental Hospital and a variety of jobs. I was parcelled off to live with various people she was friendly with and who took pity on me when it became obvious she could not cope. I seldom knew from one week or month to the next where I would be living, or with whom. Life became a blur of different people and different houses.

For some months, I stayed with Gulu and Tony Bradshaw. Gulu was then in her late twenties. Flora and she had become friends when she worked at the Red Cross. Gulu and Tony volunteered to look after me while Flora was in Tara. Periodically thereafter, whenever Flora had a breakdown and ended up in Tara or the like, I would go and stay with the Bradshaws. On one of these occasions they moved into a house in Auckland Park. For the first time, I had the luxury of my own room. Gulu was very tender towards me. She and Tony had been married for about five years without having children and I think she found in me some sort of substitute for her own lack. Tony was an alcoholic given to bouts of drunkenness when he would disappear for days on end. He too was a war casualty and was finding the peace difficult to survive. It was rather like Cape Town with my parents. The more things change ... .

I was by this time a voracious reader, but the only reading matter in the house except "*True Life Detective*" and "*Archie*" comics was a 1936 edition of the *Encyclopaedia Britannica*. I am nothing if not systematic. I started with Volume 1 and worked my way through to Volume 24. I seem to have spent quite a lot of my childhood reading various out of date editions of the *Encyclopaedia Britannica*. Whatever my academic limitations, I was rapidly developing an extensive general knowledge. My mind was packed with a mass of unsystematic information: history, geography, science, literature and art. Unfortunately, not much of it had any relevance to the school curriculum. But my reading did spark an interest in current affairs and I read the newspapers every day I could get hold of them.

If popular literature is popular because it reflects the attitudes and values of the day, "*Archie*" certainly struck a chord with me as it reflected the stable values of middle America in the 1950s. The idea of what I thought was a normal family life modelled on *William* and *Archie* was to

All the fun of the fair

remain in the realm of fantasy for many years. It took a long time before I understood there is no such thing as a normal family.

Just up the road from their house in Auckland Park there was an open piece of ground, which Pagel's Circus and Fun Fair used once a year. When Pagel's arrived that year, Tony gave me a couple of shillings and I set off to enjoy all the fun of the fair. I soon discovered a side of South Africa's life I had only been half aware of until then. Dr Verwoerd was in charge and the philosophical justification for Apartheid, along with the legislation to support it, was being put in place. Brutal behaviour was being rationalised and given quasi-respectability.

Pagel's Circus poster.

Staring Memory in the Face

The fair had a side that was not fun at all … .

The posters in the window of the Greek café announced the imminent arrival of Pagel's Fun Fair. Gaudy pictures recalled last year's visit: dive bombers, games of chance, shooting galleries, coconut shies, the giant Ferris wheel rising above the dorp, nearly as high as the church clock, a great circle of turning lights. Entertainment for the Whole Family. All the Fun of the Fair. Real Gypsy Lady Reads Your Palm Tells Your Fortune.

It was not without some disapproval that the chairman of the school committee learnt that one of the teachers had asked her class to illustrate in colour, poems about swings and roundabouts instead of, as the work programme demanded, detailing the causes, costs and damage of the drought. Dominee Prinsloo was appeased only when he was assured that Mev. Venter's class would be saying a special prayer for rain at Assembly, and would make good the time it had wasted and catch up the outstanding work. Life, said Dominee Prinsloo, is a serious business, the Almighty watches over everything, and it is important that children should be moulded from an early age in the right way. Within the dorp though, it was generally accepted that Pagel's Fun Fair would be a welcome relief and distraction from the monotony of the drought.

He, at fourteen, five foot eight, awkward and growing out of his strength, was as excited as the other boys and girls in his class. He and his friend Chris Jan and Chris Jan's sister Maria had gone to the fair together the previous year. They had been entranced by the bright lights, loud music, swirling colours, dodgem cars, the daring acts performed by the trapeze artistes (and equally daring costumes against which Dominee Prinsloo had many hard things to say) and the wonderful prizes that could be won by pitching horse shoes, flinging wooden balls, shooting and throwing darts. Each prize, to his wonderment, loot from Ali Baba's cave. Chris Jan had won a china plate with a picture on it of the Battle of Blood River.

The Sunday before the fair arrived in the dorp, Dominee Prinsloo preached a long and strong sermon on the evils of fortune telling and games of chance. Such temptations Dominee Prinsloo thundered, distracted the unwary, filling their minds with sinful thoughts. The faithful would not be led astray if they directed themselves to continual prayer, seeking forgiveness from the Almighty so that His punishment, which weighed so heavily on the district and bore everyone to the ground with its burden, the drought, might be lifted from them. Only through obedience to His Will could the

All the fun of the fair

drought be broken. Desolation was being visited upon the land because the faithful had faltered and embraced foreign ways. The volk had lost its way and was now being punished for not following the Almighty. Had not His prophet said.

> *The great day of the Lord is near;*
> *near and hastening fast*
> *And He will stretch out His hand*
> *and make a desolation*
> *A dry waste like the desert.*

Every afternoon great billowing clouds built up in the south east only to turn out a false promise. Sometimes there were faint flashes of lightning and the distant sound of thunder. In the meantime, the boreholes dried up, sucking air from the bowels of the earth; the dams merely craquelured mud flats over which dust devils whirled haphazardly.

On the day the fair arrived, he and Chris Jan arranged to slip away after supper. During the afternoon as he went about his domestic chores, (they had no servant, only an ironing girl who came on Mondays) he saw huge columns of cumulus lifting themselves thousands of feet into the heavens and wondered, half apprehensively, if the dominee's prayers were about to be answered.

During supper that evening, he watched the sky anxiously, wondering would it would rain; would he be allowed out; would it be as good as last year? The air was still, hot and oppressive. All the windows in the little corrugated iron house were open to catch the slightest breeze. The smell of stung grapes on the voorstoep hung heavy in the air.

It couldn't be put off any longer. He must ask. Choose his moment carefully. When he had raised the question a few days earlier he had not managed to get a definite answer. Chris Jan would be waiting. His father was unpredictable, alternatively authoritarian, generous, judgemental and teasing. His mother was more sympathetic. A lot depended on how long his father had spent at the Railway Hotel before coming home from work.

With thoughtful deliberation, his father drank the last of his coffee, dabbed his lips with his napkin, carefully folded it, stretching out the silence. He sighed, looked at the ceiling, fingered his moustache.

Staring Memory in the Face

Had he done his homework? Chopped the firewood? Fed the chickens? Put the bathwater on the vegetables? Tidied his room? Polished his shoes? Once he had dried the last cup and put the last knife away, his father kept him to hear his catechism and times tables. As the soft light of evening faded, the boy saw his chances of escaping to the fair fading with it.

Eventually, his mother said: "Let the child go. He's done his work."

"Have you any money?" His father asked unexpectedly.

"No, pa."

Well, here's two shillings. Mind how you spend it. And be home by nine. Don't get caught in the rain," he added as he looked outside at the darkening sky. "It looks as if the Almighty is about to answer our prayers."

The boy fled, fearful that Chris Jan would not be waiting for him. As he approached his friend's house, he saw Maria swinging on the gate, singing softly to herself. Her dark hair curled in the nape of her neck. She hung on the gate; her body arched; her face lifted to the sky.

"Chris Jan said to tell you he can't come out tonight." Swinging backwards and forwards, the hinges squeaking.

"Oh," he responded; inadequate in the presence of squeaking hinges.

Are you still going then?" She asked, not looking at him, one hand running through her hair.

"Yes. I'd better be going, or it'll be over."

The church clock chimed six. He turned away and called impulsively over his shoulder:

I'll bring you a prize from the coconut shy."

Overhead the sky continued to threaten, mutter and flicker. The moon passed behind the clouds.

"Don't get caught in the rain," she called after him; her voice lost in a low rumble of thunder.

When he got to the fairground he stood for a moment on the edge of the light and bustle, undecided. The air was thick with dust and distorted music blaring from loudspeakers on poles high above the heads of the crowd. Merry-go-rounds whirled girls high into the air, their legs and petticoats flashing into the dark. Touts advertised tombola, target shooting, the horrors of the ghost tunnel and a fabulous woman with two

All the fun of the fair

heads. Young men and women, their faces flushed with delight and fear hurtled passed him overhead clinging to chains holding their hectic swings aloft, arching over the crowd. The air was redolent with the smell of braaiing wors. The Ferris wheels rose majestic. Men threw darts, fired rifles, swaggered, won prizes which they presented heroically to the girls on their arms, flexed muscles, drank beer. Here and there a scuffle broke out. Two policemen moved good humouredly through the crowd, watchful, their biceps bared. Behind them at a proper distance a black constable followed in their footsteps.

Swept along with the crowd, the boy found a hotdog stand presided over by a huge Zulu with sombre eyes, sweating over footlong pieces of wors on a sizzling stove.

"Nes 'n bob, my basie. Mustard of tamatie sous?"

Clutching his hotdog and remaining shilling, he drifts with the crowd. Out of the night a banner proclaims: COCONUT SHY. SIX BALLS FOR A SHILLING. FABULOUS PRIZES. A crowd jostles around the stall. He has to wait while three men finish their turn. Their girls look on, faces flushed, self-conscious and proud. The crowd catches their excitement and shouts encouragement each time the target is hit.

"Mooi skoot ... Lekker ... Useless ... Amper ... Vrystaat! ...

It is sometime before he has a clear view of what is happening. A red and white target is painted on the canvas wall at the back of the stall. A coconut is fixed to the bull's eye. Smoke from the hotdog stand and flickering lights make his eyes smart. The coconut at the centre of the bull wobbles unsteadily, as if it is going to fall each time it is hit, but miraculously stays in position. As his eyes become accustom to the light the boy realises that what he took for a coconut at the centre of the target, is a man's head facing the crowd through a hole in the canvas wall. A thick pad is attached to the crown of his head to protect him from injury. Occasionally, to begin with, but with increasing frequency he misjudges the speed and direction of the wooden balls flung at him, and is hit in the face. The crowd cheers each time he is hit. And, with each succeeding hit, the target responds with:

"Mooi skoot ... More ... More ... Slaan hom my baas ... Hier ... Hier ... ," a hand waving from the canvas, pointing at the bulls eye.

Wooden balls rain down indiscriminately as the competitors abandon all restraint. The weaving head becomes more and more confused, dazed and less capable of avoiding the missiles. When the ammunition runs out there is a pause as the stunned

Staring Memory in the Face

face surveys the crowd through a blear of blood and bruise, beaten, inarticulate sounds issuing from his split lips and broken teeth.

"Your turn now sonny. A bob for six balls. I tell you," the owner of the stall says, turning to an onlooker, "this is the best idea I've had in years. You alright, Phineas? Six balls for a bob. You wanna throw next? The money I've made tonight. And, have the people enjoyed themselves?

His great belly and jovial face loom over the boy for a moment, blocking out the sight behind him.

"Fabulous prizes. Want to win a pearl necklace for your girlfriend?" Transparent paste beads cascade from one fleshy hand to the other, catching the fairground lights.

"Fabulous prizes"

Getting no response, the owner of the stall turns to find someone else eager to prove his prowess. A young man with a girl on each arm pushes forward, sweating, laughing.

"Comon Bobbie, show us what you can do."

"Later babe. Here, hold this." He passes her a half full bottle. "Right now, I'm going to throw the shit out of that bull's eye over there."

Staggering, he disentangles himself and goes through the motions of taking aim.

"Ready, Phineas?"

Later that night, I discovered him sitting bloody, bowed and beaten on a pile of circus equipment behind the stall. He stank of beer and vomit. He may or may not have been drunk, but there was no doubting the humiliation and physical pain. I stood next to him, helpless. Through his tears and anger he appealed to me to do something, anything. It was one of those situations, that cry out for justice but the means to hand are pitiful. I gave him the remaining shilling in my sweaty palm and promised to tell the police. Of course, I didn't. I made some sort of pretence to myself and slunk off home to nurse my conscience.

The episode in the fairground was the second memorable one in my growing political consciousness. The first at the Elgin had been benign, born out of kindness and tolerance. The second awoke in me a sense of injustice and of the cruelty that is the fate of all those who lack the means to defend themselves.

All the fun of the fair

There would be many more incidents, some dramatic, most barely noticeable that would gradually shape my understanding. The important point though, is that my political consciousness was never shaped by ideology, but in response to the human condition. I was never qualified to be a politician, and consequently always felt uncomfortable with those whom I met in later life whose beliefs rested on ideology.

~ 8 ~

The Rendezvous

Immediately after Flora came out of hospital she and I moved to my father's smallholding, just outside Johannesburg. The plot, about ten acres in extent, was mid-way down a two-mile red-dust road in Walkerville, between Johannesburg and Vereeniging. The railway bus dropped us off on the main road and we had to walk the two miles carrying all our possessions in three suitcases. The road, which became little more than a track after a mile or so, seemed interminable as we struggled along in the midday sun, sweaty and dusty.

Apart from the remains of a few bedraggled peach and apricot trees and a fig tree that shaded a cool room at the kitchen door the only other plants were black-jacks and khaki weed. The house was unfinished; no electricity or running water: the privy, outside, at the end of a path, hidden behind a tall stand of weeds. My father was breeding rabbits in the attic, which he hoped to sell to the restaurant trade. The house stank of rabbit pee. I had the job of feeding them and making sure they had water. For the rest, the rabbits were meant to get on with it and produce offspring that could be slaughtered and sold. During the two months we were there none of them, uncharacteristically, managed to produce a litter and several died, making the whole enterprise economically unviable.

The situation was made all the more untenable by my father moving Molly (the woman with whom he was currently having an affair) into his bedroom from whence issue nightly drunken thumpings and bumpings, cursing and shouting and the sound of breaking glass. Flora and I lay in bed in the living room listening and whispering to each other, not daring to stir. Every morning Flora walked down to the main road and caught the railway bus into Johannesburg to go to work. I spent the day bored out of my mind, tiptoeing around not to waken my father and Molly from their drunken slumbers.

The Rendezvous

In desperation, I made friends with an Afrikaans family who lived a half a mile or so away. They made a living by selling fruit, vegetables and preserves at the bus stop on the main road. Their twenty-year-old daughter ran the stall. She encouraged me to keep her company. I expect she was frantic for any kind of human contact, even from a twelve-year-old, as trade was desperately slow and there was little traffic on the road. When we had exhausted our conversation, she read a Hornblower novel. I was allowed to read over her shoulder. She had only one book, so we shared until she discovered the romantic interest, which she felt I was too young to read. I tried every argument I could muster to get her to let me read with her, but to no avail. The burden of boredom was more than I could bear. I resorted to standing behind her where she could not see how close I was and read from a distance straining my eyes, gradually edging closer and closer until she became aware of what I was doing. She banned me from standing behind her. I retreated and the manoeuvre started all over again. This went on for days until we finished the novel. I don't remember any particularly salacious scenes, but I was hooked on Hornblower and sagas of the Royal Navy. The Napoleonic Wars were a relief from rabbit pee and nightly drunken squabbles.

It became obvious that I would have to go to school. By this time, I had not been to school for about eight or nine months. We tried King Edwards Primary first. They put me through the obligatory entry test, which successfully excluded me. The next attempt was Marist Brothers in Koch Street. School fees were £5 a term. I was accepted, the brothers were more interested in our ability to pay what even in those days was a token fee, rather than in my intellectual limitations. School necessitated moving closer to town.

Flora and I moved into a one-bedroom furnished cottage at what in Afrikaans is known as a *"vakanstewund"*[17], called *The Rendezvous*. The owner ran a tea garden and provided a swimming pool, both of which were much frequented by people from the city over weekends. In the dull days of the Fifties it was one of the few places to provide entertain-

---

17. A holiday resort.

ment over a weekend outside of Johannesburg. It was still the era when people went for a Sunday drive into the country. The novelty of the motorcar had not entirely worn off. Nor were people obsessed by what they ate. Large quantities of tea and cake were consumed by overweight, under-exercised adults, reclining in the sun, trying to ignore the tedium of their lives, waiting for their first coronary. *The Rendezvous* provided a modicum of relief.

In many parts of the country Sunday swimming was not allowed, as it would divert the faithful from the proper business of the Sabbath. The dead hand of the Dutch Reformed Church lay heavily on every impulse to frivolity and pleasure, though the profit motive, to say nothing of ordinary human ingenuity and cussedness, often found a way around the restrictions it placed on social behaviour including, of course, the Immorality Act which forbade sex between blacks and whites.

The Rendezvous also had a number of cottages for rent. For the first time in four years I was in an environment where I could simply be. We were out in the country and I had plenty of space in which to roam and to explore. And, there were even horses to ride. I quickly made friends with the children on the area. We had wonderful times exploring the koppies, and playing in the ruins of an old fort build by the British during the Boer War to guard the approaches to Johannesburg.

One of my friends has a pellet gun. We are forbidden to shoot birds, but as small boys will, soon forget once we are out in the veld. As I line up a mossie sitting on a strand of barbed wire in the sights, I have a sense I am about to do something irrevocable. A wave of excitement overwhelms my scruples. I pull the trigger and am surprised to see the bird fall to the ground. Suddenly the world is different. Far from any sense of triumph, I feel empty. I've done something irredeemable and am winded. There's no turning back. Much as I try to rationalise it, it was only a mossie after all, I cannot escape from the realisation that my wilful act has changed the world, and not for the better. Questions are raised that were too big, too complex for me to understand. Vaguely, I recall something about sparrows in the Bible. I tell no one about my qualms.

The Rendezvous

There is no one to tell. My playmates would not understand. As for the adult world, hadn't I been told …?

The weekends at *The Rendezvous* are spent in the swimming pool or playing in the koppies. Nearby there is a deep water filled donga overhung by tall poplar trees. We built a *"fuffie"* slide from one side of the donga to the other. A strong wire was tied to the top of a tree and anchored into the ground some distance away. A great thrill is to plunge into the water as we hurtle down the wire holding onto a piece of greased piping though which the wire runs. There must have been about a dozen of us youngsters all of an age, black and white. On Sunday afternoons to relieve the tedium we divided ourselves into two gangs and had *"kleilat"* fights in and around the donga, which provided a ready source of ammunition. Long, thin and flexible poplars grew on the bank and were ideal for attaching a lump of clay at the thin end, which could then be flung by swinging it back over your head and then whipping it forward. With practice, one could become quite accurate. As tempers inevitably frayed (a lump of clay can cause a significant bruise) stones were embedded into the clay to make it deadlier. It is a wonder no one lost an eye. As it was, we often ended the day bleeding and bruised, limping home covered in mud. Although the air would be rich with recriminations and accusations of unfair fighting, I don't recall ever hearing anyone being singled out because of their colour. Ideology hadn't entered our account of the world. We were much more rooted in the elemental world of clay and stone.

"Kleilat" fights disappeared from my consciousness only to resurface forty years later, shortly after South Africa's first democratic elections in 1994, at a change-management workshop in the right-wing stronghold of Potchefstroom. Like so many South African stories, it is shot through with irony. I was listening to a recently enfranchised coloured Nationalist Party town councillor describe how, when he was a child his family had been forcibly removed from their home in the centre of town to a newly created township on the outskirts several kilometres away.

"My parents were very bitter about being uprooted and carted away and just dumped in the veld. After all, my family had occupied our house in town since my grandfather's time. More than fifty years ago. We owned it. It was ours. But there was nothing we could do. The authorities came with armed police and loaded all our possessions into a truck and just took us away and dumped us in the veld. But there was one good thing for us kids. The place we were moved to was next to a beautiful river and we just loved to play in it all day long. The only thing was, the white kids who used to live in that area claimed the river as their territory and they tried to stop us playing there. They would come out of town every Saturday morning and the two gangs of kids, black and white, would have a *"kleilat"* fight. I tell you, it was war."

A middle-aged white man sitting next to me had been getting more and more agitated as he told his story. Finally, he couldn't stand it any longer and leaped to his feet: "*Ek was een van daai laaities!*" ("I was one of those guys") And the whole room, black, white, coloured and Indian, exploded into laughter. We had come a long way.

∽

During the week, I travelled into school every day by bus with enough money for my bus fare into town, a ham sandwich that I bought on the way and the tram from the city hall and back. Much of my Standard Four year (1952) was spent in this fashion.

It was while we were staying at *The Rendezvous* that Flora began spending more and more time in bed. She had lost her job at the Red Cross, but got another as some sort of clerical worker. She spent nearly every weekend in bed, and with the passage of time was increasingly absent from work during the week, which she also spent in bed asleep. When she wasn't asleep she lay reading whodunits, drinking endless cups of tea and smoking.

This was to be the pattern for the next six years. I was left to my own devices. Money was left for me to buy groceries and I lived mainly on breakfast cereal, bacon and eggs, bread and jam and fruit. Sometimes I simply gorged myself on custard. Milk was delivered until the unpaid

The Rendezvous

bill became too big. Someone gave us a second-hand radio and I discovered *Tarzan, Superman* and *The Saint* on Springbok Radio, all worthy successors, in my view, to *Dick Barton*, but more important, excuses to avoid doing homework.

The residents in the other cottages gradually became aware that all was not well. One afternoon a group of women arrive at our front door. Flora had been in bed for several days and I had done nothing to keep the place tidy. Ashtrays were full to overflowing. Dirty cups and saucers were everywhere. The sink was full of unwashed dishes. The remains of inedible meals festered in unwashed pots and pans. The beds had not been made for days. Dirty clothes lay on the floor.

There was nothing I could do to keep them out. They swept past me in a gale of horrified female self-righteousness to discover Flora barely conscious in bed. While two of them tried to revive her, a third turned on me. "How long has she been like this? How could you let this place get into such a mess? Have you no respect? Don't you have any feelings for your mother?" This is one of the few questions I might have had an answer for. "Look at these dishes. They're disgusting. When last was this place cleaned?"

The litany went on and on. Though I did not know it, it was an intimation of things to come. A doctor was called (in those days doctors still made house calls) and while we waited they got stuck into cleaning up the mess. The doctor came and went. The women returned to their families, satisfied that they had done their duty, their recriminations still echoing in the now transformed cottage. Life goes on.

I sat and contemplated the clean and tidy cottage, and the now conscious tea-drinking, cigarette smoking figure in bed. I was trapped and helpless and I knew it. What was there to say? Nothing. This is how it is, and how it is going to be. I am alone. There is no one in whom I can confide. No one to whom I can turn. There was certainly no way I could talk to Flora about my fears, my deep sense of insecurity about money, my feelings of failure and lack of self-confidence. The closest we got was by playing endless games of Monopoly during which we fantasised about what we would do if we won the Rhodesian Sweepstake. I was desperately conscious we were poor. I was always aware that there wasn't enough money to pay the rent, or even the dairy account. She was earning £20 a month and I knew to the last penny how far it had to go.

But, there was more to it than worrying about money. My universe was becoming more complex. Growing self-consciousness made me more self-aware and I was beginning to ask questions of myself and my relations with other people. I once made the mistake – adolescence was beginning to bloom and acne to bud – of asking her: "Mum, am I handsome?"

She put down the whodunit she was reading and laughed.

That was enough. I do not remember her laughing very often. I did not press for an answer. Later that night some of the women, with whom I had no great reputation as a result of my inability to keep the cottage clean, dropped in and she told them what I had said. They all found it immensely amusing. I was covered in shame. Like all youngsters going through the first stirrings of adolescence I was confused and was desperate for reassurance. It was not the first time I was conscious of feeling betrayed.

I never broached a personal issue like that with her again.

~ 9 ~

"She phoned *The Star* with her last tickey"

Of course, this way of living could not be sustained. Flora lost her job again. Things were looking pretty desperate. We moved into town in April 1953, into a single room on the third floor of Boston Court on the corner of Plein and Nugget streets, just around the corner from the school. It was a gloomy concrete building that looked onto an equally gloomy building opposite and a vacant lot that served as a dump for local refuse. These were the days before Johannesburg's inner-city decay so the building was reasonably well maintained. But it was a soulless environment. It served the lowest end of the rent market. Down-at-heel flotsam and jetsam inhabited solitary rooms, emerging at intervals to buy bread and milk at the cafe across the road. They eked out their anonymous lives ignored by the rest of the city. As far as I was aware there were no other children in the building. Everyone seemed ground down, threadbare and worn out. Single rooms, each containing a washbasin, led off a central corridor. We had a room that overlooked the street and therefore a veranda. Rooms on the opposite side of the corridor were without a veranda, and therefore had a lower rent, looked onto the blank wall of the back of a warehouse. Bathrooms and lavatories were shared communally with the other residents on the same floor.

I have returned to these places. I went back to Boston Court to refresh my memory. It is now run down, disintegrating. The plumbing has collapsed and the electricity has been switched off. Never the most salubrious of addresses, it is now a decaying overcrowded slum, inhabited by refugees from the townships, Nigerian drug lords, prostitutes and hordes of snotty-nosed, hollow-eyed, emaciated and neglected children. The road outside is littered with refuse and overturned dustbins. Taxis are double-parked, blocking one side of the street, their radios on full blast in a cacophony of competing loudspeakers. At least, in my day, for all the air of depression, the building had been well looked after.

Staring Memory in the Face

To begin with, we had no furniture and I slept on an inflatable Lilo mattress on top of a trunk. Somehow, Flora managed to get some money out of Tommy and bought two second hand beds, a chest of drawers and a chair. Someone gave us a bookcase. My meagre collection of William books was my only possession. We joined the Johannesburg Public Library. I borrowed and returned our books every week, deciding for Flora what she should read. In this way, I managed to read most of the crime fiction on the shelves as well as a plethora of novels and short stories by H.E. Bates, Eric Linklater, Somerset Maugham, O. Henry, J.B. Priestly, G.K. Chesterton and, of course, C.S. Forester. These writers exhibited an ironic and pragmatic humanism with which my own embryonic understanding was in sympathy. The canvas was small enough for me to grasp and the stories followed a straightforward progression in which, even if the good did not always get their just rewards, the human spirit was vindicated in the end.

After several delays that winter, Flora managed to get a court order against my father for maintenance. It was, even for those days, a pitiful amount. I cycled down town on the last day of every month with an official letter which I presented at the maintenance department. The maintenance office was housed in the Johannesburg Magistrate's Court, a huge granite monolith built to impress the massive force of justice on all those unfortunate enough to pass through its portals.

My route took me through vast concrete canyons in the financial district down which the winter sun never penetrated and where frost lingered in the gutters well into mid-morning. Down Claim into Mooi, jumping the traffic lights at Bree Street, over Jeppe, right into Commissioner past The Empire, The Coliseum and His Majesty's, their billboards advertising the latest films ("*The Sound Barrier*" is into its record run) and into Fox to West Street where the courts occupy an entire block, and Marshall Square, the central police station, destined within a few years to become infamous for tales of torture and suspicious suicides. Number 44 Main Street, the headquarters of Anglo-American, is a short walk away. The cold is only equalled by the chilly indifference of the people inside

"She phoned The Star with her last tickey"

the centrally heated offices to the black beggars on the streets: derelicts swept up by the increasingly violent broom of Apartheid.

A queue of embittered and dispirited women and clinging snot-nosed children trails outside the waiting room door by the time I get there. Over the months I get to recognise quite a few of them. Thin desperate women, fitfully smoking, abandoned with four or five threadbare children, wrapped in their own misery and concern for their children, united in their bitterness about drunk, unemployed and irresponsible husbands. Occasionally, an elderly man or woman, an Oupa or Ouma, accompanies them. The men are always thin with their trousers hanging on their hips, their jackets threadbare. Unshaven. A felt hat over their eyes, as though they cannot dare to look at the world full on, a cigarette dangling from their lips. Silent. Their wives are big-bosomed and grim, with mouths that have never known softness. They and the younger women, the plaintiffs, engage in lengthy whispered conversations, interrupting the flow with a sigh and "*Oorja*" followed by a profound silence in which they contemplate the fecklessness of men and the desolation of their lives.

They show no interest in me and I have no desire to talk to them. I convince myself I am different from them; that they are of a world I am forced to be part of but with which I have nothing in common except our shared poverty. Poor whites clinging to the edges of survival, where even all the advantages Apartheid can afford them cannot lift them out of poverty. The overwhelming sense is that I will never escape poverty either; that I am equally doomed. I have nothing in common with these people or their children. I am not of their world. I also begin to realise gradually that poverty is a state of mind as much as anything else.

I stand for an hour or so in the freezing passage, my bare knees blue from the cold, shivering my way to the counter where an indifferent official who never looks at me takes the letter, glances at it and hands over an envelope containing a cheque. I feel humiliated. I know this is not how life should be lived. There are images everywhere proclaiming a different way of life, the South African white middle class dream on billboards, in magazines, newspapers; Springbok Radio jingles: 'living the life of Lifebuoy', 'Brylcreme a little dab i'll do ya, ya'll look so debonair'. Debonair. I've read dozens of novels set in rural middle-class England. I know there is more to life than simply surviving from one maintenance cheque to the next; of never having socks without holes or a decent jersey. The taste of poverty is bitter in my mouth.

Flora spent more and more time in bed living on sweet tea, reading detective novels, smoking. In the modern parlance, she must have been an anorexic. The word had yet to be invented. I often tried to get her to eat properly, but she seldom accepted more than a toasted cheese sandwich which I made by toasting the bread over the single bar heater in our room. She was in a state of deep depression that completely immobilised her. Sleep was her only refuge. And it was a refuge into which she retreated more and more with the help of drugs that knocked her out for anything up to twenty-four hours at a time. She managed to get a steady supply from a Chinese doctor who had his rooms just around the corner in Nugget Street. Rather than spend money on food, she relied on her supply of 'Nolludas' to keep hunger and consciousness at bay. The state of her degradation was most vividly illustrated to me one night when I woke up to discover her peeing in the washbasin next to my bed. The effort of going to the lavatory down the corridor was too much for her.

I can't recall ever eating what would ordinarily be called a proper cooked meal at home. Flora had no interest in food and assumed that it was enough that I should be provided with the basic necessities for breakfast, cornflakes, milk and sugar. Other than that, the only food kept in the room was bread and jam and custard. We had no means of keeping anything more elaborate, no fridge and not even a hotplate. Toast had to be made over the single bar heater. Whenever I was bored or preparing to settle down with a book, I made myself a large bowl of custard which I ladled into my mouth while turning the pages.

Every evening I took half a crown from Flora's purse and went across the road to the local Greek café, and had what passed for steak and egg for supper. It was a pretty rundown establishment that sold cigarettes and cold drinks over the counter. Newspapers, magazines and

"She phoned The Star with her last tickey"

dog-eared paperbacks were available from a stand at the door. The menu was limited to toasted sandwiches, steak and egg and a mix grill (which I couldn't afford), Coke, milkshakes, tea and coffee. I sat at the same table in the same corner next to the kitchen at the same time every evening. I longed to be able to afford something else. The steak was over-grilled and tough, the solitary egg, greasy, surrounded by a tired lettuce leaf and a slice of tomato. The meal was topped off with a thin slice of white bread with the merest suggestion of butter on it. Nick, the owner, got to know me as a regular and allowed me to read one of the westerns he had for sale, on condition that I return it to the stand when I had finished my meal. I got through a lot of Zane Greys. *Riders of the Purple Sage* was my favourite. Reading over my food was the only way I could prolong the meal and avoid going back to Boston Court.

I was deeply angry and afraid. Many was the time after, a session of Monopoly, we would discuss the future and how I would look after her when I grew up. Sitting on the edge of her bed, the board stacked with piles of notes, houses and hotels, Park Lane and Mayfair, Oxford Street and the Old Kent Road (*Go straight to jail. Do not pass go. Do not collect £100*) between us I could see my life stretching out before me, an endless vista punctuated by unrealisable fantasies and solitary meals in Greek cafes.

My anger surfaced one Saturday afternoon when I force her to walk something like four or five miles from the centre of town to visit friends for tea. I had it in my head that what she needed was exercise, and lured and bullied her under one pretext after another ("it's not far, we can save the bus fare by walking", "it's just around the corner", "only another block to go", "there are no buses so we will just have to walk to the next corner", "it's only a little further", "not far now") into walking the whole distance from Boston Court nearly to Turfontein, along Plein Street into Eloff and then down Eloff Street Extension.

It was a bleak journey, especially the latter half through the deserted semi-industrial area south of the city centre. She was in no condition to make such a journey on foot, nor did she have proper walking shoes. As I watched her struggle I realised I was enjoying seeing her hobble in her high heels and becoming exhausted. I was determined that she was going to walk the whole way. When we finally arrived, she was worn out. I had to endure criticism from the adults for what I forced her to do, but within me there was a bitter sense of satisfaction.

The headline opposite the leader page in *The Star* proclaimed: *"She phoned The Star with her last tickey"*. A heart-rending piece of human-interest journalism, designed to open Johannesburg's charitable pockets, recounted how Flora had fallen on hard times. Abandoned by her husband, unemployed and with a child to support she turned in desperation to *The Star* for help. It was a shrewd move. Tommy had been the chief sub-editor and there were a number of people on the paper, including the editor Horace Flather, who remembered him with some warmth.

Enough money was collected to pay our mounting debts, to buy some curtains and for me a winter jersey and a new pair of shoes. *The Star* offered her a job at a salary that made us feel rich. Monopoly took on a new impetus and we graduated to fantasising about the Irish Sweepstake. Things started to look up. The weekends were still a write off, but during the week she managed to stay off the pills enough to get through the day at the office.

~ 10 ~

School days, those Golden Rule days

In 1952 when I went there, Marist Brothers occupied a block on the corner of Koch and Claim streets over the railway line from Boston Court, not far from Joubert Park. The school resembled a Victorian prison, with the classrooms and school hall occupying two wings at right angles to each other on the perimeter. A high wall enclosed a tarmac playground opposite the classrooms. The Brothers sold the site in the Seventies and the Maristonian Hotel now occupies it, a fittingly ironic fate. What went on behind those walls could have been drawn from *Nicholas Nickelby*. What goes on behind them now would do a bordello proud.

The principal, Brother Richard, a grimly lean and handsome man, drifted spectre-like about the school, emerging like an avenging presence from the chapel on the first floor next to the Standard Four classroom looking as if he had just suffered the final privations of penance for sins unspeakable, determined to make any boy unfortunate enough to encounter him feel the full terror of his unshriven soul. His black cassock skimmed the concrete floor with a malicious hiss. A crucifix hung from his neck. He was never seen without his cane, which he held behind his back as he stooped forward in his unrelenting search for sinners. He terrified all of us. There was a school myth that he had been a sailor during the War and had been miraculously saved after his ship had been torpedoed. As the myth had it, he had entered the church in gratitude, but there were those apostate souls who had their doubts.

Brother Vidal was a much simpler proposition. Eighty if he was a day, bald headed and red faced, gnome like, he wasn't five foot tall. He looked like a caricature of Punch. He took us for gym. It was a grim affair which he drilled with a whistle clenched between his teeth and a cricket stump in one hand. Everything had to be done at the double. Anyone caught out of line or making a wrong move or talking was promptly belted with the stump. He abhorred idlers and schemers.

Staring Memory in the Face

There was plenty of interesting equipment in the gym: a horse, parallel bars and rings, but I never saw them used. We had to stand in straight lines and perform endless meaningless exercises in unison, moving mechanically to the blast of his whistle like Hitler Youth in those vast gymnastic displays in Nuremberg before the Second World War. Winter or summer it was bare feet, shorts and a vest. Gym was no one's favourite.

∼

A line of a dozen or so small boys, exercise books in their hands, stands at the front of the class waiting to have their work checked and signed off. The line moves slowly forward as each individual is interrogated, holds out his hand to be beaten by an eighteen-inch ruler that swings down from above his head, and returns to his desk, red faced, eyes awash with tears, rubbing his hands together to heal the pain. This is a ritual that takes place at least three times a day. No one escapes. Three cuts per mistake, on alternate hands.

Miss Kane, all of four foot eight, Irish, roughly square in shape with little beady black eyes. I was sure she was at least 110 years old, though she was probably in her late forties or early fifties. In any event, she was one of those ageless people who seem never to have been young. I don't recall ever hearing her laugh, and as for her smile, it was devoid of any warmth or humour; just a mechanical rearrangement of her features. She wore the same brown cardigan over the same brown blouse and a brown skirt every day. She made no compromises, not even with the spelling of her name.

To my twelve-year-old eyes she appeared immense. This impression was helped by her desk raised on a platform above the classroom floor. She sat for the most part behind her desk towering above us, rising only to write on the board. She seldom if ever descended into the class but issued decrees from on high, summoning us to stand next to the platform to learn our miserable fate. She even dealt out the daily beatings while seated. She must have hated children. She thrashed me every single day for the two years I was in her class. I'm convinced it's a world record,

School days, those Golden Rule days

and should be included in the *Guinness Book of Records*. (Teachers at Marist Brothers seemed to have a penchant for nominative determinism. I learned years later that their school at Inanda had a Mrs Baton on their staff with an equally fearsome reputation.)

Miss Kane's was a true reign of terror. For not only did she terrorise through violence (my experience was not unique) but she had her proxies who acted on her behalf, spying and reporting and playing their own little power games: who was in favour and who out; who received protection and who was fair game. Caning and public humiliation were the order of the day. William Golding's *The Lord of Flies* came as no surprise to me. The two years I was in her class provided my earliest lessons in the power of patronage and corruption. In many respects, the school as a whole and Miss Kane's class in particular was a model of what happens in a totalitarian state in which power is concentrated in the hands of a tyrant who rules by patronage and terror. It bred in me a cynical resistance to authority. Exactly the opposite it was meant to do. I bridle very quickly the moment I sense any abuse of power; something that has got me into trouble more than I care to admit. Whenever I have met anyone of my generation who endured and survived a Catholic education, it has not taken us long to discover we have a common bond.

There are 48 of us in her class. We are ranked according to our examination results four times a year. I start life in her class by coming 48th. I had not been at school for nearly eight or nine months since we left Newcastle-on-Tyne. By the end of my Standard Five year I had been terrified into coming 26th. Not a glorious career, but better than I had managed in England. Once I left her class and moved into secondary school I reverted gradually to my previous position. Never underestimate the motivating power of fear.

The top eight boys in the class monitored and policed the rest of us. We had two sets of exercise books for every subject, one of which we worked in while the other was being checked. Every exercise book was marked every second day. And reams of poetry learned off by heart: 'The Highwayman', 'If', 'The Daffodils', 'Sea Fever', 'Cargoes', 'The

Staring Memory in the Face

Lady of Shalott', 'Break, break, break', 'The Lake Isle of Innisfree', 'Vita Lampada', 'Drake's Drum'. The amount of work we got through was prodigious.

Miss Kane had the reputation of being the best teacher in the school. The only way to keep up the pressure and ensure the work was being done was to treat every lesson like a production line. Gradgrind would have been proud of her. We had arithmetic, spelling and dictation, reading and comprehension and one other subject, history, geography or nature study, for homework every day. Weekend homework also included a written composition. The only missing subject was Afrikaans, which she considered beneath her dignity to teach.

Ironically, it was at about this time the Nationalist government instituted its mother tongue language policy for education in government schools. The government was determined to use every means at its disposal to shore up Afrikaner hegemony and preserve its domination of the country. This was but one of the first moves it made to enforce its increasingly authoritarian rule. Control of education was central to their ideological struggle. What this meant in practice was that teams of school inspectors were sent out to interrogate children to find out if any Afrikaans speaking parents were sending their children to English medium schools. English medium schools were presumed to be less dominated by Afrikaner Nationalism. Because Marist was a private school (and what was worse Roman Catholic) it did not fall under the authority of the Education Department.

In another part of the city and unbeknown to me, the Fischer family with whom I would have much to do in the future, were facing choices that would change their lives. Bram and Molly Fischer deliberately sent their daughters, Ruth and Ilse, to Houghton Primary, an English medium school, although their home language was Afrikaans. They did so because they wished them to have a more liberal education than they would get at an Afrikaans medium school. In order to ensure that the inspectors would not discover that Ruth and Ilse were in fact Afrikaans-speaking they changed their home language, and the girls grew up, to all intents

School days, those Golden Rule days

and purposes, English-speaking. So, for very different reasons Ruth and I were denied access to a rich language and literature. We have both felt the loss: she by being cut off from her cultural heritage, I by my poor ability to communicate in Afrikaans.

Nor was the emphasis in Miss Kane's class simply on the quantity of work. Draconian rules were set in place to ensure neatness: no rubbing out, no crossing out, no invisible ink was allowed. Handwriting had to conform to the Marion Richards style (feint up and bold down), and this was in the era of dipping pens and blotting paper. The result was we became experts in subterfuge and could disguise almost any mistake. Some boys became so adept that the only way to find out whether they had changed anything was to hold the offending page up to the light and see if the paper had any thin spots where it might have been tampered with. Some of them became so good that they were able to exploit their skills, which they traded for extra sandwiches or sweets or even money. The entrepreneurial spirit starts early. Niche markets can be developed in the most unlikely circumstances.

And, of course, the monitors knew all the tricks as well. They examined our books every day to make sure we had not copied our homework, cheated in any way, rubbed out or crossed out mistakes or committed any criminal acts of untidiness, and recorded our marks in Miss Kane's mark ledger. Anyone contravening the rules had his name written in a book and just before break, lunch or home time (the three periods set aside for regular mass punishment) we would have to line up and be beaten with an eighteen-inch ruler, sharp or flat side depending on the seriousness of the crime ... .

Boys stand beside her desk mechanically offering alternate hands, not knowing when the beating will end, while she, a raging fury, wields the ruler from above her head.

"I…will…not…a…llow…this…sort…of…work…in…my…class."

The ruler descends on each syllable.

There were variations on this theme depending on the severity of the crime. I have an image of her to this day: a little grey-haired woman in brown sitting at her desk, the afternoon sun pouring in the window, flailing away at a line of boys drawn up in front of her, mechanically moving forward in turn like automata.

Beating was not just confined to those times. A spelling test was conducted every morning just after we had recited our times tables in unison up to 24 times 24. We corrected each other's work and punishment (three cuts for each spelling mistake) was meted out immediately. I still have a spelling problem. Whenever I am stressed and I have to write my spelling goes to bits. I never once managed to get full marks in the daily spelling test in two years. It did not matter how well Flora drilled me before school, I knew I would make at least one mistake; a self-fulfilling prophecy. I also developed calluses on my hands.

Of course, the system was open to corruption. Bribes, as are consistent with schoolboys' finances, were given and taken. Sandwiches, sweets, fruit and sometimes money changed hands. Scores were paid off, or alternatively, friends covered up for each other. But, the books had to be handed in and checked by the monitors who duly reported any inconsistencies. Some of them had friends who didn't qualify to become monitors but whom they tried to protect. And, of course, they protected themselves. Nor were the monitors immune from investigation. Once or twice a year Miss Kane would rouse herself and check on them. On one occasion, she discovered that they had been covering up for each other. Because they were the clever elite, their sins were not the sort we lesser mortals were usually guilty of, falsifying marks or changing answers. Theirs were lesser crimes such as rubbing out or using invisible ink to remove evidence of mistakes or inkblots. Nonetheless, they were arraigned, accused and made to confess their crimes in public before the rest of the class.

Show trials weren't in it. Stalin might have learned a thing or two. Twenty odd years later, I was destined to encounter a much more dangerous form of surveillance with much more devastating consequences.

School days, those Golden Rule days

We sit in stunned if satisfied silence. At last there seems to be some justice in the world after all. Many of us have been victims of the monitors' capriciousness. Miss Kane rants on and on like a vengeful goddess, betrayed by false prophets. They will roast in hell. They have committed a mortal sin from which there can be no escaping the worst punishments of hell. Their souls will be damned forever if they do not go immediately to confession. And, in order to make sure they spend several harrowing hours on their bare knees, she calls in Brother Richard and makes them confess again. He stands on the platform at the head of the class, his white face seeming to hover in space, the pulse in his jaw visible even from the back of the class, with his back to the blackboard, his crucifix gleaming against his raven cassock as he listens to the catalogue of tearful, burbled confessions. Through the snivelling he makes the point that no matter how clever they or we for that matter think we are, we will always be caught out in the end. There is no way of avoiding punishment for our sins.

"Do you know what it means not to be in a state of grace, boy?"

"Yes, brother."

"It means," he went on ignoring the response, "that if you die, you will go straight to hell and you'll lie in torment in the everlasting flames forever. Lies, deceit, cheating will lead you to the Devil. Can you imagine that?"

"No, brother."

"Don't give me lip, boy. I want to see you in confession at break."

One of the monitors was Neil McGurk. He was without doubt the cleverest in the class getting top marks for whatever he did. He is the only one of those whose fate I shared during those two years I ever met again in adult life. Neil came from a staunchly Roman Catholic family and entered the church as a novice as soon as he could. He had a brilliant school and university career and by the time he was ordained had two doctorates. He eventually became the principal of one of the first white private schools in Johannesburg, Sacred Heart, to confront the National Party on Apartheid in education. Long before the Apartheid laws started crumbling his school admitted black children. He was at the forefront of opposition in education to government policy and certainly showed more courage then, than he had when he was in Miss Kane's class – which suggests something about the terror she managed to inspire.

I met Neil several times during the mid-Eighties but I could never get him to talk about those years when he had been one of Miss Kane's monitors. Every time I brought up the subject he turned it aside, refusing to be drawn. I was deeply disappointed. There were many ghosts I wanted to lay to rest. I don't know what I expected, but I had hoped we could share our memories and that I at least might be able to see them in a different light.

Nor was it just Miss Kane. She was but one significant thread in the fabric. Was Neil still too traumatised? Was the pain of reliving those experiences even thirty odd years later too agonising? Perhaps he felt guilty about his own moral role; his complicity in what was a corrupt rule by terror. In many ways Miss Kane paralleled the way the Nationalist Party ruled the country, by patronising a small group who carried out her commands and intimidating the rest and ruling through fear. Perhaps the pressures from his family and the church had been too much. He was certainly regarded as the golden boy and shining example of how a Catholic should dedicate himself from an early age to his vocation. He had several uncles who had entered the church. So, the pressure was on him from every side. Miss Kane definitely knew what to expect from him.

Neil faced his devils. I faced mine, and as usual I escaped into fantasy.

The sea haunted my waking and sleeping. Images of surging waves charged with monstrous energy, restless, uncontrollable, limitless filled my imagination. Gazing out of the classroom window *I feel the deck roll beneath my feet as I stand on the bridge of a corvette in the middle of the Atlantic, a storm beginning to rise and the sound and sight of gun fire on the horizon. U Boats lurk in the dark and a convoy scatters under cover of night and the changing weather. The salt spray in my face, I cling to the rail and face mountainous seas. The corvette, a fragile vessel in the midst of tumult, a north Atlantic storm in the height of the war.* Miss Kane's voice drones on like the sound of an incoming dive bomber, berating some child for having used a rubber or a ballpoint pen. The

School days, those Golden Rule days

Battle of the Atlantic as it plays itself out in my imagination is a sweet relief. At night, I lie in bed drifting off to sleep, my hand at the tiller, *turning into the wind and waves, canvas flapping loud as the boat comes about. The weather is closing in. The swell begins to crest. Foam flies in the wind.* If only I could run away to sea. It was the last of these fantasies that brought me up sharp against the realities of the world in which running away to sea was no longer the easy option it had once been. Passport and immigration control were now at levels of sophistication Robert Louis Stevenson could never have imagined, to say nothing of the power of juvenile courts and social workers.

The news was full of Stalin's death. His death was the first international news story I can consciously recall. The press carried articles on his career and crimes, which I read avidly. A man as evil as Hitler, though to some, Uncle Joe. I thought the world would probably have been better off if Miss Kane and not he had died. But it was not to be. I still had six months of my sentence to serve.

One morning we troop into class, all of us, Catholics, a handful of Protestants and a single Jew, Zimmerman, dipping our fingers into the bowl of holy water at the door and dutifully crossing ourselves in the name of the Father, the Son and the Holy Ghost.

"*Holy Mary, Mother of God, pray for us sinners now and at the hour of our death. Amen*"

Brother Richard appears in front of the class. Some boys, we are told, have desecrated the chapel the previous afternoon, and as our classroom was next door to it they could only have come from our class. None of us is in a position to query this strange assumption, nor would we have dared if we had been. Flowers had been taken from a vase on the altar and scattered about the floor. The vase was broken and a pool of water had soaked into the carpet. The boy or boys responsible are told to stand and confess. There is no point in trying to hide their guilt as God knows who they are and he will reveal them for the scum they are if they did not have the guts to stand up and take their medicine. They have committed a mortal sin (we often heard of mortal sins) for which the punishment is eternal hell fire and damnation if they do not confess. We sit in silence, not moving an eyelid as Brother Richard patrols the rows between our desks looking for the least indication of guilt. Boys are interrogated at random. Where had they been at such and such an hour? How can they account for their movements? When last had they been in the chapel? They had been seen walking passed the chapel that afternoon, what had they been doing there? Miss Kane stands next to her desk her arms folded over her ample brown bosom, grimly watching for the slightest sign. Her beady black eyes glinting in the weak winter morning light. Every now and then I fancy I see her tongue flicker across her lips. I shiver. No one moves. I feel both hot and cold at the same time as Brother Richard approaches me from behind.

"You, boy, you're looking very guilty. Are you sure it wasn't you?" he barks at the back of my head. "Why are you blushing like that?" Ice-cold water drenches me.

He hauls me out of my desk by the scruff of my neck and deposits me in front of Miss Kane. I am mesmerised. My throat constricted. I am bright red with terror. Try as I might I can't get a sound out. My mouth opens and shuts, but no words come. What is worse, I know I'm guilty. I had not been anywhere near the chapel when the crime had been committed and had no knowledge of it until Brother Richard appeared that morning, but I know, and I know God knows, I am guilty. I hang my head and wait to be sentenced. Darkness at noon.

Fortunately, Brother Richard misunderstands my shame and tells me to return to my desk. I know I've been given a dreadful warning and the next time I avoid the bowl of Holy Water at the classroom door my miserable Protestant soul will not survive. It is enough to effect an almost instant conversion.

"Holy Mary, Mother of God, Blessed art thou among women and blessed is the fruit of thy womb, Jesus Christ." The fruit of thy womb?

I do not pause for a moment to consider what the words mean, or if in fact they mean anything. It is sufficient that I learn them as a recipe against further terror. The only boy who shows any sympathy when it

School days, those Golden Rule days

is safe to do so later during break, is Zimmerman, who understands the nature of my suffering, if not my guilt.

The end of my Standard Five year approached. This is the most important moment of our school lives we are informed, as we will be writing the exams that will see us move from primary to secondary school. On the Friday before the exams, Miss Kane issues a decree that no one is allowed to go swimming over the weekend, as she doesn't want any of us absent with colds during the during exam time. The following Monday morning just before we wrote our first exam she orders all those who had gone swimming over the weekend to stand. I rise trembling to my feet. Not a soul stirs around me.

"So, you disobeyed me," It is not a question.

I hang my head.

"Why?"

There is nothing I can say. There is no point in trying to excuse myself. I have admitted my guilt. Then follows the usual explosion of rage and questions that have no answer.

"Didn't I tell the class before you went home on Friday that you weren't allowed to go swimming this weekend? Why do you think I said that? Just to amuse myself?"

At that, try as I may, I can't stop myself from grinning like an idiot.

"Come here. I'll give you something to grin about."

This time, perhaps remembering that I will need to use my hand to write, she turns me over and gives me six cuts on my backside with the sharp edge of the eighteen-inch ruler. I return to my desk, sit down gingerly and wait for the first exam paper to be handed out. During all this time, the class has not uttered a sound or made a move. I know nothing of scapegoats, but I do know in some obscure way I have taken the punishment for just about everyone in the class that day.

∽

Staring Memory in the Face

Years later, when I thought I had learned a thing or two about educational theory and psychology, I decided to pay Miss Kane a visit and confront her with my newly acquired insights into what she had done to me during the two years I was in her class.

As I walked down Claim Street to the school, from the Johannesburg College of Education where I was a first year student, I rehearsed what I would say and how I would make her grovel and weep for forgiveness. By the time I got to the school I was panting for revenge. It was late in the afternoon when I knocked on her classroom door, the same classroom in which I had spent so many unhappy hours. Not a soul was around. I opened the door. The little bowl of Holy Water was still in its place. I had to catch myself from dipping my fingers in it and making the sign of the cross. *"Holy Mary, mother of God, pray for us sinners now ... ."* Miss Kane was still at her desk, still dressed in her uncompromising brown. She did not appear to have aged a day. She looked up from her work. I explained who I was. She remembered me.

"Yes, you had a very soft mother. She was always making excuses for you."

This was the first I had ever heard of it. As far as I could remember Flora had never interfered with what was going on at school. In fact, I had always known that school was a place where I could expect no help from anyone. I had to endure it alone.

I looked at her, rage burning in my soul and discovered a pathetic little woman. In a moment, all the built-up emotion in me evaporated and I realised the futility of saying anything. Somehow, when confronted with the opportunity of destroying her I couldn't do it. I left after five minutes feeling empty and frustrated, full of impotent rage. I decided to pay Miss Fairfax a visit. I hadn't thought about her for years, but as I was in the vicinity and was revisiting the past as it were, I thought it appropriate. She was still there.. Still serene and unblemished. She still had the capacity to make me feel whole and clean.

~ 11 ~

Miss Fairfax

Not everything about those years in the mid-Fifties at Marist Koch Street was utterly dire. The highlight of my day admittedly came after school, but if I had not been at that school I would not have had the opportunity, nor I suspect would it have meant as much to me if I had, of visiting the Joubert Park Art Gallery on my way home from school in the afternoon. It was there that I met Miss Fairfax. It is fitting that the Gallery which played such a formative role in my life, should also have provided my daughter Dammon with the opportunity to develop her interests in art and education many years later, and launched her on her career as a museum educationalist.

The gallery building is a very beautiful yellow sandstone structure designed by Sir Edwin Landseer Lutyens, architect to the Edwardian Raj, who was responsible for planning New Delhi. It is one of his gems, although much desecrated in recent years by additions and alterations which became necessary as the collection grew. Founded by one of the Rand Lords, Sir Lionel Philips, it houses a substantial collection of international and South African Art, including a number of fine Rembrandt etchings. It was there that I saw my first original van Gogh, a tiny scene of a Provencal orchard in blossom.

It was there, as I said, that I met Miss Fairfax. She provided me with my first conscious aesthetic experience and came to symbolise everything that beauty meant to me. Her bust carved in pure white marble stood on a plinth at the entrance to the main gallery just inside the front door. Remote, ethereal and exquisite, inviolable; self-contained, serene and pure in an aura of timeless silence. She took my breath away. She made no demands. She never passed judgment. She was always there. She soothed my soul. She never failed me. There was nothing smudged about her. Pure form in pure white flawless marble. Rodin at his most sensual. She has remained with me all my life.

Staring Memory in the Face

Miss Fairfax (Rodin)

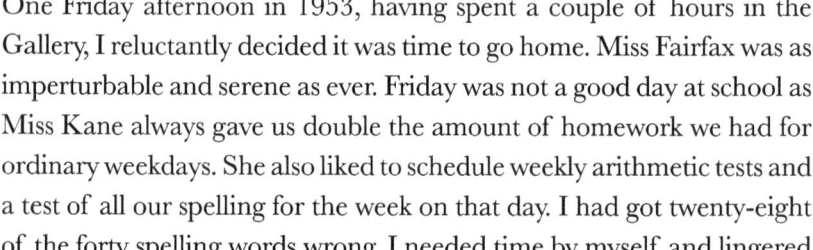

One Friday afternoon in 1953, having spent a couple of hours in the Gallery, I reluctantly decided it was time to go home. Miss Fairfax was as imperturbable and serene as ever. Friday was not a good day at school as Miss Kane always gave us double the amount of homework we had for ordinary weekdays. She also liked to schedule weekly arithmetic tests and a test of all our spelling for the week on that day. I had got twenty-eight of the forty spelling words wrong. I needed time by myself and lingered in the Gallery until closing time.

I knew I wiould not be missed because when I left for school in the morning Flora had not stirred even for her obligatory cup of tea, and I doubted she had come to consciousness during the day. I was now well versed in reading the signs. Occasionally, I'd find her pills lying next to the bed and I would flush them down the sink, thinking they deserved

Miss Fairfax

to be peed on. I knew all her hiding places and searched them regularly. My feelings were at best ambivalent. She was my mother. I loved her. But there was no escaping the fact that she was dragging us down. Something had to be done. But what? I had no idea.

When I got home she was, as I had anticipated, still unconscious. A cold half-drunk cup of tea stood on the floor beside the bed. Her false teeth sat in half a glass of water, a mute testimony. A far cry from Miss Fairfax. The smell of smouldering blanket permeated the air. I knew immediately what had happened. She had woken sometime during the day, lit a cigarette and made a cup of tea to wash down another dose and had fallen unconscious before she could stub out her fag. Fortunately, the blanket hadn't done anything more than smoulder. This sort of thing had happened several times and I had established a fairly efficient regime for dealing with it. First find the pills, then phone the doctor. I hunted around and found a container half full of pills hidden in the folds of the blankets. I then stripped the bed looking for more, and found another cache under the mattress.

I stood looking down at her not knowing whether to be angry or worried. She had done this so many times. It was routine. She lay on her back, her nightie half off her upper body. Her hair stuck to the sweat on her forehead. I looked dispassionately at her emaciated torso, her withered breasts, listened to her laboured breathing, half choking sounds coming from her throat every so often. Mucus dribbled from the side of her mouth. She had wet the bed.

I went downstairs to the public phone in the lobby and phoned the General Hospital for an ambulance. The casualty duty doctor was sympathetic when I explained what was wrong and he undertook to get an ambulance to us as soon as possible. Once he arrived, Flora was given a stomach pump, put on stretcher and taken off to the General Hospital. I then contemplated what needed to be done next. There was no way she would be well enough to go to work by Monday. I would have to phone *The Star* and tell them she was sick.

Staring Memory in the Face

I went to see her in hospital the following afternoon. I had spent the whole of the morning putting it off, trying to avoid doing what I must. She smiled at me wanly when I got to her bedside. It had been decided by a psychiatrist, she said, that she should be sent to a sanatorium in the Karoo near Three Sisters to recover. She was going down to the Karoo by train the following morning and I must look after myself in the meantime. She would not be away long. She had £17.7s.6d in her purse, which I must use for food while she was away.

Events were happening too rapidly for me to take them in properly. I had no idea where the Karoo is, much less Three Sisters. Whether the money would last long enough was not a thought that occurred. I was incapable of contacting any of the adults I knew who might be of assistance. I went home and made myself a large bowl of custard and wondered what to do. I woke up later that night shivering and climbed into bed.

The following morning, I walk to Park Station to see her off from Platform 13 on the 11.30 train. It is bitterly cold. Dressed only in a pair of rugby shorts and a thin shirt I can hardly stop my teeth chattering. The wind rushes through the streets and around corners in a swirl of leaves, grime and old newspapers. I am on my way to say good-bye, I don't know for how long.

In those days access to the platforms was via a bridge which extended from one side of the station to the other. Signs everywhere: Net Blankes/Europeans Only. I got to the stairway to Platform 13 and looked down. The ambulance had already arrived and was parked next to the train. As I watched from above the ambulance doors opened and Flora, now strapped into a stretcher was placed on the platform before being put into the train. I looked down. This was the moment when I should descend and say good-bye. She looked pitiful. I wasn't sure if she was conscious. I couldn't move. I must have stood there for five or ten minutes before I managed to rouse myself. With a shudder. At what? Her degradation and helplessness? My own lack of courage, compassion?

Miss Fairfax

The cold? I turned away and walked back to Boston Court, buffeted by the freezing winter wind.

I did not go to school the following week. I hardly stepped out of the room, not even getting dressed in the morning, but just lay in bed eating bowl after bowl of custard, reading one whodunit after another, and slept. I hardly gave Miss Kane a thought. School, Miss Kane, Brother Richard, the world outside for that matter, ceased to have any significance. The week passed. I spoke to no one. I saw no one. I sought my refuge in Agatha Christie and Dorothy Sayers.

On Saturday morning I was woken by Flora's voice. She stood in the dimly lit passageway in her nightie and a hospital dressing gown, clutching a brown paper bag. She told me, once I had made her a cup of tea and she had settled herself into bed, that she had managed to convince one of the nurses at the sanatorium to lend her some money to help her get back to Johannesburg. Addicts can be very manipulative. Even experienced hardened nurses are not immune.

We had a long session that night in which I pleaded with her to give up taking drugs. She said she would, but we had had this discussion too many times. I had flushed too many pills down the drain to have much faith in her word. With the right equipment, I could have given her a stomach pump myself and saved the doctor the trouble. She was at work the following Monday. I have no idea how she explained her absence or her sudden reappearance.

A dismal routine sets in. During the week it begins with a bowl of cornflakes followed by reluctant walk to school. Miss Kane occupies most of the day. There is a short respite in the late afternoon with Miss Fairfax. Half a crown for supper and a chapter of the current western consumed over cardboard-like steak, egg and a slice of bread. Homework, avoided for as long as possible. This is made easier because lately we have acquired a second-hand radio, an emblem of, ironically, our improved financial situation as a result of Flora's job at *The Star*. I've become addicted to fifteen-minute serials on Springbok Radio: *Tarzan of the Apes*, *Inspector West* and *The Saint* are my favourites. Anything, in fact, to postpone the awful moment when I will have to settle down to LCMs and HCFs, compound interest, the seventeen times table, twenty words to be learned for the following morning's spelling test, and a passage prepared for dictation. My self-pity blooms. I affect a limp like a character in *Oliver Twist*, a not very artful dodger, too timid to ask for more. The beginnings of what will become a dramatic white streak appear in my hair.

Weekends weigh heavily. Sometimes I am invited to spend the weekend with one of my classmates, Bennie Piel, but for the most part it means staying at home, reading, playing Monopoly, making tea and little else. There is no money for movies or any other entertainment.

Bennie lived on a farm outside Alberton, way beyond my cycling range. The weekends I spend with Bennie show me that what I had come to regard as a normal life exists outside of novels. His family was extremely wealthy and among other things trained racehorses. On one occasion, I was invited to spend a week of the July holidays with Bennie on his parents' bushveld farm adjoining the Kruger National Park. This truly was an adventure. They used the farm once a year during the hunting season. It was my introduction to the bushveld and it stimulated a love of the bush I have never lost. In those days there were no phones, no electricity, no tarred roads. We were as cut off from civilisation as it was possible to get. Once we left the tarred road north of Warmbaths, we had a journey of seven or eight hours over rough sand roads through miles and miles of mopani and thorn bush. Four by Fours did not exist and the deeply eroded tracks and dry river crossings had to be negotiated in the Piels' Nash.

Bennie's father shot a wildebeest. Bennie was allowed to shoot an impala and I shot a baboon, about which I had mixed feelings, which I kept well hidden. This was not a moment in which to appear squeamish or ungrateful for the privileges I was enjoying. One of the black trackers took me under his wing and began to teach me how to read the signs of

Miss Fairfax

the bush. How to recognise impala, bushbuck and baboon tracks. How to read an elephant's tracks, which way it was walking, whether the tracks were fresh or old. How to distinguish a hippo's tracks from a rhino's. I was thrilled by my first sighting of a lilac breasted roller; the glossy starlings with the bright orange eyes; the ubiquitous hornbills, looping from tree to tree. And, of course, the colours of the mopani trees, the knobthorn and baobab. We went out tracking every day and got back to camp in the evening exhausted and ravenous and full of stories.

Much as I enjoyed these weekends away from home, I never felt completely at ease. I was always aware that this world of wealth and privilege, to which I am periodically admitted, is not my world. I felt vaguely uneasy, always on the alert not to displease or disappoint. Sometimes I found myself in situations where I am forced to act against my instincts. There are no free lunches.

Saturday morning at the Alberton bioscope. A competition has been organised by the management for the interval at which prizes will be awarded for the most imaginatively decorated bicycle. Bennie has entered and his bike looks resplendent, profusely decorated with silver paper and old Xmas decorations. His mother is going to drive him into Alberton on the back of the farm bakkie so his bike could arrive unblemished. As these arrangements are being made, it suddenly occurs to someone that I am being left out of the fun and games. Bennie's sister has an old Humber; perhaps I could use it and enter the competition as well. My initial response is to shy away, but after a great deal of persuasion I allow myself to be cajoled into agreeing to be a late entry. All the decorations have been used up for Bennie's bike. A search reveals some scraps of coloured paper which are hastily wrapped round the frame of the Humber. The result is tattered and tawdry rather than festive. My heart sinks: it looks terrible, the pathetic attempt of some poverty-stricken kid. I know I am trapped. The more I try to resist, the more pressure is put on me not to be a spoilsport. I am under an obligation to people who have shown me great kindness and generosity. Had they not had me for weekends? Taken me to the bushveld? Allowed me to ride their horses? How could I disappoint them?

We line up in the wings. The other seven bikes are magnificent, festooned with baubles, stars and flashing lights, glittering under a canopy of silver and gold. One youngster has even gone so far as to turn her bike into a mobile South African flag. Pedalled patriotism on the platteland. There is only one word to describe mine, pathetic. A recorded fanfare is sounded. Drums roll. The competitors are announced to enthusiastic applause. Caught in a spotlight, they wheel their bikes out onto the darkened stage. I am last in line and have plenty of time to contemplate the next few minutes. My stomach churns. There is no escaping. My turn comes. I am caught in the spotlight and reeled into the middle of the stage. Mercifully, I can't see the audience, but I can hear the embarrassed silence broken by "shame, shame" as it is whispered around the auditorium. I am stranded, gasping on a bank of public humiliation and there is nothing I can do about it except endure.

~ 12 ~

On His Majesty's Service ???

By the end of Standard Five, in 1953, I managed to come 26th in class. The first year of my high school life loomed. I was quite excited. We would be doing Latin and geometry and algebra. I came 10th in class at the end of the first term in Standard Six and immediately had an exaggerated view of my own ability. What I failed to acknowledge was that I was in the dummies class. The Brothers believed in putting like with like. All the bright boys are in Six A. I am in Six C. After Miss Kane, it took no great intelligence to see that Brother Owen, nice and gentle as he was, was no great shakes as a teacher. I knew what controlling and drilling a class should be like. His discipline was appalling and the class ran riot for most of the day, only being brought to heel when Brother Richard happened to be passing and dropped in to put the fear of the Almighty God into us.

In truth, I was bored with Latin declensions. Flora taught me a little Cockney Rhyming Slang which I found much more entertaining. I couldn't see the point of algebra, though geometry had some marginal interest. The idea of having to use logic to prove something had its appeal. Afrikaans appeared on the timetable for the first time. It held no attractions for me as I had absorbed the English-speaking prejudices against it and become resistant. In any event, Brother Owen's Afrikaans was not much better than the class he was supposed to be teaching. Even I could see that.

One afternoon I got home before Flora had returned from work. I was idly looking through the cupboard next to the basin when I noticed a small cardboard box lying on the floor. It contained a number of documents, all tightly rolled up, old birth, death and marriage certificates and an assortment of other official-looking papers. A tatty old brown envelope, On His Majesty's Service embossed with an impressive coat of arms, a lion on one side a unicorn on the other. Dieu et Mon Droit printed in elaborate script. The word "Adoption" catches my eye. Disbelief gives way to relief. I had stumbled upon my own adoption papers. This means, I realised, as I read and re-read the document in my hands:

"None of this has anything to do with me. I am not responsible. These people are not my people".

My drunken, wife-beating, family-abandoning, useless, feckless father, Tommy is not my father. Drug-addicted, depressed, tea-drinking, chain-smoking, Flora is not my mother. I do not have their blood. I am not of them. Nothing is foreordained. I am not responsible for their failures, their lives or their addictions. I am not doomed to pre-ordained poverty and failure, drugs or alcoholism.

"No matter what happens, this isn't part of me".

There are words you think or say that never leave you.

Wave after wave of relief swept over me. Of course, it was not as simple as that. I was emotionally bonded to Flora. I had a deep sense of responsibility for her. But, there was now space between us. The objective facts of my daily life were not going to change. My dismal school career was not likely to get better. Nor did it: but at least now I feel that change, however remote, is possible. Nothing goes on forever.

I quickly became in my own eyes a romantic and mysterious figure like so many young heroes I had read about in novels and the *Boys Own Paper*, another David Balfour as in *Kidnapped*. I convinced myself that my true parents were landed aristocrats with a castle in Scotland and that I would be discovered to be the heir to a vast fortune. Here was food for my wildest adolescent fantasies. I was, as I had always suspected, special. If all this was so, what was my destiny? There must be a point to it all. Was I being tested for higher things to see if I was worthy?

Existential questions about the purpose and meaning of life have haunted me for as long as I can remember. They didn't start then, but they certainly took on a new intensity, troubling my sleep as they would, as they continue to do so. The mirage of understanding ever receding. Sometimes sharper, most times dissolving into the mist. We all blunder in the dark.

On His Majesty's Service ???

I now embark on a life of deception. I now truly have a secret life. There is no one I can confide in, no secret sharer. There is no way I can confront Flora with what I have discovered. I am alone with my new knowledge. Over the next few weeks, whenever I get the chance, I re-read the notice from the Home Office to reassure myself. Of course, the affairs of daily existence have to be dealt with and the feeling of exhilaration gradually fades, but not the sense of relief. Then, one day, the document is not there. Everything else is in place, but the one piece of paper on which I have built so much is missing. Had I dreamed it all? Was it all a fantasy?

Walking up the passage my head is still full of Miss Fairfax, and romantic landscapes. It had been a particularly torrid day at school. I had made a blot in my arithmetic exercise book and had tried to disguise it with invisible ink. One of the most accomplished criminals in the class assured me he could remove all the evidence of my crime. Instead his efforts had caused the ink to spread spidery legs over much of the rest of the page. There it sat in the middle of the page, a black widow of a blot. Grotesque evidence of my ineptitude. I resorted to scraping it delicately with a razor blade and was in the process of shining the roughened paper with my nail when Miss Kane, in one of her rare sallies into the body of the class happened to be passing my desk and saw what I was up to. My ear felt as if it was about to be wrenched from the side of my head as I lurched out of the desk twisting in agony to see her face contorted in rage, a blood red moon rising over the two immense brown mountains of her bosom. The rest of the afternoon was spent nursing my swollen hands and writing a thousand times: 'I must not blot my work or rub out'.

I put my key into the lock. As I open the door I can sense something is wrong. Flora is sitting up in bed, a cigarette in one hand, a cup of tea in the other, a purposeful expression on her face. A notebook lies in her lap. I recognise it. Shortly after I had discovered my adoption papers I started my first attempt at autobiography. I dropped my school satchel on the floor and guardedly said hello.

It was Friday night. By Sunday night we had exhausted ourselves.

Staring Memory in the Face

"Is this yours? Did you write this? How did you find out? Why didn't you tell me?"

Unanswerable questions. I wait dumbly for the interrogation and the inevitable emotional blackmail to gather momentum.

"We could have talked about it if you had asked. How long have you known? Do you hate me for not being your mother? Does this mean you are going to leave me?" Her voice begins to tremble. "Are you going to leave me? Where would you go? You don't think Tommy would have you, do you? He's abandoned you once already. You know how he resents having to pay anything towards your maintenance. Do you think he would be willing to take you on now? Anyway, where would you live? He doesn't have any room for you and I'm sure whoever he's living with won't want you hanging around. And, what do you think will happen to me? Why do you think I continue working? Why do you think I continue living?"

She is becoming shrill, and I realise I will have to respond if I wanted to avoid a hysterical breakdown.

"I was looking in the bottom of the cupboard and found the papers by accident." Hoping to break through the monologue and avoid tears.

"Haven't I told you never to go looking through other people's private things?"

She is sufficiently distracted to register indignation, which she uses to bolster her feelings of uncertainty and loss of control. One of her favourite tricks whenever we have a disagreement is to latch onto one or other of my moral failings and swamp me in a morass of self-justification in which the original issue is soon lost. On this occasion, I had gone snooping where I had no business and was therefore being underhand and dishonest, reading confidential documents. Things that have nothing to do with me. My moral standing is undermined before I can open my mouth.

She turns to the notebook.

"Is this yours? Did you write this? When did you do it?" Pointing at my pathetic efforts at composition. "How long have you known? How did you find out?"

On His Majesty's Service ???

The questions quickly escalate into accusations about putting my nose into other peoples' things, and defensiveness and tears. All my dammed-up anger and frustration at our way of life, of the pressure she put on me to succeed at school and my humiliation at being a failure, the degradation I have felt at being dragged from one place to another, of perpetual poverty, the drugs, of living in one room, of never being able to bring any friends home, of always being dependent on charity, and so on and so on, all flood out. Something in me gives, and I discover a dagger of ice I have never suspected. I had always allowed her to get away with emotional bullying and had bitten back on what I wanted to say. Not now. I was not going to let her get away with the usual denials and feeble explanations and excuses. I didn't ask to be adopted. I remind her of all the humiliations I had faced in England. She is not going to dodge the full truth of what I feel and with what I have had to cope every day.

"I'm stupid. I know I'm stupid and I resent you trying to force me to be what I can't. I'll never be good at school, never pass matric, never go to university, never be good at anything. I know. I know."

It all comes out in an inarticulate jumble. We fight all night and skirmish for the rest of the weekend.

The point is though, which she cannot deny and to which I cling, I am not her flesh and blood. "This isn't part of me. This isn't part of me." It is my only lifeline, to what I have no idea. But at least I am not doomed to this existence. "I'm not responsible. I'm not responsible." There is a glimmer of hope. I can escape; to what, I have no idea. Whatever my life is to become, at least it will be of my own making.

I was, of course, caught in a terrible but unacknowledged contradiction. I knew I was stupid and a failure. There was no denying the evidence. But I suddenly had a sense of liberation. Life was there for the taking and making. I was also terrified of the implications of cutting myself adrift from Flora. For, no matter how insecure our life together was, it was what I knew. Paradoxically, it did provide a modicum of security and predictability. Normality is what you're used to. There was also the emotional and moral bond. I couldn't just abandon her. Cutting myself off from Flora meant taking my chances in the unknown. I wasn't ready to risk that yet, but I knew that at least now it was a possibility. The gutter, as I envisioned it and as she had so often predicted, was not my inescapable fate. The first faltering steps of separation had been taken.

As with all these kinds of outbursts, nothing was resolved, nothing really explained, nothing really understood. Confusion and guilt cast their pall over everything. We never mentioned the subject again. I retreated into fantasy. *Grey sheets of rain swept across the island. The sea sounded louder than usual. It was unusually cold and dark, even during the day. Listening to the wind gusting outside, the cries of storm swept gulls. Could it be that a tidal wave would engulf the island? This was not the first time the island had been blasted by a storm.* In the morning, not even a footprint in the sand.

We may have been struggling in the turbulent current of our life together, but there was another flow within which we both participated, and about which I was beginning to become more aware. I was now fourteen and puberty was beginning to press. The more aware I became of the forces beyond my immediate existence, the less equipped I felt to survive in the crosscurrents I sensed awaited me. The fall of *Dien Bien Phu* in the middle of that year sparked an awareness of the world beyond Boston Court. Vietnam entered my vocabulary.

Notwithstanding my seeming improved position in class, I knew I could not rely on my brains. What could I rely on? University was too remote even to consider. I had no special talents. I had no interest in making or fixing things, though I once bought a model aeroplane kit, determined to be, as I thought, as other boys of my age, and nearly cut off my thumb. I was not interested in engines. I could draw a little, but lacked real passion and technical ability. I had a drawing book full of sketches and watercolours of ships at sea, usually in storms. The psychological symbolism is obvious now. It wasn't then.

∼

On His Majesty's Service ???

My first year in secondary school in 1954 forced upon me the realisation that in the not too distant future I would have to make my way in the world. The only thing I could think of was joining the Royal Navy. As what, I had no idea. I vaguely thought of myself as an officer, but what officers did was beyond me. The navy was attractive because of what it represented to my imagination: freedom, independence, expansiveness and the romantic potential for adventure. I had read numerous accounts of the battle of the Atlantic by such men as Commander Walker RN, novels such as *The Cruel Sea, The Caine Mutiny*, and of course the Hornblower series. The navy fitted in well with my fantasy life. My ambitions were the ambitions of avoidance.

The year came to a close, and I was promoted to Standard Seven C at Marist Observatory at the beginning of 1955. The Koch Street school only went as far as Standard Six. I could feel that I was slipping further and further down the slope of irredeemable failure. Nor was I wrong. Within a term I managed to come 49th out of 49 in the class. I was completely bewildered. And my bewilderment was compounded by my inability to organise myself. I truly had no idea what was required of me. I sat at the back of the class and everything passed before me in a blur. I understood nothing. I felt utterly helpless. The election of class monitors reinforced my sense of failure and rejection. I was the only boy of 49 who did not receive a single vote in the class. Physics and chemistry, two new subjects, were presented as a series of formulae to be learned off by heart. Experiments that should have been conducted in the laboratories were blindly copied out of textbooks into exercise books. The Periodic Table made no sense whatsoever. There was no point in turning to Flora for help. She was asleep shortly after she got home from work and was unconscious for most of every weekend.

There were two bright spots. I had long harboured a fantasy since my time at SACS Junior in Cape Town that rugby was my game. I was small, therefore a scrum half. Scrum half is probably the most vulnerable position on the field. The theory was that a small quick link is needed to deliver the ball from the forwards (big and slow) to the fly half (fast and tactical) who would then distribute it to the back line whose job is to score tries. A simple philosophy, but like so much philosophy that has to be translated into practical action it does not take into account the fact that the scrum half cannot be guaranteed to always evade the supposedly lumbering forwards or the opposite scrum half who was, in my case, invariably bigger, stronger and faster than I was.

It was not long before I ended up in hospital, having torn the muscles in my right thigh. It was one of those glorious moments. I intercepted a pass and was dashing for the line when two of the opposition tackled me. I went down in a howl of pain and was carried from the field. I thought I had broken my leg. Brother Gerard drove me home. I prayed that Flora wasn't there when we arrived. As luck would have it, she wasn't, but even so, Brother Gerard was visibly shaken at seeing for the first time the conditions in which his least promising pupil lived. He left as soon as he had seen me safely onto my bed, but not before he had dashed downstairs to the café opposite and bought me a Coke which he left on the table next to my bed. The injury proved much more serious than anyone realised and I had to be taken to hospital where I spent the night being X-rayed and strapped up. Fortunately, it was the last match of the season.

I had been looking forward to Shakespeare, but was disappointed. Our first experience was *Henry V*. The language was impenetrable, the plot unfathomable and for all the promise of the battle of Agincourt and sword fighting, nothing happened. There was too much talk and too little action. The ringing appeals to English patriotism failed to move me. Nonetheless, the idea of drama intrigued me. Brother Gerard discovered I could do Scots, Irish and Welsh accents, so I was roped into reading Bardolph, Pistol and Nym as the class worked its way laboriously through the play.

Having struggled through *Henry V*, our next play was *Julius Caesar*, which he decided should be that year's school production. Auditions were held. I was not chosen, but I could not resist going to watch rehearsals in the afternoon. I attended every rehearsal and gradually ingratiated

On His Majesty's Service ???

myself into helping backstage. Here was another world; a world which gave new life to the stories I acted out each night in my imagination as I lay in the dark listening to Flora's laboured breathing.

"The fault ... is not in our stars / But in ourselves ... ."[18] Certain words and phrases once encountered become embedded in one's consciousness. They orientate one's moral compass and enter one's working vocabulary. I was beginning to find words for the unarticulated feelings I had about life and growing up. Cassius gave expression to my scepticism and fumbling need to take charge of my life.

My moment of glory came when I was chosen to hold one of the curtains open to reveal Brutus and Cassius before the Battle of Philippi. The curtain opened briefly for me too: *"There is a tide in the affairs of men, which, taken at the flood, leads on to fortune."*[19]

All too briefly; after that it was back to the Periodic Table and Latin verbs. Miss Fairfax passed from my life. Even so, the seeds had been sown. Seeing the language in action made all the difference and fired – perhaps fired is too strong a word – sparked a love of poetry and drama that has sustained me all my life.

---

18. Shakespeare: *Julius Caesar* Act 1 Sc. 3.
19. Ibid. Act 4 Sc. 3.

~ 13 ~

Longwood House

By the end of the second term in 1955 when I had managed to come 49th out of 49, Flora decided I should go to boarding school. Unbeknown to me she had been in contact with Bennie Piel's father. Bennie had left Marist a month or so earlier for Longwood House, not on St Helena, but a boarding school just outside Meyerton on the road to Vereeniging. Vereeniging was where the Peace Treaty had been signed that brought the Second Anglo- Boer War to an end in 1902, of which, naturally, I knew nothing. Flora announced one afternoon that I would be going to Longwood the following week. My immediate response was to ask how was she going to pay the fees. They were £50 a term, including books. She assured me that now that she was working for *The Star* and had a regular income it would not be a problem. In fact, she paid the first term's fees, but never a penny more for the three and a half years I was at the school.

Lynn Cloete and his wife Joyce, Sir and Ma'am to us, founded Longwood House in 1949. They started the school with eight pupils, two of whom were their own children, Jocelyn and Pauline. Within a couple of days five parents gave notice that they were going to withdraw their children at the end of term. Everything hinged on his personality and his wife's ability to balance the books. She was the stabilising force. He provided the vision and inspiration.

Joyce was a true eccentric. Many years later, after I had left school and had come to know and appreciate her as an adult, I remember her telling me how she had lost the ruby in her engagement ring but had made good the loss by breaking off and melting a piece of a red plastic toothbrush which she had fitted into the setting. She was very proud of herself. "You wouldn't know the difference. It's just as good as the real thing, and now I don't have to worry about losing it," she said, as she held up her hand to the light so I could see it better. I didn't have the

Longwood House

Joyce (Ma'am) and Lynn (Sir) Cloete

heart to tell her it looked exactly like a piece of melted red plastic. Every year until she died she sent me an old used Christmas card with 'Happy Birthday Michael' scrawled across the original message.

It is no exaggeration to say that Longwood House was the most important influence in shaping my life and values during my adolescence. Although I did not improve academically and ultimately failed matric, the school provided me with stability and continuity I had never known. More importantly, I found myself in a place where I was not terrified into submission. The conformism demanded by a Catholic education, and the retribution that reinforced it and which killed off creativity and individuality, was replaced by a chaotic and unpredictable system loosely aimed at stimulating and developing individual talent.

My indiscriminate reading that supported a wide and undisciplined range of interests and general knowledge was now recognised and applauded. I might not be able to decline Latin verbs or solve quadratic equations, but I could discuss books and ideas with my teachers which made me feel I was being taken seriously. For the first time, I felt valued. Miss Kane and Brother Richard's influence did not entirely dissipate. I retained an exaggerated though cynical respect for authority while at the same time resisting it, and a capacity I came to recognise and value only much later in life for intense and systematic concentration. But, for the first time in my life, I felt I belonged, that I was part of a community. I sang in the choir, acted in school plays and played in the First Eleven cricket and soccer sides. I was known, though not especially liked. In the parlance of the day I was a "square", and as I grew in self-confidence, an intellectual snob.

Not that it was all roses and honey. Cloete was charismatic, erratic, unpredictable and a Francophile, given to violent outbursts and mood swings, and for the times was wildly unconventional. Periodically, he would insist that we do cadets, and we would be marched up and down the cricket field for an hour before breakfast. I hated it. Resistance can take many unconscious forms.

∼

Years later at an 'Old Boys' reunion one of my school mates from those far off days asked me with genuine concern: "Michael, Michael are you alright? Are you alright?"

I looked at him quizzically.

"You know, since we left school I've often thought about you and worried that you would have a really hard time."

"Why?"

"Because, whenever we did cadets you were the only one who could never march in step. I always thought you were going to have a hard time. You were always out of step. Are you sure you are alright?"

I was touched. There is no telling what sort of impression one makes on other people. I had no idea that I was so obviously or memorably rebellious. My resistance to conformity and much else besides

Longwood House

must have been pretty well bedded down by then. It would prove to be a hair shirt I would wear for the rest of my life. Just how uncomfortable that shirt has been I tried to capture one rainy afternoon over 50 years later, when instead of paying attention to the financial director during a board meeting, I sat scribbling what I would call 'Bored Room Blues':

'And now, madam chair, we turn to the Monthly Management Accounts, otherwise known as Financial Statements.'

'It's fascinating how figures can tell a story.'

Adamastor stirs, uncomfortably, after a corporate lunch, belches.
Gloom descends.
Her tangible assets
rest
on the boardroom table.
Gratis.
Bottom lines and gross margins swell,
dyspeptically.

The mountain is wreathed in mist.
Rain beats at the windows
knowing nothing of income statements;
obliterates margins between earth, sea and sky;
gurgles in gutters.

'Consider the income statement:
I would like to draw your attention to our cash-flow'.

Go with the flow.

'Just to remind you:
NLV is a function of RP, less trade discount and VAT at 14%.
Our overheads continue to be well covered.'

I am over my head.

'The negative variation
between actual and budgeted turnover, expressed as a percentage,

Staring Memory in the Face

is better than it seems
considering fluctuating exchange rates
covered by buying forward.'

A continent declines.

What interest received?
What interest paid?

~

One of Cloete's eccentricities was that every evening we had to change for supper, boys into navy blue suits and polished black shoes, and girls into evening dresses. He believed that changing into formal clothes in the evening would give us a sense of style, self-discipline and respect for the opposite sex. Inspection took place as we lined up for supper. Anyone found inappropriately dressed or without shining shoes would be sent away, and on bad days go without supper. On the one hand, Cloete was extraordinarily advanced for his time in advocating democratic school government, on the other he harked back to an era of discipline when everyone knew his place. With the exception of evening dress, none of these eccentricities lasted for any length of time. If nothing else they were an expression of his confused notions of social order.

In those less regulated days it was possible for teachers and schools to shape the curriculum to individual interests and whims. Cloete ensured we were exposed to a surfeit of French culture, everything from Victor Hugo to Juliette Greco. The school was named after Napoleon's house on St Helena. The fact that I had been there and could describe it gave me some standing. His son Jocelyn was named after an obscure French composer; his daughter Pauline after Napoleon's sister. He was also an alcoholic. During the last two years of school when I came to know him and his wife very well, they were drinking at least a bottle of brandy a day between them.

In my matric year, and much of the year preceding it, we spent every evening in his study smoking his cigarettes, listening to Beethoven,

Longwood House

Mozart, Bach and Handel, and talking until the small hours about the meaning of life, living to the full of one's potential, "*drinking life to the lees*", and drinking much else besides, between liberal doses of Rimbaud, Edith Piaf, Sartre, Camus, Proust, Zola, Balzac, de Maupassant and Saint Exupéry. These nightly seminars inevitably concluded at around two or three in the morning when he and we would repair to the kitchen where we made ourselves elaborate omelettes and toasted sandwiches.

Cloete's seventy-eight-year-old mother, known to all of us as Nana (she had nothing in common with her namesake in *Peter Pan*), had a room near the kitchen so we had to be especially quiet. She was the keeper of the keys. Bizarre as it may seem, the headmaster together with his, often tipsy, prefects and matric class would break in and raid the pantry. We tiptoed around the kitchen fearful that Nana would wake and discover us. And, inevitably she did. Nana was a fierce old battle-axe who had everyone in fear and trembling, including her son. Her face looked as if it had been chiselled out of ice. I saw her smile on two occasions, neither was a warming sight. She was a bitter old woman who took no pleasure in her family, the children she taught, or the world at large. She and Miss Kane had a lot in common. Fortunately, she did not teach me, but the stories emanating from her classroom were as terrifying as anything I had endured. The night she caught us, we heard her coming down the passage before she opened the kitchen door.

On this occasion, there were five of us and Cloete in the kitchen. We had just finished making a feast of bacon and eggs and toast. At the first sound of her approach all evidence of our meal was hastily hidden in a cupboard under the sink, the light switched off and we hid where we could. Cloete squashed into the broom cupboard. Bromfield managed to escape through the open window. Pike and Chan slipped into the pantry. Jones and I hid under the kitchen table in the middle of the room.

A large plastic tablecloth hung nearly to the floor. Through a tear I saw the door open and Nana switch on the light. She stood in the doorway like some latter-day Miss Haversham, her hair in curlers, clutching a huge bunch of keys. Something had been going on. She was sure of it. Brian and I watched her slippered feet circle the table to the open window. She slammed it down muttering to herself, and turned to see Cloete barely concealed in the broom cupboard. How he thought he could remain undiscovered is anyone's guess.

"Lynn, what on earth do you think you are doing? What is going on?"

He emerged from the cupboard, several brooms and mops crashing to the floor, compounding his guilt. His explanation, which I recall had something to do with having spilled some water in the study and looking for something to clean it up with, would have convinced no one. It certainly did not mollify Nana. They disappeared down the hall, Nana scolding her son for crimes she had no trouble imagining, he trying unsuccessfully to placate her. When they were safely out of earshot we emerged from our hiding places and escaped through the window into the blessed dark of the night.

Occasionally, Cloete indulged himself in fits of erratic self-righteous discipline that left us all gasping. We regularly smoked his cigarettes and drank his beer in his study. It was our unofficial common room. Sometimes he would, without warning, ban smoking on pain of six cuts if anyone were caught. Unexpected raids on our lockers would reveal the guilty and guarantee the thrashing that ensued. I was not a smoker, but on one of his raids he discovered a packet of cigarettes in my locker. I was hiding it for Pike. Honour demanded that I take my punishment without a murmur. Might as well be killed for a sheep as a lamb I thought, and promptly started smoking. Nor were the girls any less likely to feel the lash of his tongue and the cane. Diana Bennett was paraded in front of the whole school one morning and told she was a slut and a whore, the whole performance culminating in her being slapped in the face. What she had done I can't remember, but it could not have been all that heinous. It certainly had nothing to do with errant sexual behaviour. She was known as the ice maiden by all the senior boys. Pauline, his daughter, was frequently berated and humiliated in front of the school. We were

Longwood House

never sure what she had done wrong either, but the ferocity of his attacks left everyone gasping.

His treatment of his wife Joyce was equally appalling. She had the unenviable task of trying to keep the school on an even financial keel, which forced her into a position where she was constantly trying to limit his capacity for spending money. There was nothing Cloete enjoyed more than taking the matric boys out to the theatre in Johannesburg and then drinking with them in a pub afterwards, all at his expense. Naturally, we all saw her as a spoilsport. It was only much later after I had left school that I came to appreciate her true worth. Although I recognised the contradictions in his behaviour I could not confront them, preferring to worship him. Which was all very well as long as I was in his good books, but if I fell from favour, as inevitably happened from time to time, I was thrown into a state of utter confusion and remorse, assuming, as I had with Miss Kane, that I must be the guilty party.

I learned reams of French poetry off by heart, not understanding a word of it. While the rest of the class was doing French (I had arrived in the middle of the year too late to catch up). I was supposed to be doing extra maths. Instead, I imbibed the sonorous rhythms of Victor Hugo and Paul Verlaine read aloud to the class. The music was enough.

Cloete claimed he had modelled his school on Summer Hill, and certainly there were similarities with the emphasis on the arts and developing the pupils' creativity. Every year he produced a Shakespearian play and an operetta with an orchestra he recruited from members of the SABC Symphony and which he conducted himself, as well as an evening of choral music. And everyone had to take part. There was no choice: art was a compulsory subject. Democracy was not one of his failings. For all his promotion of individual talent there was no doubt where authority lay. Such was his charisma that we seldom challenged his arbitrary and erratic judgment or opinions. The only exception to this was my refusal to accept that French culture was superior to English, which led, of course, to nightly debates into the early hours about the relative virtues of English and French literature, art and music. My position was no less chauvinistic than his, but my wide if indiscriminate reading gave me sufficient confidence to challenge him. From one point of view these sessions were at several removes from the real world we inhabited. From another, they played a vital role in helping me to imagine the possibilities life might hold. It was, after all, South Africa in the mid 50s firmly in the grip of the Nationalist Party. The United Party had split with the founding of the Progressive Party with Helen Suzman as its sole representative in Parliament. Sometimes, we could imagine seeing Sputnik high in the night sky.

The school was small. So, I had the opportunity to play in the First Eleven cricket and soccer teams which I would never have had at any other school. I also had the opportunity for the first time to start discovering the opposite sex. Shy romances bloomed and died in a week. It was all very innocent: ours must have been the last generation that believed in marrying virgins. The height of passion was to sit holding sweaty hands during the weekly film, usually some French art movie deemed to be improving. We saw *Monsieur Vincent* about a dozen times. It was the age before the Beatles. Elvis Presley was only beginning to make his presence felt. Cloete's attitude to this, as with everything else, was unpredictable. He would alternately ban, without warning or explanation, Pat Boone, but allow Presley, or vice versa. He was absolutely committed to the principles of co-education but he clearly had little time for the girls. He allowed us to have a dance every Saturday night, even tolerating some rock and roll as long as there was a predominance of waltzes and foxtrots.

The school was unique too in that it admitted Chinese children. The thumbscrews of Apartheid were being tightened and Cloete was determined to resist where he could. He was a mass of contradictions. We had it drummed into us that people should be judged by what they did, by their actions, not by the accident of their birth, religion or colour. Yet, by today's standards he would be regarded as a racist. He divided the world into aristocrats and the rest. He was no democrat. He believed in an aristocracy of creative minds. It was an elite he had little trouble convincing us we were all destined to be part of. Gifted, creative indi-

Longwood House

viduals, artists, musicians, writers, philosophers, regardless of who they were held the key to and were the guardians of the highest expressions of civilisation. Nobody else mattered. There were exceptions, of course, Napoleon, de Gaulle, Louis XIV, Joan of Arc.

He inspired an appetite for life. Blake and Keats were his starting points: *"Oh for a life of sensations."*[20] Yet, at the same time he stimulated intense intellectual curiosity. What is the meaning of life? Who am I? Is there any purpose? What is truth? Beauty? Is that *"all ye know on earth and all ye need to know"*?[21] How should we judge art? What is great art? Are there any absolutes? How should we understand and judge human behaviour? Good and evil? Is there a universal basis to morality? Does God exist? What do we mean by exist? All the questions that awakening adolescent minds find fascinating. These sessions went on until the early hours of the morning, night after night, the air thick with cigarette smoke, and as the year progressed the beer and cider flowing ever more freely. Many was the time I arrived in class the following morning with a severe hangover.

Cloete despised politics and politicians. "The only talent a politician needs is the ability to lie", he said. I had no trouble in accepting his dictum that politicians and patriotic tub-thumping were to be treated with the utmost suspicion. He liked to quote Dr Johnson: *"Patriotism is the last refuge of a scoundrel"*[22]. E M Forster's essay *Two Cheers for Democracy* was required reading. Forster begins it by saying that if he were forced to make a choice between betraying his country and betraying a friend he hoped he would have the courage to betray his country. I had just discovered Orwell. *Nineteen Eighty-Four* became the focus of many of these late-night sessions.

Cloete's views on Apartheid, as on everything else, were contradictory. On the one hand, he held many of the prejudices of the times. Yet at the same time he was absolutely committed to the view that all men are born equal and that they should only be judged by their actions.

---

20. John Keats: *Letters*.

21. John Keats: 'Ode on a Grecian Urn'.

22. James Boswell: *Life of Johnson*.

Staring Memory in the Face

The school motto was *"facta non verba"*, deeds not words. Politically, he had not moved much beyond a romantic view of the French Revolution: Liberty, Equality and Fraternity, waving flags and the Marseillaise, paying lip service to democracy but in reality, he was an unreconstructed autocrat. A commitment to abstractions rather than concrete reality, to ideas rather than living breathing human beings leads to show trials and the concentration camps, he claimed. Yet, at the same time, he fed us liberal doses of Sartre and Camus.

Heady stuff. Many of these attitudes became, albeit unconsciously, the confused foundations on which I began to build my understanding of what it is to be human. Faced with a choice of acting out of ideological belief or responding to human need there has never been any doubt in my mind which should take precedence. These ideas complemented my acquaintance with totalitarianism at Marist Brothers. As a result of my experiences at the hands of Brother Richard and Miss Kane with her rule by terror through, what in another system would be described as the vanguard of the party, I developed attitudes to authority and power that have remained with me all my life, and were to lead to my, admittedly minor, involvement in the struggle against Apartheid years later, which came close to having fatal consequences.

My Catholic education also gave me a deep distrust and cynicism about publicly proclaimed ideals, be they religious or political. Neither Miss Kane nor Brother Richard and the system they upheld were prepared to tolerate human imperfection: not a blot, not a mistake. Ironically, this was an attitude they held in common with the Communist Party. Surviving a Catholic education was the best training I could have had for resisting the seduction of the Communist Party with its promise of creating a utopia, just as soon as all the doubters, class enemies, running dogs and other anti-revolutionary elements had been eliminated. Both systems demanded total control over the inner lives of their adherents and utter conformity to the abstract systems they created. Both were ruthless in rooting out non-conformists. Miss Kane had shown me how imperfect and unworthy I was. Longwood House, with all its imperfections, was to

Longwood House

show me how important intellectual independence and the imagination are for human survival. *Darkness at Noon*[23] confirmed my suspicions.

The paradox, for all my rejection of authority, was that I longed for a father figure. Cloete, for all his flaws, supplied that need. He was inspirational and I was all too ready to be inspired. What I would struggle to understand was that his imperfections were his, not mine; that his rejection of me, when it came, said more about him than it did about me. Vance Packard's *The Hidden Persuaders* had just been published. I was appalled to discover the power of advertisers and the use they made of the latest advances in psychology to manipulate consumers. I was oblivious of the irony that saw me seduced by Cloete's charisma while resisting everything else I thought would subjugate me. My reaction to advertising, once I finished the book, was similar to my feelings about drugs. I was determined to resist any attempt to manipulate me, anything that would compromise my autonomy. A fond hope.

Longwood House began my rehabilitation. I was in a social environment that accommodated a great degree of eccentricity, but still required a wide variety of conventional social skills, many of which I had had no cause to learn or practise before I arrived there. I began to enjoy school, at least the social aspects. It was a relief from what awaited me at home. When I was at Marist Brothers, except for the hours of school, I had spent most of my life in the company of one person, who for the most part was there in body but not mind. I was used to being solitary and amusing myself, relying on myself. I had developed the skills of survival. Now I discovered that I was quite gregarious. My broad but completely unsystematic general knowledge was acknowledged and valued, though it continued to have little immediate relation to the curriculum. Our classes were small; ten was big. So, we got to know one another very well, and in the process had to learn to tolerate each other.

---

23. Arthur Koestler: *Darkness at Noon* (1954).

Staring Memory in the Face

It was at about this time, when I was reading Packard, that I encountered Victor Frankel's *Man's Search for Meaning*. Of all the books I read at that time it was the most influential. Much of the book is taken up with Frankel's description of how he survived Auschwitz. In it he examines what he believes are the essential characteristics for survival. To his surprise it was not the big and the strong who necessarily fared best. He watched strong healthy men wilt, turn in on themselves and die within a short time of entering the camp. He saw others, a very few, whom he expected to die within days, survive against all the odds. What made the difference?

The manuscript of his book was discovered and destroyed several times. Each time he rewrote it on whatever scraps of paper he could find. And herein lies part of the answer to why he, who was not particularly robust, survived. He was determined that his book would not be destroyed. It was this determination that sustained him. He believed in the worth of what he had to say to the world. That gave him meaning and it was this meaning that enabled him to endure. And so, it was with all of those he observed who survived. They believed in something outside of, beyond themselves, usually in the need to be of service to other people. Those who did not have a central motivating meaning in their lives succumbed rapidly.

Much of what Frankel had to say resonates with Desmond Tutu's views on *uBuntu*. The book is a tribute to all those who had everything taken from them except the final freedom; the freedom to choose their own way. These ideas, as I say, had a profound effect on me and have sustained me throughout my life. Religion, at least in the forms I had experienced it, had not provided the basis for anything on which I could build my belief in myself, in life, or God. Needing to have a sense of purpose seems a pretty universal desire.

I needed a life-raft, and if there wasn't one to hand I would build my own. Once it was created I clung to it. Repaired it after every storm. Added to it when the means came to hand. Although it was some time in coming, Gloucester's remark in *King Lear*: *"As flies to wanton boys are we*

Longwood House

to the gods; they kill us for their sport"[24] was to hold a special significance for me. I realised he was wrong. We are the authors of our own misfortune. The gods are indifferent. We have choices. While events over which we have no control may devastate us, it is how we choose to deal with those events rather than the events themselves that determines the trajectory our lives take. This realisation did not come to me in a flash, nor have I always been able to live up to it, but somehow, as I began to construct my ramshackle life-raft it became one of the main spars holding the whole construction together. Others were an ironic eye, a sceptical view of human institutions and humbug, and a sardonic sense of humour.

Closely allied, and perhaps in partial contradiction to these notions, I felt I had to justify my existence, and that I could only do so if I had an enthusiasm for living. It was a circular argument and full of contradictions. But that was not the point. The point was that I gradually began to experience and then explore and then embrace and celebrate what life had to offer. I must open myself to experience. And, that meant opening myself to other people. Of course, there were failures and disappointments, but there were enough positive experiences to become self-fulfilling and keep the raft afloat. To this day, I tend to accept people at face value, though when I'm disappointed the hurt takes a long time to heal. I still have a capacity to fling myself into new challenges without considering too closely the possible consequences. It is an aspect of my personality that is often misinterpreted and misunderstood, and has sometimes got me into trouble. Reticence is not one of my strong points.

Many of us grew up at Longwood House believing that we were about to take the world by storm as writers or actors or singers when we left school. Cloete convinced me that I had a "great voice" and that I could become a "great actor". During my three and a half years at Longwood I played in *San Marino, Gretchen, The Mikado, Oklahoma* (all operettas) *Hamlet, Macbeth,* and *The Tempest.* Shakespeare began to mean something to me. As I learned my lines it seemed as if they became part of me and that I could feel my understanding of the human (and by that I understood my)

---

24. Shakespeare: *King Lear* Act 4 Sc. 1.

condition growing within me. The words, their sounds and rhythms were becoming a palpable part of my consciousness. All this was, of course, at the level of intuition. I would have been hard pressed to explain what I meant, but essentially, I was realising that I was not alone in the world, that my life and shame and inadequacy were not unique. I could rise above my circumstances, or sink into the gutter. The choice was mine.

Every year we produced an evening of sacred choral music which toured the churches in Three Rivers, Van der Bijl Park and Vereeniging singing carols, choruses and arias from the Handel's *Messiah* and Mendelssohn's *Elijah*, and sacred songs such as *Ave Maria* and Gounod's *Jerusalem*. When performing, I felt as if my very soul was struggling to burst out, reveal itself and take flight. There was also the warm glow that accompanied applause. The need for affirmation is universal.

The challenge was to be *"strong in will to strive, to seek to find, and not to yield."* [25] This line from Tennyson became my mantra. In fact, art was becoming a substitute for religion. I was finding something that gave my life meaning. Something through which I could experience and express my own existence. All this might be dismissed as clumsy but exuberant adolescent passion. Art had not only become a substitute for religion but for a great deal besides. Nonetheless, it was something beyond myself waiting to be explored and which, I thought, had the practical value of enabling me to celebrate, fulfil and justify, and sustain my life. As Romain Gary says in *La Nuit Sera Calme*: *"if you take poetry and imagination away from people, all you're left with is hunks of meat."*

Lessons were unsystematic, chaotic. The timetable was ignored for the most part. During the summer, lessons were often abandoned in favour of the swimming pool. One afternoon I rushed into my Latin class still dripping wet from swimming, my sodden shirt barely covering my swimming costume which I had not had time to change. Dr Thomas took one look at me and roared in her thick Neapolitan accent:

"Get out-a my class. I don't-a allow-a sex-a maniacs in my class."

---

25. Tennyson: Op.cit.

Longwood House

She was always calling us "sex-a maniacs" which was a bit rich coming from someone who taught us about the Impressionists by highlighting the more dramatic episodes in their sex lives. Gauguin and Toulouse-Lautrec received special attention. Brothels featured briefly in our essays after that, until we were dismissed as "sex-a maniacs" who deserved no more than two out of ten for our "immature and boring" literary efforts. On another occasion, she was teaching Romeo and Juliet, the balcony scene. She turned to Jocelyn and asked him what he thought Romeo and Juliet were doing when they disappeared behind the curtain. He looked at her blankly.

"What do you-a think they're doing? Playing-a marbles?"

Whatever her limitations, she was never boring.

She opened my eyes to the visual arts, politics and organised religion. Our textbook was Helen Gardner's *Art Through the Ages*, which I had already read from cover to cover, more for the history than the art, by the time I ended up in her class. She was a fount of information not only about the Italian renaissance, but of ancient Rome, Greece and Egypt. Her lessons on Egyptian sculpture and architecture had me entranced. A civilisation that stood almost unchallenged for 3000 years seemed to me to be worthy of admiration. Over a period of several weeks she covered aesthetics – Nefertiti's bust has provided a standard for beauty and power that has lasted over three millennia; Pythagoras and the building of the pyramids – the square on the hypotenuse, it would seem, had some practical application. She also covered, as an atheist and lapsed Catholic, the emergence of monotheism under Akhenaten and related topics such as death and immortality; all fascinating to a malleable adolescent mind. She laid the foundations that have lasted a lifetime of many of my attitudes to art, religion and politics, especially a scepticism of high-flown social theories and utopian ideologies.

Central to it all was language. She had grown up during the last days of fascism just before and during the Second World War in Naples, and knew how language could be manipulated for corrupt ends. One of the most enduring lessons she taught me was that the corruption of language is inseparable from the corruption of human beings. Hence, to this day, my abhorrence of the language of con men of whatever stripe: advertising, political rhetoric, public relations and what is known as 'management speak'. This lesson was to stand me in good stead in the 1980s, when I was writing a regular column called *'Our View'* published in *The Star* on behalf of the Detainees Parents Support Committee at the time of the Free the Children Campaign. I had to resist pressure from the ideological purists with whom I had to work who wanted to inject the rhetoric of the Left, jargon laden with adjectives and adverbs, into my text in order to, as they asserted, emphasise our message. The raw account I wanted to give was dramatic enough without embellishing it. Certainly, these columns had an impact as far afield as the United States Senate and the United Nations. But that is a story for later. In the meantime, the world hovered on the brink of nuclear confrontation. The Russians invaded Hungary. One of the families that managed to escape to South Africa sent their son to Longwood, where he held a special fascination for adolescents harbouring romantic ideas about war.

Teachers, with some exceptions, taught what they felt like, when they felt like it. I spent most of my time reading everything I could get my hands on. Some days I forgot to go to class I became so absorbed. No one missed me.

It was at about this time that I had a conversation with one of my schoolmates, Brian Jones, who provided me with an image that has remained with me all my life. Like me, he came from a broken home, but unlike me he had no difficulty talking about it. He was angry with his parents, frightened about what might happen to him and his brother Trevor, bitter with his mother for abandoning them. I was intrigued and surprised that he could talk so openly about things that I would have regarded as shameful and would never have revealed. (In fact, I never had revealed my own shame.) He said he had realised that if he suppressed his feelings they would grow like a boil which it might be possible to disguise for a while, but which would eventually burst. His was a pragmatic choice. If we don't manage our circumstances, our circumstances will manage us.

Longwood House

Of course, living in an age of ubiquitous psychotherapy such views are no longer surprising, but in the mid-nineteen fifties and especially from the lips of a seventeen-year-old, they were a revelation. I understood what he was saying, but it would take me another thirty years to trust it.

~ 14 ~

"Hambakahle"

She sits opposite me in the high-backed chair, her hands resting in her lap. Her face, relaxed and sagging, wrinkled with old age, asleep. The sleeve on one of her arms has run up and I can just see the tattooed numbers on her forearm. She has sat there every day now for a week. Whenever I emerge from swirling nightmares, always of torrential rivers, she stirs herself and mops my brow with a damp cloth. The heat is stifling, mid-summer on the Highveld.

Ten days earlier I had suddenly developed an agonising pain in my stomach that doubled me up and kept me awake at night. A burst appendix. I spent my seventeenth birthday on an operating table. Three days later I was released from hospital and returned to Boston Court to convalesce. Because Flora was at work during the day there was no one to care for me while she was away. My sudden illness at least had the salutary effect of keeping her off the pills.

Hanna Rubenstein lived by herself just down the hall. She must have been in her late sixties but looked much older. She and Flora had struck up a nodding acquaintance as they passed each other infrequently in the passage. It was to Hanna that she now turned.

I was not recovering as well as I should. For much of the following week I drifted in and out of consciousness, incapable of helping myself. Nightmare followed nightmare, as I seemed to be plunging down one vortex of chaos and pain after another. Periodically, I recovered consciousness enough to recognise my surroundings. It was on one of these occasions that I woke to discover Hanna asleep in the chair next to my bed. It must have been towards the end of my relapse and the beginning of my recovery because I remained awake long enough to notice her forearm, and thought it strange that such an old woman should have a tattoo. Gradually my resilience asserted itself and I began to spend more time awake and less asleep.

"Hambakahle"

One afternoon, shortly after she had fed me on a cup of chicken soup I asked her about her tattoo. She grasped her wrist as if to hide the mark, tugging down her sleeve, stammering. She had a thick Polish accent that was sometimes difficult to follow because she spoke so softly. Her voice represented another world I had only read about in books. She pulled herself together, obviously thinking about how to answer me and sat down clasping her mug of soup between her hands and asked me if I had ever heard of Auschwitz. The tattoo marked her forever as an inmate. Evidence that could never be removed.

I had never met anyone who had been in a concentration camp. It had never occurred to me that there must have been millions of people scattered all over the world in the aftermath of the War who had survived the Holocaust. The Holocaust and the camps were an abstraction. They were the stuff of grainy photographs; pictures which filled me with a kind of awe at the fact and magnitude and casualness of death. Piles of emaciated naked dead bodies, shapes hanging from gallows, gaunt figures in striped pyjamas, pictures of gas ovens and shower rooms, they bore no relation to anything I knew. My father's explanation of why we had come to South Africa had included the highly unlikely story that when he had been invalided out of the army he had returned to Fleet Street and had been one of the first journalists into Buchenwald and Auschwitz.

So, I knew about the camps and what they had been used for. But meeting someone, someone whom I had passed in the passageway every day, who was familiar to me as part of the recognised but unacknowledged landscape, came as a shock. Her story, as she related it to me that afternoon must have been a fairly typical one. Her family had been rounded up at the beginning of the War. They had lived in Warsaw and were among the first to be transported to a slave camp after the invasion of Poland in 1939. Her parents and brothers and sisters all perished.

After the War, she managed to find her way to South Africa. She had a pension that was just enough to pay the rent and feed her. And now, like us and many others, had been washed up into the shallows of Boston Court: one room with a basin, sharing the lavatory and bath with the others on the same floor, where she lived her anonymous life. Her memories were her only bulwark against loneliness. Her story had a profound effect on me. I was no longer capable of regarding the camps and the persecution of the Jews as something that had nothing to do with me. As I listened to her tale my own existence seemed by comparison nothing to complain about. There was no denying our circumstances, but we did not have to fear for our lives. There was no question of the Gestapo beating on our door at four in the morning and dragging us off to the gas chambers. At least, that is what I knew I should be thinking and feeling.

My political education still had a long way to go.

I started to become consciously aware of the greater political world in which we lived. The United Party, the official opposition to the Nationalist government, split with the minority under Jan Steytler leaving to found the Progressive Party in 1956. I was very excited by these events. Firstly, I was anti-Nat simply because the Nats represented the ruling party and Afrikanerdom. I had been schooled from an early age into being against the government. My experiences at the hands of Mnr. Oosthuisen, our Afrikaans teacher at Longwood, had done nothing to change my mind. He was a tall pale man with a pedantic air about him who set himself the task of beating his language into us *"rooineks"*. He did not endear either himself or anyone associated with him or his language. But more than that, I knew that the reason black people did not have the vote, the reason they were treated so badly and were so poorly paid was because of Nationalist Party policy.

Even then, I could not understand the economics of it. For it seemed to me that it would be to everyone's benefit if they were treated and paid like white people. Without the benefit of a degree in economics it was obvious to me that the more people were paid the more they had to save and spend. Surely, this could only be of benefit to the economy? As for voting and the rights of citizenship, it was perfectly obvious that depriving people of things that everyone else took for granted could only build up resentment. It was just a matter of time before the pressure became

"Hambakahle"

too great. In any case, excluding so many people meant there must be an enormous waste of human talent. None of my friends were interested in these things and the few adults with whom I tried to discuss them simply said I was being impractical. Blacks were unskilled and uneducated. "You can't simply make them free. There would be chaos." Chaos, a favourite word that stopped all further discussion.

That was then. Chaos would come again and again. The Treason Trial, Sharpville, Rivonia, Dr Verwoerd's assassination were just around the corner. The lull before the storm. The deadly days of the Sixties and early Seventies when the Nationalist government strengthened its grip on power and drove the country relentlessly towards the Soweto uprising of 1976 and the gathering revolution of the Eighties were undreamed of. Little did I, could I realise that the time would come when my phone would be tapped, friends would disappear, and some of them would die in a hail of bullets.

~

Benjy lived with us for about six months in 1987 as one of our family while he was on the run. Ruth was deeply involved in the Detainees' Counselling Service and had met him during a visit to Wilgespruit, a facility just outside Johannesburg that provided temporary refuge and counselling for young activists. These were the early days of psychological counselling for political detainees. The Detainees' Counselling Service was a living laboratory for victims of torture and post-traumatic stress and much pioneering work was done by dedicated social workers and psychologists who risked a great deal. Although never documented, there was no time for that sort of thing, Ruth's work with torture victims suffering from post-traumatic stress was at the forefront of clinical understanding at the time.

Benjy was brighter and more articulate than most and harboured ambitions of going to university and studying law. He was tall, good looking and charismatic. A natural leader, idealistic and committed to the cause. It always amazed us that a youngster like Benjy could emerge from the brutal experience of growing up in the townships and survive with the values and attitudes he had. Nor was he the only one we met in those years. He and many like him, youngsters whose idealism overcame the circumstances of their lives gave us hope for the future, making the struggle we had embarked on seem all the more necessary and worthwhile. Benjy harboured no racial resentments and was passionately committed to the creation of a non-racial democratic South Africa. *'The Freedom Charter'* was his creed. Ruth brought him home because Wilgespruit could no longer guarantee his safety. Nor would he be the only youngster we would provide a safe house to in those years. Much as we took him into our family (our children, especially Gretel, included him in their lives) he was desperately homesick.

One Friday Benjy disappeared leaving us a note saying he was going home to Potchestroom to see his grandmother. He would see us on Sunday night. He was found on that Monday morning in a ditch with five bullets in the back of his head. We never did find out who murdered him. He became just another statistic in the official files, but at least six months of his life are remembered by those who lived with him through those times.

Hambakahle, Benjy.

Nor would Benjy be the last.

~

Chance would see me involved in the struggle against Apartheid. And chance, I believe, kept me safe. One Saturday afternoon in the late-eighties David Webster and I arranged to run one of our "tea parties" on behalf of the Detainees Parents Support Committee in Brakpan east of Johannesburg.

The gatherings themselves were perfectly legal. The churches provided the cover. Not even the Nationalist Government was prepared to ban church tea parties. We used these opportunities to communicate and

"Hambakahle"

motivate people in their struggle against Apartheid. They also allowed us to establish an extremely efficient network which fed us information about numbers and patterns of arrest, police harassment and torture.

We picked up the combi and drove out to the East Rand on the N17 turning off at the Helderberg interchange, threading our way along the edge of the suburbs, yellow brick, manicured lawns and swimming pools to one side, burned veld and mine dumps to the other, a bleached sky overhead. As we reached the intersection between Van der Walt and Voortrekker streets we sensed something was wrong. There was virtually no traffic on the road except for military and police vehicles parked on the verges. Police waved us through as we drove the combi through several roadblocks to the church hall where the meeting was due to take place. Armoured troop carriers and jeeps were parked at every intersection. Not a soul was on the streets. All the shops were closed. Some were even boarded up. Not a car moved. There was an eerie stillness. Our vehicle was waved through red traffic lights and stop streets as David and I joked that we were being treated like royalty.

There was no doubt the police knew who we were and why we were there. To someone looking for revolutionaries we must have looked the part. I with my beard, David his balding head and intense face framed by steel-rimmed glasses.

It was very flattering, but quite frightening. To think that two obscure academics in jeans and *'Free the Children'* t-shirts could generate this amount of attention! I was beginning to understand power: guns count, but without conviction they are nothing. We were witnessing the beginnings of unbelief, of a crisis of conviction that would lead ultimately to a failure of nerve. Doubt, like running water, can undermine the most solid defences. The show of firepower that Saturday afternoon indicated weakness born of a lack of conviction. It was a massive overreaction. And, as history was to show, this was one of the first minute cracks to appear in the edifice.

When we got to the hall a small crowd of black women who had braved the siege had already organised the chairs and tables. Groups of people stood around chatting, drinking tea and eating biscuits. In the main, they were poor people dressed in their best, for whom our tea party was one of the few social occasions they could look forward to in their otherwise bleak lives. Poor people for whom David and I represented the only possibility of help in their endless struggle with the pass laws, the security establishment, and grinding poverty. The little we could offer by way of advice and support was a testimony to their desperation.

In my revolutionary mode. Drawing by Greg Kerr, (1985)

Just as we were about to start the proceedings the Special Branch arrived. Three or four young men who looked as if they could have been rugby forwards entered the hall (in fact, one or two of them had played

"Hambakahle"

provincial rugby) and stood in a line at the back, flexing their biceps and waiting for the opening prayer to finish. The final "amen" was still echoing as they surrounded me. I am not a big man. David, who was if anything slighter built than I, forced his way into the middle of the group.

"Can I help you?" he said in his firm, but polite way. "This is a legal gathering. We are not breaking the law. Need I remind you that this is church property?"

One of them turned away from me and said to David: "This is the last tea party you will give."

And with that they turned on their heels and walked out.

Three weeks later David lay dead in a pool of blood, gunned down outside his house in Johannesburg. A week or so later I discovered I was on the same hit list. My stomach turned over.

David Webster. Murdered 1989.

Why David? His research as an anthropologist had taken him into the remote regions of northern Natal, near Kosi Bay, right on the border with Mozambique. There had been suspicions for some time that what came to be known as the 'third force' was running guns across the border into Natal where they were being distributed to the Inkata Freedom Party. Natal had been in a state of civil disorder for years with pro and anti-government factions engaged in a low intensity war. There was little doubt that the government was fuelling the unrest as part of its divide and rule strategy. David had come across evidence and had taken statements from witnesses that confirmed the security police and the army's involvement in these 'third force' activities. He had also been heavily involved in organising the unions in Johannesburg. On both counts he was a prime target. He was a good friend and I miss him.

But, I'm getting ahead of myself.

15

A long weekend

Once a term we were allowed to go home for the weekend. I dreaded those times as they meant returning to a world I could not blot out and pretend did not exist. I arrived home to find Flora comatose. Friday evening and the weekend stretch before me. Am I going to spend the whole weekend reading in a room with an unconscious woman who will only recognise my presence long enough to demand that I make tea? I don't want to but it looks as if there is no option.

Since I had gone to boarding school I had lost touch with my friends in town. There was no possibility of being able to drop in on any of them. We lived in different worlds with different interests. Anyway, I did not have any transport. Johannesburg is a big city. Its public transport system was created on the premise that every white person owned a car. I go out and walk the streets to kill time. Rush hour. I lose myself in the crowds going home to proper homes and proper families and proper suppers.

Up Plein Street past the Union Grounds and the Drill Hall, destined to have its moment of fame when the Treason Trial is held there, past the Elgin Hotel in which we had stayed when we first came to Johannesburg and the bookshop across the road where I had struggled for hours to spend a book token I had been given. It is too late to drop in on Miss Fairfax; the Gallery will be closing now. Left at the Technical College into Eloff the main street downtown past John Orrs, the OK Bazaars, Pollyacs and Markhams now beginning to close their shutters; their windows full of things I could never buy, to Commissioner Street and His Majesty's, The Coliseum and The Empire where I linger reading the billboards, looking at pictures of the films now showing, and back up Nugget Street to Boston Court. I manage to drag out three hours, passing big department stores, book shops, cinemas and hotels with their uniformed commissioners ushering beautiful women and rich men who live normal lives through the lobby to a tantalising world of light and music.

Staring Memory in the Face

When I got back Flora was still unconscious. Something was different though. Something was missing. I looked at the bookcase that stood between our two beds. My *William* books! They're gone. I did not have much that I could call my own, but my complete set of *William* books, that I had spent years collecting, was my most cherished possession. I returned to the stories again and again, finding solace and security in the world they portrayed. Their very physical presence in the bookcase gave me a sense of continuity and stability. I read and reread them over and over. I could quote at length from many of the stories. William's gang and Jumble were as alive in my imagination as they were on the printed page. In fact, I created innumerable stories of my own at night lying in my bed, the lights from the traffic outside flickering against the ceiling of our one room, imagining English villages and country lanes, woods and farmyards, proper families in proper houses living proper lives punctuated by fathers returning from work at the end of every day. Endless adventures in which I took on the stupidity and obduracy of the adult world. It was above all a predictable and safe world, where mothers were not drug addicts and fathers did not abandon their families. Flora had sold my books, she said, because she had no money and needed to buy food. I knew she had sold them for drugs, and in fact found some crushed pills in her sheets the following morning.

I know I have to confront her. Since our row, when she discovered I knew of my adoption, I have avoided any direct confrontation with her. I know she can twist everything I say so that it ends up meaning the opposite of what I intended. The anguish I feel beforehand, trying to get everything ordered in my head and the guilt afterwards when I have been convinced that I was fabricating a tissue of lies are more than I can bear. But now, I am in the grip of emotions that are driving me in a direction that cannot be avoided. This is the one weekend of term when I am at home. The least she could do is to keep off the pills for these two days.

I had dreaded coming home: I knew what to expect. I do not want to spend my only free weekend with an unconscious body that simply requires me to make tea whenever it wakes up. This is not how normal

A long weekend

people live. I am determined to have a proper Sunday lunch with roast lamb and vegetables and gravy. We will be like ordinary people just for one day and eat proper food in a proper way. And, what is more, it has been agreed she and I are going out to the bioscope on Saturday night. *Shane* with Alan Ladd and Jack Palance is on at the Coliseum, and it will do her good to get out.

Flora denies she has taken any sleeping pills. She had run out of money and had been forced to sell the books to buy what little food there was in the room. It is all too pat and I do not believe her for a moment. She has had a heavy week at work and fallen asleep as soon as she got home, and is sorry she wasn't awake when I arrived but she had obviously been too exhausted. She is not prepared to discuss sleeping pills or any other kind of pills with me. So, what about the books? They were only books and I had outgrown them anyway. And the pills? She takes only what her doctor prescribes and obviously, if he prescribed them, she needs them. She is not going to have me tell her what she should take and what not. She flatly refuses to consider going to a film. She has no clothes. We cannot afford it. She isn't feeling well enough. There are no buses running late at night and how will we get home? Anyway, she doesn't like rubbishy westerns.

Recognising that she would not give in on the film I said I would go and see it by myself. Would she at least agree that we have a proper Sunday lunch for a change before I go back to school? Yes. Could I please have some money to buy what is needed for our lunch and for the bioscope?

I was desperate to see *Shane* as I had heard all about it from my friends at school, and anyway I was absolutely determined to have something out of the weekend that approximated to what I believed was a normal experience: bioscope on Saturday night and a proper Sunday lunch. She reached for her bag and gave me ten shillings. I went out immediately to get to the butcher before he closed for the weekend. I had never done shopping of this kind before and had no idea of what sort of quantities to buy. A leg of lamb for two proved beyond my budget if I was going to stretch the money to include vegetables, tinned peaches and custard for pudding and have one and tuppence left over for the film. I settled for a knuckle of lamb and then went to the greengrocer where I bought potatoes, cabbage, squash, carrots and peas; enough vegetables to feed a family of four for a week. Food was incredibly cheap in those days.

By the time I got back Flora was asleep. She had obviously taken something while I was out at the shops. I can get nothing coherent out of her. I search and find a half full container under her pillow, and flush the pills down the sink. At least she would spend Sunday awake.

I spend the rest of the evening riding the range, a solitary and mysterious gunman confronting a killer who dons black leather gloves before he draws his Colt 45. When the gunfire ceases he rides off without saying goodbye, his name echoing in the hills. Shane, … Shane … .

The following morning, she did not wake and ask for her morning cup of tea. That should have alerted me, but in pursuit of a normal family Sunday I went out and bought *The Sunday Times*. The main story was about a group of white female political prisoners in The Fort who had gone on a hunger strike. I was not the only child not having a normal family weekend.

By the time I finished the paper it was eleven o'clock. It was time to start preparing lunch. Flora had not stirred all morning. A little searching revealed another lot of pills in the folds of the blankets on her bed. She was completely unconscious, but I knew the signs well enough to know that she was in no danger. I was still determined that we would have a proper Sunday lunch and set about cleaning the vegetables and preparing the meat. There was much too much food. Even I could see that. But I went ahead anyway and got pots bubbling away on all the plates. The meat went into the oven. I hoped that what I was doing would not ruin it. I was also worried that nothing would be ready before I would have to leave to catch the 4.00 o'clock train back to school. Everything seemed to be taking much more time than I imagined. By 2.30 I decided I could not wait any longer. The vegetables were cooked. Of that I was sure. The meat still looked a bit raw but I could not carry on waiting. There was no gravy: I had been relying on Flora to help me with that part but she

A long weekend

was beyond helping anyone. I served myself, sat down with the remnants of the Sunday paper in front of me and polished off as much as I could. To hell with the washing up. She could do that when she woke up. Half an hour later I closed the door behind me without saying goodbye. My name not echoing in the hallway, I left the building.

I got to the train just as it was about to pull out of the station. Fortunately, two of my friends, Chan and Ah Lee Ah Moy from school were on the train. There was no time to feel sorry for myself. Chan and I were in the same class. I helped him with his English essays and he helped me with my maths. Chan always brought me Chinese food from home at the end of each free weekend. Ah Lee was a very pretty girl with, in my view, wisdom beyond her fifteen years. Delicate, with perfect skin, she was outgoing and had what I thought was the most beautiful voice. I had long wanted her as a girlfriend but was too shy to ask. They opened their tuck boxes and pressed spring rolls on me.

The train pulled out of Park Station passing through the eastern suburbs of Johannesburg. When we reached Germiston a ticket inspector came aboard and started working his way through the carriage. He got to our compartment, took one look and belligerently demanded that Chan and Ah Lee get off the train. First in Afrikaans then in broken English.

"No Chinks. No Chinks on this train. Get off. Get off the train. You get off. This train for whites only. No compartments for other races. You get off, or I call the police."

It was Sunday afternoon, but his breath smelled of drink. We were all in our school uniforms so there was no mistaking that he saw we all went to the same school. When Chan protested saying they were returning to boarding school and that he had been travelling on this train for three years, he was told,

"Don't talk back to a whiteman. You get off now."

Staring Memory in the Face

At this point, something in me snapped. The accumulated emotions of the weekend and outrage at the injustice I was witnessing prompted my outburst. I rose to my feet trembling with rage, terrified by my own audacity at challenging an adult, and one in an official uniform at that, who had the power to detain us if he liked.

How dare he speak to my friends like that. Who did he think he was? He had no right! His job is to check that people have tickets not stop children from going to school. Couldn't he see they went to the same school as me? Wait till I reported this to my school principal. Then we'd see who would be in trouble. How would he like it if his kids were thrown off a train and left by themselves without any way of telling their parents where they were? Who did he think he was treating school children like that? Didn't he know that even the government regarded Chinese as whites? The Chinese had been civilised for thousands of years before whites. What right had he to think he was superior to them? Who did he think he was? I would report him to his superiors. See what the newspapers would make of that. Would he like to have his name splashed all over the *Sunday Times*? If he was going to throw them off he'd have to throw me off too. And, if he was going to call the police I would make sure they arrested me as well and see what the papers made of *that*.

I don't know if it was the ferocity and unexpectedness of my attack, but he retreated from the compartment muttering vague threats and disappeared. The train pulled out of the station a few minutes later without any sign of the police or the inspector. We sat in stunned silence: Chan and Ah Lee fearful of what might happen when the trained stopped at the next station, I at my own audacity. And nothing happened. It was a salutary lesson in the power of confrontation. We pulled into the next station and there were no police waiting for us. No officials came to our compartment.

The train made its way over the Highveld, the stations punctuating a blazing afternoon: Natalspruit, Klipriver, Daleside and Henley-on-Klip, eventually stopping in Meyerton two hours later without incident. It was only when we had put the station well behind us that we found the cour-

A long weekend

age to talk. I was still burning with righteous outrage. Chan and Ah Lee took a more pragmatic view, saying there was no point in complaining. There was nothing we could do. A shroud of fatalism descended as we walked the two miles back to school, the late afternoon sun streaming through the bluegums lining the road that stretched before us, dust and eucalyptus thick in the air.

My first overt and deliberate political act.

16

L'Albergo di Luigi

Flora lost her job at *The Star*. She had been ill too often and had exhausted their patience and charity. She moved out of Boston Court into a boarding house in Hillbrow but neglected to tell me. It was the end of the 1957 school year. Sputnik had circled the earth. The Christmas holidays were looming. I had lost my only pair of shoes two days previously. As it was summer and we spent most of our time barefoot, I was able to manage. Fortunately, I had an old pair of sandals and so, in my school uniform, suitcase in my hand and broken sandals held together with string I boarded the train back to Johannesburg. I was acutely aware of how poor I looked, and sat with my suitcase covering my feet.

When I reached Boston Court I discovered Flora was not living there any longer. Our room was occupied by a strange woman who had no idea where she had gone. What to do?

I am in the middle of town. I have no idea where she is. No money and no shoes and no one to whom I can appeal.

Friday night. I was sitting on my suitcase just inside the lobby wondering what to do next when Hanna Rubenstein, looking much older and frailer opens the front door. She has an address, a boarding house near Barnato Park in Hillbrow. There is nothing for it. I pick up my suitcase and start walking. An hour and a half later … .

"*O mio babbino caro*". "*E lucevan le stelle*". "*La Paloma*". The warm summer night is alive with sobbing sopranos and heroic tenors, Callas, Gigli, di Stefano. Italian opera and Neapolitan folk songs. Is this the place? *L'albergo di Luigi*. A constant stream of people coming and going through the front door. The street is loud with Italian voices. I check the address: no mistake. This is it. I go inside and ask for Flora. Christmas decorations festoon the walls and ceilings. A large Christmas tree stands in the corner of the dining room. I stand irresolutely in front of her door, suitcase in hand. I knock. No answer. The light is on. She is asleep. A

L'Albergo di Luigi

cigarette smoulders in saucer next to the bed. An empty teacup. The signs are all too familiar.

A head appears round the door.

"Are you OK?" She asks. In the gloom, I can just make out an over made-up female face, lips, cheeks and eyes and unruly dark hair.

"She said you'd get here OK."

So, my existence is known. I have been expected. I look down at the still sleeping figure, shrug my shoulders and put my suitcase on the bed against the opposite wall.

"Have you eaten? You'd better join us. We are about to eat. I'm Maria."

I follow her to the dining room and am seated at a vast table where I am introduced to the fifteen or so people sitting down to supper. A huge steaming bowl of pasta is brought in and placed in the middle of the table. We help ourselves as carafes of Chianti are passed around. No one takes any special notice of me. Everyone is too full of talk and food and wine. A man sitting next to me fills my glass. Mario. He tells me he and his friends work on the mines, Carletonville. They were all recruited in Italy and are in South Africa on a three-year contract. They spend every weekend here. They all belong to the same soccer team that plays in a Johannesburg league every Saturday. They are celebrating their win this afternoon.

"You play, … calcio, … a futabal?"

"Left wing."

I am beginning to relax. Imagination is beginning to give way to fantasy. Someone at the end of the table begins to sing "*La Paloma*" followed by "*O Sole Mio*", "*La Serenata*" and "*Non ti scordar di me*". And everyone joins in. Song follows song with different singers taking up the challenge. No need for Gigli now. *Nessun dorma* … .

Maria and the other girls, Sophia, Miranda, Rosa and Renata disappear from time to time with Mario, or Giulio, or Giovanni, or Riccado or Enrico or Renaldo or Paolo. I lose track of the names. Besides

Staring Memory in the Face

I am now into my third glass of wine and am beginning to have enough courage to sing along when I can.

"Ah, you can-a sing ... Sing for us ... Come, anything ... It-a doesn't matter."

Wothell. Embarrassed but determined to show off. I've got nothing to lose. I'm surrounded by expectant faces. I look into the eyes of the girl nearest me and draw breath.

"*My desert is waiting, Dear come there with me, I'm longing to teach you love's sweet melody ... .*" I serenade Maria, or is it Renata?

Applause. Inspired, I turn to Rosa.

"O, *Rosemarie I love you, I'm always dreaming of you ... .*"

More applause. It goes to my head and then it's,

"*Jerusalem sing for the night is young. Hosanna in the highest Hosanna for evermore ... .*"

I fill the room with hosannas.

"Bravo, bravo."

The room is cleared and the dancing begins. "*The Merry Widow*". "*Voices of Spring*". "*The Blue Danube*". One waltz after another. I am now drunk with song and dance and wine and the joy of being alive and surrounded by people who think I'm marvellous. And the girls are beautiful. Their breasts bounce tantalisingly in three-four time. Invitation to the dance. To what else? For the first time in my life I'm the centre of attention at a party. And it's wonderful. And what is more, a party at which before this evening I didn't know a soul. They insist that I waltz with Maria. It's my performance. They leave the floor to us and I spin her through the *Vienna Woods*.

Miranda sits next to me. Recklessly, I begin ...

"Do you remember an inn,
Miranda?
Do you remember an inn?
And the tedding and the spreading of the straw for a bedding
And the fleas that tease in the High Pyrenees?

L'Albergo di Luigi

And the wine that tasted of tar …?[26]

I am plied with more wine. This is Life. This is how it should be all the time. The *joie de vivre*. Laughter. Dancing and singing. I am vaguely aware that Riccardo and Paolo are having an argument about Sophia. They disappear but the party continues. The girls make a fuss of me and I am flattered and excited. The room is a blur of sound and motion. It is beginning to revolve of its own accord. Suddenly, I am exhausted. I get up and try to make my way to the room. I feel Maria's arm around me, for which I am very grateful. I am conscious enough to appreciate her breast against the side of my chest. I know I'm drunk.

And I don't care.

Maria helps me to the room. She opens the door and helps me to the bed where I throw up. I lie half on the bed incapable of helping myself. She gets me onto the bed and rolls me over. Nimble, knowing, practised fingers; damp cloths on my forehead. I am unbuttoned.

I am undone.

The following morning, I wake with a splitting headache and nausea that has me retching again. As I become aware of my surroundings and begin to remember the previous evening, I realise I'm naked. The sheets and pillow are clean; a glass of water is on the chair beside my bed. There is no trace of vomit, though a lingering taste in my mouth. If I move my head the world reels.

And, Flora is still asleep.

When eventually she wakes, she is not surprised to see me. She had to leave Boston Court. She did a flit because she owed four months' rent. The money she gets from Tommy is just enough to cover the rent here with a little over for food. Is she eating? Not just drinking tea? Is it going to be enough for me too? Don't worry, we'll work something out. She's already spoken to Luigi and he's agreed to let me stay for the holidays at a reduced rate. What could she possibly promise to get him to agree to that? Has she got another job? Not yet. There's no point in looking for one until after the New Year. Everyone's away on holiday. Anyway, she

---

26. Hilaire Belloc: 'Tarantella'.

Staring Memory in the Face

is going to ask the courts to increase what she gets from my father every month. I sense a disaster in the offing.

Luigi takes an interest in me. We talk *il calcio* (futabal), opera, Michelangelo, Verdi. He tells me to read Dante. I try to explain cricket. He tells me I shouldn't drink too much.

"But remember Mike, always have-a couple a-glasses a-water before you a-go to a-bed. Then, in the a-morning, no hangover."

It's good advice.

I am beginning to have more than feelings of friendship for his girls, especially Maria, but know there is a limit beyond which I cannot venture. In any case, I am too unsure of myself. Their concern for me is maternal. I meet them in the passage coming from the bathroom, emerging from their rooms, in various states of undress at all times of the day and night. Dishevelled, firm breasts and slim thighs. Bruised lips and necks. They are always friendly and kind. I bemoan my immaturity. Their kindness is the kindness of women to a child, not of young women to a young man. Careless of their dress: I struggle not to stare. Once, coming back from the bathroom without a shirt I bump into Maria and Sophia.

"What's with the build, hey Mike?"

Confused and blushing, I stumble away.

I started to pick up a little Italian. It was to become a lifelong ambition, culminating many years later in a two-month stint at the *Instituto d'italiano a Firenze* where, surrounded by nubile twenty-year olds from northern Europe and Scandinavia, I struggled, not for the first or last time, unsuccessfully to marry competing fantasies with reality.

December is an endless party. Enrico and his friends are on leave and are spending it at Luigi's. Every night there is a feast, Chianti and singing.

∼

The weeks pass and Christmas approaches. I am called to the phone. It is Tommy. How did he know where we were living? Would I like to come

L'Albergo di Luigi

over and spend Christmas Eve with him and Pat (the new woman in his life) and her family? I don't know what Mum has got organised: I'll give him a ring (buying time) as soon as I know. I tell her about the phone call. What should I do? Would she mind if I went? Maybe I could persuade him to give her a little more money.

"Tell him your shirts are full of holes. You have no shoes. I have no money to get you any new clothes." She is already a month behind with the rent.

A new year dawns.

I am eighteen. I am tired of sharing a room with Flora. It occurs to me that I have never had my own room. I have shared a room with Flora, often sharing the same bed, since we went to England nine years ago. I am tired of finding her unconscious, a sodden cigarette in a saucer and a cup half full of cold tea next to the bed. I am tired of always having to hunt for pills. I am tired of the broken promises. I am tired of the squalor of our lives. I am tired of having to tell lies.

She has noticed that I have been coming to bed smelling of alcohol.

"I hope you are not going to become like your father?"

The accusation hangs in the air.

It is eleven o'clock in the morning. She is lying in bed smoking. There has been a heavy silence since she woke at eight when I brought her first cup of tea. Last night, New Year's Eve, had been a great party. I had got to bed at four, exhausted from dancing, my throat raw from singing, my head spinning, but this time I had managed to get there by myself. Maria, Sophia, Rosa, Miranda and Renata had disappeared long before I staggered off. I had been hoping to celebrate the New Year with the loss of my virginity, but the girls had been preoccupied, coming and going, and I didn't get a chance to persuade any of them to change their maternal concern for me into something more exciting.

What right has she to comment on what I do? I am eighteen. I can vote. I am old enough to make decisions about what I want to do. I am also consumed with doubt and guilt. I know that if it hadn't been for drink Tommy would not have abandoned us. She would never have taken to drugs. And yet, and yet … .

The morning dawns. I get up, get dressed and make tea. The house is still quiet. There is no one in the kitchen. I help myself to a slice of toast and a glass of milk. When I am finished I put the teapot and a cup and jug of milk on a tray and take it through to our room. As I put it down next to her, she stirs. I sit down and wait, knowing she will first have to light a cigarette. I feel a great black hole opening up inside me. It gave no warning. Something is happening and I am powerless to stop it.

"I've had enough. I'm leaving you. I'm sick to death of everything about you."

I launched into and was committed to a headlong course of action before I had thought of the implications, but was determined to see it through.

I dragged out the suitcase from under the bed and began cramming my clothes into it, repeating, "I'm sick of it. I'm sick of it. I've had enough." I was no longer able to contain my anger, no longer able to douse the flames of rebellion with guilt.

My anger works itself up as I pack; Flora does not respond beyond, "Where do you think you are going?"

"To my father. At least I won't have to live with you."

Trembling with rage and fearful of the course on which I have set myself, I slammed the case shut and walked out.

"Goodbye."

By the time I knocked on Tommy's door two hours later I had calmed down and was concerned about the reception I would get. Would he reject me? If he did, how could I return to Flora with my tail between my legs? What would Pat's reaction be? Did they have space? He opened the door. He took one look at my suitcase and led me through to the spare bedroom.

"You can unpack here. This will be your room."

There were no questions. No call for an explanation of why I had arrived or why I had left Flora. We went into the living room, "Michael

L'Albergo di Luigi

has come to stay. I've shown him his room." As if they had been expecting me.

I managed to hold out for about ten days before I went to see Flora. I had spent the better part of the time alternatively reinforcing my determination to make a clean break and worrying how she was. Finally, I compromised by deciding I would simply visit her to see if she was coping. I was determined not to live with her again. The end of the holidays was close at hand, and I would be returning to school anyway. It was Saturday morning. I arrived at Luigi's just after nine. No one was around. The house felt almost abandoned. Flora was awake, sitting up in bed smoking a cigarette. A half cup of tea stood on the table next to the bed.

"How are you?"

"Fine, and you?"

"Fine. How is Tommy?"

"Fine."

"How do you find living there?"

"Fine."

"When do you go back to school?"

"In two weeks."

"I always knew you'd abandon me in the end."

What can I say? The silences drag out. The territory between us is too terrifying to test. She is gaunt, almost skeletal. Her eyes are dark hollows. Blue veins run down the side of her head. Her hair is lank and unwashed, streaked with grey.

"Are you eating?"

"No, I'm taking Tommy to court again on Monday to see if I can get the maintenance increased. I want to lose weight to get the magistrate's sympathy."

I left shortly afterwards, confused and consumed with guilt, but determined that my survival depended on not going back.

On Monday morning, the phone rang. I heard Tommy put it down after a few minutes. He came through to my room.

Staring Memory in the Face

"Flora was taken to hospital last night. She died early this morning. It seems she took an overdose."

Relief floods through me. It is over. I am no longer responsible. A weight lifts. I feel giddy, light-headed. Empty.

And then, guilt that I do not feel remorse, but relief.

Later in the morning I go out and find the most dismal place I can, the parking garage beneath the flats, and force myself to cry. I don't believe in what I am doing. This is what is required. This is what people do when their mother dies. It is a ritual that has to be endured. The garage is an empty concrete shell. There are no witnesses. Once I have satisfied myself that I have done what is necessary, I leave the building and go for a long walk. It is finished. A door has closed. There is nothing I could have done. It was inevitable. I recognise all that. But still, I am appalled with myself for feeling as little as I do. All those years of degradation, the hunting for pills, phoning doctors and ambulances, the squalid rooms we shared are all being stripped away. I have my life before me.

Flora was forty-eight when she died at the beginning of 1958; a young woman. The marriage had broken irretrievably when she was in her mid-thirties. She had never managed to make a new start and had been caught in a downward spiral of drugs, depression and poverty.

I didn't go to her funeral.

~ 17 ~

A life sentence

A few weeks later I was back at school for the beginning of my matric year. I told no one, except Cloete, what had happened. There was no question of my leaving school. The fees hadn't been paid for three years and he had no expectation that they ever would be. I was taken back under no obligation. Nor was I the only or first child he took under his wing like that. There must have been at least half a dozen or more of us in a similar position at any given time. He was no businessman but had a deep commitment to education and young people. He certainly had an enormous influence on me. More than anything, he imparted an enthusiasm for life, by stimulating my curiosity and imagination in exciting ways through art and music and philosophy, the theatre and literature. He taught me to read and love poetry; to delight in the seeming limitless possibilities of life. He had my complete loyalty. I worshipped the ground he walked on. I owed him everything and forgave him everything. And there was much to forgive. He was erratic and unpredictable and cruel. I was never quite sure if I was in favour or out. I could never really understand his motives.

A month after I returned to school all the senior pupils wrote a standardised IQ test. This event was preceded by much discussion and speculation about the meaning of IQ, its accuracy, reliability and predictive value. Above all, what were our individual IQs? Late into the night over beer and cigarettes we discussed the nature of intelligence. Verbal and non-verbal intelligence. Could it be defined? Was it possible to measure something about which so little is known? Do we really know what we are trying to measure? To this day these questions are still matters of controversy. We were told about normal distribution curves and the norm of 100 and shown lists of the great and their IQs. It was impressed upon us that the multiple-choice questionnaires used in the tests couldn't be fooled. There was, of course, no way you could prepare yourself for the test. Intelligence had nothing to do with knowledge. This was the ultimate exam that assigned a value beyond what could be learned. This sort of thinking was, of course, reductive, narrow, simplistic and hopelessly unscientific, but it did reflect the understanding of the times.

No one was allowed to see the results of the test because of the possible psychological damage it might do if the results did not meet their expectations. The argument was that everyone thinks they are more intelligent than they are. A result which was perceived as infallible could do psychological damage by branding a person for life as below normal, stupid. The tension was between professional understanding of what the tests were and what they were not, and the layman's understanding. The tests, while not infallible, were perceived by the professionals of the day as good indicators and predictors of success. The professionals, especially the academics who designed and administered them and interpreted the results, were much more confident of what they were doing than they had reason to be. The methodologies they were using were badly flawed. The definition of intelligence was extremely narrow. It boiled down to little more than the ability to recognise number relationships, word patterns and spatial relationships on a given occasion. Nonetheless, the tests were widely used and the results accepted. In the hands of teachers who had only the slightest understanding of what they represented, untold damage was done to thousands of children who on the basis of what they had scored were treated as if they were sub-normal. The so-called bright children were no better off. They had unreasonable expectations foisted on them, which many of them could not meet.

We were told the results would be entered on a green Ed-lab card in an office in Pretoria containing our entire school record. This card would follow us to the grave. Big Brother was watching us, and he had all the evidence he needed for any assessment of our abilities. That is, our worth. There was no escape. I had just read Orwell's *Nineteen Eighty-Four* and Huxley's *Brave New World*. The message was all too clear.

My three years at Longwood had done a great deal for my self-confidence and self-esteem. We were all quite excited at being tested and

A life sentence

having our genius confirmed. Like everyone else in school, Cloete had me convinced that I was gifted. It was simply a matter of time before a grateful world discovered me.

The tester from the Human Sciences Research Council distributed the question papers and I sat feeling as if I was being drenched by bucket after bucket of ice-cold water. Pages of geometric shapes that had to be categorised. Questions that went round in circles and left me feeling utterly confused. Lists of numbers and words containing hidden patterns. And all against the clock. I was in familiar territory. Panic caught me by the throat. I could hardly breathe. At the end of three hours I staggered out and put on a brave face. There was nothing to it. Simple. And everyone agreed with me, which just made it worse.

One night several weeks later, while we were ostensibly doing prep in his study (we were actually listening to music, talking and drinking beer and smoking) Cloete announced that he had received the results. Of course, we all wanted to know how well we had done. No, he couldn't tell us. However, as the night wore on and the brandy bottle got lower, Pike managed to get him to tell him his IQ. Pike was the brightest in our class. There was no harm in confirming what we all knew. Pike was also his favourite and usually managed to get what he wanted. He asked to see the official results and in a little while we were all crowded around the study desk reading the HSRC official report. My eye went down the page. There it was. Verbal and non-verbal scores and the aggregate. That was it. There was nothing I could do. The ultimate confirmation of what I had always known. Science could not be wrong. I was trapped in this body and this brain. This time there would be no escape. It was a life sentence.

The year that had started so precipitously with Flora's suicide, 1958, saw me fail matric. More than thirty years later I returned to the school, now long closed. The buildings were still there, but strangely still, bereft of life. The soccer field and cricket pitch were also surprisingly still there, but the goal posts had been removed: a bare open space separated from the road on the boundary by a tall line of blue-gums. The smell of

Staring Memory in the Face

eucalyptus still lingers in the air. Faint echoes of bat on ball. Memories of long summer afternoons lost in a book, oblivious of the world. The only sign of the plantation we called the forest was the straggled remains of burnt stumps. The school hall had been turned into a fundamentalist chapel. The murals with which we had decorated the interior, scenes copied from postcards of rural France, were still there. Evidently, they were bland enough not to offend the religious taste of the present occupiers. Cloete's study bereft of books and music, where I had listened to the *Arch Duke Trio* night after night, after hours of talk, lying on my back on the veranda, the Milky Way and Southern Cross wheeling overhead, was now a store room for *The Watchtower*. The old fake Cape Dutch house which contained the dining room and kitchen we had raided on so many occasions was now, fittingly, a casino and a brothel.

I suspect that for some of my readers the question must arise during the course of this narrative: what made it possible for me not only to survive but also to find intellectual and emotional fulfilment? The clues, if they are that, are sometimes obvious, a person, something said, an insight drawn from observation, something I read, a lucky accident.

Luck. Never underestimate luck. What are not so obvious are the influences that worked below the level of consciousness, the feelings and emotions that made me open to such influences; that enabled me to pick myself up, dust myself off and start all over again. I puzzle about it to this day. There are a multiplicity of ironies and contradictions. On the one hand, I suffered from an appalling self-image and lack of self-confidence; on the other, I believed the world was my oyster. It was there waiting for me to make of it what I will. Whatever the case, I was determined to avoid what I melodramatically described to myself as the gutter. This decision has often resulted in a failure of nerve, and I have pulled back from the consequences of risk. The two opposing poles of my personality, my capacity for fantasy and my pragmatism, have constantly been at war with each other. As I have got older pragmatism has usually won out. So, where did I get my exuberance from, my zest for life? I can't answer that

A life sentence

question. The best I can offer is this text, incomplete as it is. In writing we discover ourselves.

~

I spent most of that year at school, not even going home for weekends or the holidays. As a result, I hardly saw Tommy or Pat, only returning home for one weekend during the year, after I had written my final exams. It was this weekend that convinced me that I needed to spend as much time away from home as possible. Tommy was determined to have a heart to heart talk with me, now that I was about to plunge into life, as he put it, and found an opportunity one Saturday morning. What I had been doing up to that point was a moot question. He obviously wanted to unburden himself about the past, about his failed marriage and his failure as a father.

The physical details are sharp. Tommy's bald head, florid face, pale grey eyes, hunched shoulders and stooped frame. His hands clutching the veranda rail as though to keep himself erect. Puffing nervously on a cigarette. Nicotine stained fingers. His jersey has a hole in one of the elbows. A thread has come loose in one of the sleeves. We are overlooking a vacant plot of land tangled with weeds. The clear Highveld sky, tufts of brown winter grass. Someone has used the space as a dumping ground for building material and garden refuse. A cat is slinking through the dusty undergrowth of khakibos and blackjacks, hunting field mice.

It is the first opportunity we have had to talk about Flora since her death. He breaks down and begins weeping, begging me to believe that he is my father. No matter what I think, no matter what has happened, I must believe him, I am his son.

My reaction is neither disbelief nor relief. I stand next to this weeping man whom I hardly know, but about whom I have heard a great deal, most of it negative, for almost nine years not knowing what to think or where to look. I had only turned to him as a last desperate resort when I could not bear living with Flora any more. His reputation as an alcoholic, wife abuser and abandoner of his family has been too deeply ingrained for me to regard him with more than suspicion. I see him through the cruel prism of youth as weak, ineffectual, a failure and maudlin. I was also seeing myself. This holding up a mirror steeled my resolve to keep my distance. It is easy to judge at eighteen.

He then told me about my mother. As he tried to justify why he had an affair so soon after marrying Flora, I found my mind wandering, half listening, trying to imagine her, who bore me, who now has a name, Mary Edna White, a Canadian nurse, but no reality beyond these broken sobbed words on a Saturday morning, recalling events ten thousand miles away, twenty years previously. The marriage had obviously been on shaky ground from the beginning. The intervention of the War had probably kept it going longer than it should. Peace, a new country and a new life had dealt the deathblow. He had tried unsuccessfully to trace her after she had been wounded in North Africa and repatriated to Canada. But, as I discovered many years later, it was all a lie: there had been no Mary Edna White, no Canadian nurse, or if there had been she was not my mother. But it made a convincing tale at the time.

The monologue, for that is what it was, lasted a long time. And the longer it lasted the more uncomfortable I felt. He was deeply ashamed of the past, of the fact that he had not been a better father, of my having had to deal with Flora's drug problem for all those years. But I knew he had no idea of what it was really like. How could he? How could anyone who had not grown up during those seemingly endless days and nights, sharing one room, often the same bed with a woman who was for the most part unconscious, wondering where the next meal was coming from, whether there was enough money to pay the rent? Lurching from one failure at school to the next. Empty. Alone. I watched him cry and felt no pity, as only a callow youth can.

I subsequently learned many years later, more or less at the time I discovered that Mary Edna was a figment of his imagination, that my birth was a source of much conflict in the family. It is not clear how I was explained away except that just before the war my father and Flora had

A life sentence

gone to Glasgow to announce my impending arrival to the family. My father announced Flora's pregnancy. How he persuaded her to go along with the deception, why he did so, and why she agreed to are mysteries that tease and invite my sense of melodrama. My aunt Winnie remembered her mother, Mina, seeing her off at a bus stop in Glasgow, when my father and Flora encountered them in the high street. The news was greeted with joy. I would be the first grandchild.

Some forty odd years later in 2004, when all the main actors were long since dead, I decided to try and unravel some of the mystery. As might be expected, I got both more and a lot less than I hoped for. More in the sense that I learned for the first time what my mother's name was and where I had been born; less than I hoped, because I soon ran into a blank wall beyond which it has proved impossible to go. Too much time had passed. Records had been destroyed, and those who might have provided information are all dead or have disappeared.

My mother, I discovered, was Elizabeth Fenton. I had been named Alan Chadwick Fenton at birth; strangely, as a child I had often wished I had been called Alan instead of Michael. Who Elizabeth Fenton was or what her relationship with my father have remained a mystery. Birth certificates of the illegitimate in those days did not reveal the father's name, so I have to take his word for it that I am his son. But Chadwick? It was obviously a family name of some significance, but what, I have not been able to uncover. Nor is there any record of where I lived from the time that I was born until I was adopted over a year later.

But even so, some interesting if not helpful information has come to hand. I learned that the nursing home I was born in at 27 Riverleigh Avenue Lytham St Annes, just south of Blackpool, was run by one Mary O'Boyle who took in young girls who had, to use the quaint expression of the day, "got themselves into trouble" and provided them with a haven in which to have their babies. She also helped arrange adoptions through Nazareth House, a Catholic orphanage in Burnley. From the little I have been able to glean, she must have been a remarkable woman. Christine Woods, who told me about Mary O'Boyle, was also born in Number 27 and later adopted by Mary O'Boyle. Unfortunately, by the time I made contact with Christine, Mary had been dead for many years. Her story deserves to be told.

A hiatus was caused by the war. This may have been fortuitous as it provided the cover for my birth and adoption. My grandmother did not see me until two or three years later when we visited her in Glasgow.

My cousin Kathy discovered this picture in 2020 of Elizabeth Fenton (left).

My cousin Kathy Trevelyan, an indefatigable researcher of our genealogy, is convinced she has discovered who Elizabeth Fenton was, and even a photograph. Kathy has searched the Lancaster municipal records of the time and has discovered two candidates with the right name. She has

A life sentence

eliminated one of them on the grounds of age. The other was an anaesthetist who served in Normandy and later emigrated to New Zealand. She never married. Kathy is convinced she must be my mother. In her words: "The reason Ruth and I got excited about Elizabeth Fenton is that she is the only person of that name and the right age who was living anywhere near where you were born. She was also training as a doctor. I found her in the 1939 Register, so near your birthdate. She had no children that her relative I contacted knows of. We will probably never know for sure unless one of her family would be willing to do a DNA test." So, the dates are right and there is the coincidence of her profession and emigration after the War. I'm rather more sceptical.

The afternoon following my father's revelations, I boarded the train to take me back to school. The compartment had one other occupant, a youngster of about my own age who was also returning to school, but in a different town. I didn't like the look of him. He sat in a corner with a scowl on his face slumped forward with his head bowed over his legs. As the train pulled out of the station he rummaged in his bag and brought out a small envelope. He emptied the contents onto the seat and began rolling a zoll, a cigarette made from brown paper and raw tobacco. He opened the window, lit up and the compartment was filled with a strong pervasive smell, not of Horseshoe Tobacco, but dagga. I sat in silence. Here was someone of my own age, making choices that could only, in my experience, lead to addiction, squalor and degradation.

As soon as the dagga began to take effect he offered me a drag. He tried to convince me of the pleasures and virtues of smoking pot: "Don't believe all that shit you get from teachers."

I had never encountered anyone who was prepared to argue the advantages of taking drugs. My experience of the drug world was limited to Flora. My understanding of the effects and consequences were immediate and undiluted. I had no time for an abstract philosophical debate. My choices were stark and immediate. I had no coherent philosophy, only a set of loosely, not too rigorously examined beliefs born of experience to which I clung. Life was a leap of faith. Anyway, it was a leap. And, so it has remained.

Under Cloete's tutelage, I had come to believe that everyone had a responsibility to awaken and develop their own innate creativity. To suppress it in any way or cut oneself off would be a denial of life. Thus, the idealism of youth.

In mitigation, I must say I was eighteen. I had also recently discovered Zen. In my immature understanding, art became a substitute for religion. I was desperate to *"drink life to the lees"*[27]. I was excited by what I thought were the limitless possibilities of life. I was burning *"To follow knowledge, like a sinking star, / Beyond the utmost bound of human thought."*[28] I would be a poet, an actor and singer, perhaps a novelist. For someone whose intellectual self-image had recently taken a severe battering, this was no small ambition. I was oblivious of the contradiction between my lust for life and the limitations imposed on me by my supposed intellect. Though, I must say in my own defence that my magpie curiosity never faltered. I continued to read voraciously and indiscriminately.

Reviewing those feelings today they are touchingly idealistic, and yet at the same time conservative and conventional. On the one hand, I longed for creative fulfilment, but could not risk moving out of the safe havens I had discovered in the value system I had created for myself and had had reinforced by Cloete. It was, of course, a failure of imagination.

I looked at my young companion in the railway compartment and realised the futility of trying to warn him about what I knew would be his fate, and felt a great emptiness as the dismal landscape rolled by.

A life sentence indeed.

---

27. Tennyson: 'Ulysses'
28. Op cit.

Part Two

~ 18 ~

In the deep end

My matric results came as no surprise. I re-wrote the supplementary exams a few months later with no better result. In the meantime, I had my first experience of living for an extended period with my father and Pat. A routine was quickly established and to begin with, although it took some getting used to, I appreciated the regularity. But the honeymoon period did not last much beyond the New Year.

My father and Pat started drinking as soon as they got home from work on Friday night. By eight o'clock they staggered off to bed where they remained for the better part of the rest of the weekend drinking themselves insensible. Some things never change. Occasionally, I heard voices raised in anger, shouting, a couple of dull thuds and silence. One night, Pat locked my father out of the bedroom. He found an axe and smashed a hole in the door. The hole was never fixed and remained a mute reminder of their drunken violence for the rest of my stay, which lasted another six months.

Their drunken squabbles became almost a nightly affair. I closed my door and buried myself in a book. Though the walls I could hear Pat's voice whining on and on until my father could stand it no more. His voice would rise to a crescendo. There would be a few dull thumps, then silence, then sobbing. Gradually, I realised that I was the subject of most of their fights. Pat felt I was usurping her place in my father's affections. Nothing could have been further from the truth. I contrived to live as separately from them as possible, coming home only when I could be fairly well assured they were asleep. But to no avail. The weekends were the worst. Pat began to turn her anger directly towards me and I had to endure her vitriolic tongue as she lashed into me at every opportunity. It is not difficult to humiliate a youngster with a poor self-image, little self-confidence and a dramatic record of failure.

Staring Memory in the Face

Soon after I failed matric for the second time I applied for a job at the SABC as a trainee journalist on what was then called *The Radio Bulletin*. The year was 1959. The Treason Trial, which I followed avidly, was well underway. I had been at school with Peter Berrangé, a nephew of one of the defence lawyers, Verron Berrangé. Another member of the defence was Bram Fischer who was destined to be a star performer in the Rivonia Trial a few years later and leader of Mandela's defence team. His defence saved Mandela from the death penalty. Bram (everyone called him Bram) was ultimately to go on trial himself after a year spent underground avoiding the security police. He received a life sentence. Wheels worked within wheels. Much into the future, my own life would be even more deeply entangled with the Fischers when I married Bram's daughter, Ruth. When Sharon Farr made her documentary film in 2006: *Love, Communism, Revolution and Rivonia, Bram Fischer's Story*, I played him in the re-created court scenes. Another of my schoolmates had been David Joffe. (We opened the first team batting together.) His brother Joel was Bram's attorney in the trial. Joel eventually became Lord Joffe and chairman of OXFAM. How little we know. Many years later he generously funded a project I ran from 2015-19 in the Western Cape. The web becomes ever more tangled. With the Rivonia Trial, and the revelations by police who had managed to infiltrate the inner circles of the Communist Party, the drama reached heights that Hollywood would find difficult to emulate. The country held its breath.

But at the time of the Treason Trial I was not yet politically active or sophisticated. Far from it: my mind was pre-occupied with my own survival. Nonetheless, I rejoiced when the defence showed up the holes in the prosecution's arguments. I knew I was 'agin' the government and that was enough. My mind was enflamed with idealistic notions of the innate goodness of all human beings and of the imperative to oppose tyranny. The drama of the times demanded a theatrical response. *King Kong* was playing to packed houses. *Back of the Moon* became a hit. Of course, I had a vested interest in supporting the oppressed and downtrodden. At one level, and a not very sophisticated level at that, I identified with them.

In the deep end

I was outraged by what I perceived to be injustice. My own battles to preserve my identity had given me a fine appreciation of what it took to oppose the powerful. Unfortunately, I quickly became inarticulate when confronted and found it difficult to argue coherently. The stage was the one venue I could appear clear and coherent. Other men's words.

Verron Berrangé's first speech in defence of the accused in the Treason Trial was fully reported in *The Star*. The accused, he asserted, had always striven in the interests of racial harmony and cooperation. They had worked for world peace and the resolution of disputes by peaceful means. They were opposed to the use of violence. If this amounted to treason Berrangé said: "then I can only say my clients stand convicted".

The accused represented a complete cross section of South African society, blacks, whites, Indians, coloured, Jews, Christians, atheists, rich, poor, professionals and labourers, but they all held one thing in common: "Despite the fact…that they have different and differing political affiliations, at least they believe in the brotherhood of man…. this case arises out of a political plot of the type that characterised the period of the Inquisition and the Reichstag fire trial. We believe, that in the result, this trial will be answered in the right way by history." I followed the proceedings avidly. They had all the trappings of great drama. Good versus evil. Heroes and villains easily recognised. Dramatic revelations. And finally, those on the side of the brotherhood of man, triumphant. Sharpville was a year away.

The Radio Bulletin had its offices in SABC's head office in what had once been John Dale Lace's mansion, Northwards, designed by Sir Herbert Baker. Dale Lace had been one of the original Randlords and had hobnobbed with the likes of Rhodes, Barney Barnato and Sir Ernest Oppenheimer. The house was bought in 1911 by Sir George Albu, the founder of General Mining. He and his family lived in it until 1951 when it was sold to the SABC. *The Radio Bulletin* had a staff of five people

Staring Memory in the Face

when I joined, a general editor, Awie de Swardt, and four young female editorial assistants, Shirley, Hope, Pam and Karen. All of them in their mid-twenties. They were all attractive, and to me incredibly sophisticated and confident, and certainly not interested in me in any way. They quickly established a pattern of patronising me and treating me as a child who had to be protected from learning anything about the adult world. There was a heady but unarticulated suggestion of sex in the air most of the time. I knew something was going on, but what, I was not quite sure. Four young women, ripe for marriage; the pheromone factor. I was excited but bewildered.

The political issues of the day hardly figured in our conversation. We were part of the news service, but somehow what was happening in the country hardly impinged on their consciousness. Nationalist Party hegemony was being extended into the Corporation so that it was not possible to talk openly. I felt constrained by my own immaturity and lack of confidence. A great drama was being acted out, but I knew no one with whom I could share my excitement. In any event, there were other distractions in the office. There was no doubt that careers hinged on toeing the party line. Not that many people had much difficulty toeing it. Lives were becoming more and more compartmentalised and sealed off from one another. Apartheid was being screwed down.

Because I was not considered as a sexual prospect and therefore kind of neutered, and taken for granted, the girls were frequently quite careless about their talk and dress in front of me. I learned to dissemble and retreated behind an innocent façade from which I listened and observed. What I heard intrigued me. I had no idea that women talked about sex and what is more told each other about their experiences. This was a salutary lesson. Don't kiss and tell. Not that I was doing any kissing, but the lesson served me well in the future. My fantasy life had ample stimulation as I saw more than enough healthy young female flesh every day. Significantly, my fantasies were less and less preoccupied with desert islands. This was my first experience of the adult world as an adult. More was to come. A large proportion of the male announcing and technical

In the deep end

staff was gay. I was fair game. I learned not to go into recording booths alone with a number of the leading broadcasting celebrities of the day. On the positive side, I learned what many women must feel like having to fight off unwanted sexual advances. My experiences on the sand dunes in Cape Town and in Eric's bed in Canterbury were confirmed during that year. Of one thing I was sure: I was not homosexual.

In the midst of the Treason Trial on the 21 March 1960 police shot and killed 69 and wounded another 187 in a township south west of Johannesburg. Pictures of the Sharpville massacre were flashed around the world. Suddenly, there was a stillness, a strange quiet, as if we all recognised that a significant moment in history had occurred. It seemed to me that people were walking on tiptoes, talking in whispers, hoping not to disturb what remained of a fragile façade that had been shaken to its foundations. That weekend there was hardly a person on the streets. Johannesburg seemed all but deserted. A week later there was a nation-wide stay-at-home strike and a massive march on Parliament in Cape Town. Betrayal was in the air. The organisers of the Cape Town march led by Philip Kgosana a UCT student, who were negotiating with the Minister of Justice, were all arrested. Africans were burning their passes. A State of Emergency was declared. And then, barely two weeks later, the first assassination attempt was made on Dr Verwoerd the Prime Minister at the Rand Easter Show. These were stirring times.

I went to my first political meeting organised by the Congress of Democrats to protest the Emergency. Solemn men and women sat on the stage. Rev. Beyers Naude (ex-member of the Broederbond and now an embarrassment to the Afrikaner establishment) opened the proceedings. Fiery speeches were made denouncing the government. It was exciting but at the same time alienating. Everyone seemed to be rushing about with a wild light in their eyes speaking a language that I only half understood. I remained on the periphery, half detached, half intrigued. Policemen lined the back of the hall, a menacing khaki presence.

A police officer climbed onto the stage and grabbed the microphone and announced that there had been a bomb scare and he was ordering the evacuation of the building. Without thinking I started chanting: "Out. Out. Out." One or two people near me took up the chant and soon the hall was filled with the sound: "Out. Out. Out...." He gave up and left the stage. My first deliberate act of political dissent. My first taste of inspiring a crowd. It was exhilarating.

Years later, when opposition to Apartheid had taken on a much more serious form, I would experience the same feeling but with a lot more anticipation and achievement. Power is seductive. When the meeting broke up the police had regrouped outside. Dog handlers were positioned at regular intervals on the opposite pavement. Police vehicles had been parked strategically to break up any kind of demonstration, while the police themselves, armed with rifles, truncheons and sjamboks waited in the shadows. Confronted by such a show of force the mood in the crowd was decidedly subdued.

It did not take me long to realise that I was completely out of my depth at work. I had none of the journalistic skills necessary for the job. My spelling was appalling. I had no idea of how to structure a story or how to conduct an interview. My proof reading and editing skills were non-existent. But, the promise was that I would be trained. It did not happen. I spent a year floundering from one assignment to the next until I was entrusted with only the most menial office tasks. Nonetheless, it came as a painful surprise at the end of twelve months to discover that the SABC had decided it could do without my services.

My first attempts at making my way in the world were no different from my efforts at school. What should I do? I was paid out about R1000 by way of pension benefits and severance pay. What could I do? The future looked decidedly grim. I was qualified for nothing. My on-the-job experience (there had been no training) had left me with little or nothing anyone would be interested in. Whatever I applied for would reveal that

In the deep end

I had been found inadequate in my first attempt. But work I would have to get. R1000 would not take me very far.

I could not appeal to Tommy. As far as he was concerned, I was not his responsibility any longer. Not that I had ever been, but there had been a time when he had evinced some sort of maudlin emotional tie, and he had provided me with shelter for about a year. Instead, I turned to the man I worshipped, who had provided for me for nearly four years, who had been the only father figure I had ever known, Cloete. I was still a frequent visitor over weekends. The weekend following my notice of dismissal I went down to Longwood House to get advice. Cloete's response was immediate. Come back to school as a housemaster and odd job man on no salary for the rest of the year and at least I would have a roof over my head and three proper meals until I had worked out what it was I wanted to do. Which is what I did.

I found very soon that I was more than an odd job man and housemaster. I was quickly drafted into teaching some of the junior secondary classes English and maths. The irony did not escape me. I, who had just managed to scrape a pass in English in matric and who had failed maths dismally, now found myself in front of a class talking about literature, grammar and creative writing, to say nothing of converting vulgar fractions into decimals and the beginnings of geometry and algebra. Much to my amazement I was enjoying what I was doing. I was in control of the subject matter and enjoyed the logic of the systems I was explaining: if this, then that. I enjoyed the elegance of finding solutions. And the exceptions intrigued me. It was new and fresh. Of course, it was all very simple too, but I had never had to think about the underlying logic of grammar or the angle on the hypotenuse. And, there was a logic. Something I had never before suspected.

When I had been at school these were things one had to learn, which for me meant memorising. And, when my memory failed or I began to doubt, as inevitably happened when I was stressed, any understanding I might have had evaporated. I now had to explain, and I had to use my own language to do so. I did not articulate my experiences in these

Staring Memory in the Face

terms, but I was aware that I had discovered a talent; a significant first that was to bear fruit. Even though I was barely older than the kids I was teaching, I had no discipline problems. Coaching cricket and soccer in the afternoon was fun. I loved to see talent in others beginning to flower and derived immense pleasure from the achievements of the youngsters I coached, most of whom I had known at school a year or so previously.

Even so, it did not occur to me that a career in teaching might be possible. I had not passed matric. I had no money and no prospect of getting a bursary. Besides, the world was waiting for me to discover it; to say nothing of the world waiting to discover me.

Summer changed to autumn and winter and with the change of seasons came the bitterly cold Highveld nights and white frosted mornings. My twenty-first birthday loomed. One morning at the staff tea, Sally Dudgeon, who had taught me biology, invited me to spend the weekend with her and her husband Doug at their house on the banks of the Klip River. Away from school for the first time in five months I was able to contemplate my future as they questioned me about what I wanted to do with my life. They were unequivocal. "You can't stay at Longwood forever. You must get away. Go overseas. Explore the world and discover what you want to do."

It emerged during the course of the weekend that I harboured ambitions to be an actor and a singer. I had been taking singing lessons for a year while I had been at the SABC, but had had to give them up once I had moved out to Longwood. Cloete was currently in the midst of producing *Oklahoma* and I was to play the leading role. I had played the lead in *Macbeth* earlier in the year. "Why don't you go and study music and drama in London?" The question hung in the air all weekend. My destiny seemed unavoidable. It was obvious. A glittering career awaited me on the London stage.

By Sunday night it was decided. I would leave for London as soon as it could be arranged. There was much to do. Letters to write applying for a place at the Royal Academy of Music and the Guildhall School of Music and Drama as a part time student. A berth to book on a Union

In the deep end

Castle liner. Application to be made for a passport. Endless forms to fill in. The earliest I could leave would be late September. It was now May.

I was deeply frustrated at not being able to go immediately. Everyone I spoke to approved. It was the great adventure waiting to happen and I was bogged down by bureaucracy. I had a sense that a new dawn was about to break.

∼

I decided to learn French in preparation for my life overseas. Cloete suggested I join a private student he taught who lived in the village. Her name was Dawn Parker. She was seventeen and had written matric the previous year. She was between school and starting work: her father was going to set her up with a little dress shop in Vereeniging. She was having time out, getting her driver's licence, learning French, having an extended holiday. She lived with her parents and a younger sister in the village. She was very attractive, with long dark brown hair and dark brown eyes, poised, self-assured and with a deep vibrant voice. I was intimidated and sure that she would not look twice at me. I spent the lesson surreptitiously glancing at her, feeling inadequate and stupid. She seemed able to remember all the declensions. Her vocabulary made mine pale into insignificance. All I could do with any self-assurance was recite stanzas of Victor Hugo and Rimbaud I had learned off by heart, none of which I understood.

At the end of the lesson when we were left alone for a few minutes before her mother fetched her, she invited me to supper. I was amazed. I had never met her before and I was conscious of not having shaved that morning. I had spent most of the day burning firebreaks near the school buildings. My clothes were filthy. I had not even had time to wash the soot and grime from my face before the lesson. I was sure I stank of sweat and smoke. Mrs Parker arrived at that moment and Dawn repeated the invitation. I stammered an acceptance but insisted that I change into clean clothes and join the family a little later. A hasty bath, shave and change of clothes saw me on the road down to the village. My mind in a whirl. My emotions confused. My heart racing. I arrived just after sunset, hardly aware of the winter evening's chill.

We ate in the kitchen. Mr Parker said little. He was an accountant in Vereeniging and seemed interested in little beyond the financial pages of the evening newspaper. Mrs Parker busied herself about the range serving food, all the while asking me about myself. What had I done since I left school? Why was I back at Longwood? What were my plans for the future? I talked about my experiences at the SABC and told them censored stories about the various broadcasting celebrities I had known, straining all the while to make a good impression. I dwelt at length on my plans to study music and drama in London. The evening was a strain. I had never been in this kind of situation before and felt very unsure of myself. Except for mild flirtations at school I had never had a girlfriend. I had never been in a position where I was being scrutinised by adults who were monitoring their daughter's boyfriends to establish their suitability. I must have come across as hopelessly naïve and certainly not a prospect for their daughter. Fortunately, I was about to go overseas.

After supper Dawn and I moved to the living room. I know I dominated the conversation with my vision of the future and my barely articulated views on life and art. Tennyson's *Ulysses* figured large in my conversation and I quoted liberally to emphasise my belief that life should be an adventure. I wooed her with poetry: *"So we'll go no more a roving so late into the night…"*, *"The marriage of true minds…."*, *"To his coy mistress"*. I was amazed by how much I could recite. One poem led to another. My imagination was on fire. The London stage was waiting to be conquered. Ten o'clock came and it was time to go. We went through to the kitchen and I said good night and thanked Mrs Parker for the meal. Mr Parker hardly looked up from his paper. Dawn said she would see me to the front door. The family remained tactfully in the kitchen.

Dawn led the way up the passage, and instead of turning towards the front door grabbed my hand and drew me further down the passage and through a door into an inter-leading room. She opened a third door

In the deep end

and I discovered myself in her bedroom. Putting her finger to her lips she whispered: "wait here". She switched off the light, closed the door behind her and left me standing in the dark. I stood still, my heart pounding. A few moments later I heard her open the front door and the murmur of her voice. The door closed and the light in the living room was switched off. The only illumination came from a streetlight across the road. In the gloom, I could just make out a bed in the far corner, a wardrobe next to the door and a dressing table beneath the window. I was in such a state of amazed agitation every muscle in my face felt tense. My kneecaps were jumping up and down uncontrollably. My throat was dry but I dared not cough. I did not know what to do with my hands. I could not believe what was happening. Ten minutes later, wondering what I would say if either of the parents discovered me in their daughter's room, wondering if I was dreaming, wondering if I could escape through the window, the door opened silently. Dawn slipped into the room without switching on the light.

"Sssh," she whispered, taking my hand.

When I climbed out of her window at 4.30 the following morning, the moon was long gone. The glow from the street lamp across the road cast a small pool of light beyond which all was darkness and vague shadows. My feet crunched across the frost-hard grass, leaving black footsteps in the dark before dawn. A blast from a train's hooter in the shunting yards a couple of miles away echoed mournfully. I was unaware of the sharp pre-dawn cold.

19

The Crucible

I disembarked from the *Stirling Castle* in Southampton on the 10th September 1960 with £22 in my pocket determined to conquer the stage. I was convinced that I was about to be discovered. A life of fame and fortune awaited me at Covent Garden, la Scala, the Metropolitan. In the event, I discovered that my lack of musical education, and even more important, my lack of genuine musical talent, could not be gainsaid.

Auditions followed one upon the other at the Royal Academy for Music and the Guildhall School of Music and Drama. I was accepted by both institutions but could not afford fulltime fees. The Guildhall offered the cheaper part time courses. I duly enrolled for two voice classes of half an hour each, and one in theory. The voice classes were rigorous individual sessions. The theory class had about twenty odd deluded aspirants like me who had no background to speak of and similar hopeless ambitions. Still, it was exciting to have got this far.

In the meantime, my £22 did not take me very far and I had to find some way of earning a living. I had no qualifications of any sort, and so I found myself at the very bottom of the employment ladder. Eventually, I got a job as a hall porter at the Overseas Visitors Club in Earls Court at £9.10 a week. I arranged my shift for midnight to eight in the morning. Not only was it the quietest shift and in all probability, I would be able to spend much of it asleep, but the days would be free to practise, study the history and theory of music, and on Mondays and Thursdays go to college. I arranged with my aunt Joyce who lived in Primrose Hill to use her piano every afternoon to practise my scales. I also hoped to be able to teach myself enough on the piano to turn the theory I was learning into some sort of practice.

What with rent, Tube fares to college and Primrose Hill, food, and saving to pay my fees, £9.10 a week did not go very far. There was nothing left over for entertainment, emergencies or clothes; and winter

The Crucible

was coming. The end of every week saw me with at most a couple of shillings in my pocket. My dreams of going regularly to the theatre had to be shelved for the time being. But no matter, I was doing what I believed I was destined for. If starving in a garret was part of it, so be it. The important thing was to risk everything. And, I convinced myself, this was life. *la Bohème, Tosca, la Traviata, Aida, Carmen.* They were all waiting. I had been thoroughly brainwashed into believing that I had the talent and that I would be discovered. It did not matter that I could not read music, that I had no contacts in the theatre world, and that I would never, at this rate, earn enough to study full time.

My fantasies received further fuel when I auditioned for a Royal Academy of Music production of *The Crucible* by Arthur Miller and landed a part even though I wasn't a registered student. I had managed to worm my way into the play shortly after I auditioned at the Academy to study for a teacher's and performer's diploma in drama. I was hoping that if I was accepted I would qualify for a bursary. I duly prepared and presented myself to the auditioning committee. I was required to recite a piece of poetry of my own choice. The rest of the audition tested my ability to tell an unprepared story, read a part from a play and do a mime exercise. The piece of poetry I chose was John Donne's *The Sun Rising*. I worked on it for over a week becoming word perfect, the delivery honed to perfection. Rhythm, diction, dramatic irony, had been polished to the point I could recite it in my sleep. It would be a definitive performance.

I sit in a room adjoining the hall in which we are to be auditioned with a number of other aspirants, three girls and a young man, clutching in their sweaty hands the rapidly crumpling copies of the poems they are about to perform; all of us putting on a brave face. It docs not take much to sense the rising level of terror. Each audition takes about half an hour, so we have ample time to get to know one another.

Staring Memory in the Face

I look around. A September sun slants through high windows. Two of the girls are pretty. The third is overweight and acned. The young man, affecting an Oscar Wilde manner, wears a black velvet suit with an elaborate lace handkerchief tumbling out of his top pocket. He looks at us with disdain. As we are competing for a limited number of places the conversation is stilted and guarded. No point in giving too much away. The girl sitting next to me confesses that her O levels had not been good and she is worried that this will count against her.

"What were your results like?" she asks.

"Oh, in South Africa (I quickly established myself as an exotic and therefore exempt from the laws governing ordinary mortals) we have a different system. We have matric exam that's the same as your A levels. I did six subjects and so have the same as six A levels."

I'd failed in both my attempts at matric, but I wasn't going to let on now. Nor was matric the equivalent of A level. This was the first hurdle. I must persuade everyone that I have the talent and then hope they do not enquire too closely into my academic record. If I can bluff my way past this girl, perhaps I can bluff my way past the people who make decisions about bursaries and scholarships.

"You're so lucky," she sighs. "I want to do drama more than anything."

The others in the room share similar anxieties and look on me with envy which turns to admiration when they ask which poem I'm going to do. The velvet suit is visibly taken aback.

"John Donne. Isn't he very difficult?"

"Oh, I like the metaphysicals. I think it's important to do a poet you like. You can put so much more into it if it means something special to you. Do you know *The Sun Rising*?"

"We had it at school, but I never really understood it."

My confidence is beginning to swell to bursting point.

"I had thought of doing a couple of the sonnets such as *Batter my Heart* and *Death Be Not Proud*, but they seemed too gloomy, or even Andrew Marvell's *To His Coy Mistress*, but it's too long."

The Crucible

The door to the audition room opens. "Thank you, we will be in touch. Next please".

I stand. The moment of truth has arrived. There is no backing away now. Two men and a woman sit behind a long oak table at the end of the hall. I advance, stop and wait for them to acknowledge my presence. They are engaged in earnest conversation about the previous candidate. I try to look as if I'm not listening, but it is clear she has not done well.

"Poorly prepared. Weak academically. Little understanding of what she was reading. Voice quite nice. But that's not enough. I'm afraid not. Yes. Yes. No. Are we agreed?"

As they talk among themselves, I have an opportunity to observe them. The main speaker, and therefore I assume the chairman of the committee, is a neatly dressed diminutive man, not five foot tall. His neat little feet dangle a few inches above the floor. Everything about him is pressed and precise from his polished diction to the parting in his hair, his trimmed beard, meticulously pressed trousers and shining shoes. His colleagues, who defer to him all the while, sit on either side of him. The woman looks like all middle-aged women look to me. She is conservatively dressed in a twin-set with pearls. Nothing distinguishes her from the hundreds of similar women I pass in the street every day, except her voice which is remarkably deep and sonorous and beautiful and modulated. The third member of the committee, a large shambling man with bright red face, unkempt hair and beard, wears a bright purple corduroy suit with a white carnation in his buttonhole and a scarlet cravate. They are a curious group.

"Ah, yes," says the chairman, glancing down at his notes, "I am sorry to keep you waiting." He makes the introductions. The only name that sticks in my mind is the woman's, Greta Colson.

"Well, what have you for us? But first tell us a little about yourself."

I'd been expecting something of the sort and launch into a set piece about growing up in South Africa, and my ambitions to be a singer and actor.

Pause, take a deep breath.

Staring Memory in the Face

"Would you like to start? I see you have chosen a most interesting, and from our point of view, unusual poem. Why did you choose it? We don't often hear Donne at these auditions, do we?" He turns to his colleagues for conformation.

"Well, I ... er ... like Donne's poetry ... very much."

"Oh, that's interesting. What do you like about the metaphysicals? What do you think of Donne as a poet? Do you prefer him to Herbert? His religious poetry I mean. What do you think of Marvell?"

The rapid-fire questions save me. I mutter something about liking Donne's sonnets, avoid saying anything about Herbert of whom I know next to nothing and latch on to Marvell's *To his Coy Mistress*, quoting the most famous lines with enthusiasm. The existential despair fits my self-image as a brooding Byronic genius.

> *"But at my back I always hear*
> *Time's winged chariot hurrying near;*
> *And yonder all before us lie*
> *Deserts of vast eternity."* [29]

This goes down well, and the purple suit chimes in:

> *"Thy beauty shall no more be found,*
> *Nor in thy marble vault shall sound*
> *My echoing song; (and with evident relish) then worms shall try*
> *That long preserved virginity*
> *And your quaint honour turn to dust.*
> *And into ashes all my lust."*

Is it my imagination? Are these last lines addressed to the only female member of the committee? I do not have time to speculate. In any event, I have been rescued from revealing the abysmal depths of my ignorance.

"No. No. Please start." The chairman interrupts.

A deep breath: *"The Sun Rising"* by John Donne[30]

---

29. Andrew Marvell: 'To his Coy Mistress'.
30. John Donne: 'The Sun Rising'

The Crucible

> *"Busy old fool, unruly sun,*
> *Why dost thou thus, ..."*

Words fail. I'm blank. I've lost the impetus. I haven't a clue what comes next. Panic. The room seems to reel. "I'm sorry. May I start again?"

> *"Busy old fool, unruly sun,*
> *Why dost thou thus, ..."*

I've hit a blank wall. I can't for the life of me remember what comes next. The more I try, the more I realise how hopeless it is. Blushing furiously, I start again.

> *"Busy old fool, unruly sun,*
> *Why dost thou thus, ..."*

Then Greta Colson takes pity on me. She prompts: "Through windows ...."

"*Through windows and* ... er."

"curtains ...."

"*curtains call on us? ....* er, ... er."

"Must ...."

"*Must to thy motions lovers' seasons run?*"

I've got it again. It's come back. Relief sweeps over me. I surge forward on a wave of relief and optimism, hoping that the impetus of the poem will carry me through:

> *"Saucy pedantic wretch, go chide*
> *Late school boys and sour prentices,*
> *Go tell court huntsmen that the king will ride*
> *Call country ants to harvest offices.*
> *Love all alike, no season knows no r... er, ... er."*

Another blank. She prompts: "clime ...." "*clime* ...." "Nor hours ...." "*Nor hours* ...." "days ...." "*days* ...." "months ...." "*months* ...." "which ...." "*which are the rags of time.*"

And there are still two stanzas to go. She helps me through them. As I stagger to the conclusion, I know that there's no hope. No redemption. The audition could not be more of a disaster. I'm bathed in sweat.

Staring Memory in the Face

It feels as if buckets of ice have been thrown over me. I can hardly speak. My tongue feels like a dead piece of leather in my mouth. I've an almost overwhelming need to curl up and go to sleep. I'm overcome with embarrassment.

All I want to do is escape, but they insist on keeping me. I'm asked to read an extract from *Romeo and Juliet*, Mecutio's Queen Mab speech, something from *Murder in the Cathedral* and a piece from Shaw's *Arms and the Man*. At the end of what seems like never ending humiliation, I am asked to remain in the waiting room. I wonder why they bother. I've obviously made a complete hash of the whole thing. Why drag it out? An hour passes and the door opens again.

"Ah, Michael," begins the dapper little man, "we have consulted with the bursar about your status as a South African and regret to inform you that you will not be eligible for a bursary or a scholarship. Hence, we cannot admit you to the Academy as we understand you do not have any independent financial means. However, we would like to encourage you in any way we can. Mrs Colson has suggested that we could use you in our production of *The Crucible* which is about to go into rehearsal. She also has a few private voice and movement students and is willing to take you on if you are interested."

I'm stunned and splutter my incoherent thanks. The ways of the world are more and more mysterious. Eight weeks later, in an obscure corner of the arts page in *The Times*, a review of *The Crucible*: "*Michael Rice is a budding talent. We look forward to seeing him fulfil his promise in the future.*"

It was not to be.

Eighteen months later, in September 1961, I faced the unavoidable truth. I would never be able to finance my ambitions on my wage as a hall porter. Not only did I not earn enough to study full time, but lack of sleep made it virtually impossible to concentrate. I had no skills and no education that would enable me to get a better job and earn more money. I had one brief foray as an office worker at National Cash Registers, but the mind-deadening work was more than I could tolerate (I told my supervisor I'd reached saturation point) and I left after two months.

The Crucible

Rev Samuel Parris. The Crucible (1961) London

The *"winged chariot"* was pressing at my back. I was 22. Virtually middle-aged. I needed a break to reassess my position. Should I take my chances and join a repertory company, get a proper job, or give the whole thing up and return to South Africa? If so, to do what? The insecurity of the theatre world was looking less and less attractive. On the other hand, nothing else appealed. It was the familiar tussle between fantasy and pragmatism. Spring turned to summer and I got a job on a farm just outside Faversham in Kent. Three months of fresh air, regular farm-cooked meals, plenty of exercise looking after pigs, sheep and a pack of Beagles, and scandalising the locals by driving a tractor without my shirt on.

~ 20 ~

A certain smile

And so, …

It is eight o'clock of a late summer's evening in 1961. President Kennedy is in the White House and earlier in the year Patrice Lumumba had been assassinated in the Congo.

I am sitting in the saloon of the cross-channel ferry from Dover to Calais learning French from a menu.

Bread	*pain*
Cheese	*fromage*
Coffee	*café*
Sugar	*sucre*
Ham sandwich	*ham sandwich* – ham sandwich?
Salad	*salade*

It's not much, but it's enough. British Rail fare in the early 1960s. Nothing fancy. Prices quoted in sterling, new and old francs. I work out the conversion rates and add them to my new store of knowledge.

I'd decided on the spur of the moment to spend a week in France, to go to Paris, see the sights and do the Louvre. I was between jobs and had a week to kill and £10 in my pocket. It seemed enough at the time. It would cost me £1.10s to get across the Channel. £8.10s seemed more than enough to live on for a week. I didn't reckon in the cost of getting back. That was a problem I would face when it arose. I had no idea how I was going to get to Paris. Once the ferry reached Calais there would be no question of catching a train. I would have to trust to lifts and luck.

The ferry casts off and moves slowly away from the jetty. Through the saloon window, I can see cranes and warehouses slip past into the lengthening shadows. The white cliffs glimmer and begin to fade. Lights are already beginning to come on in the town. As I sit trying to memorise

A certain smile

the menu it begins to occur to me, I'm hungry. I have to make a choice. Eat now and spend half a crown, or wait till morning. The logic of delayed gratification wins. I drink a glass of water and contemplate my fellow passengers clutching their beers and stuffing themselves with crisps and soggy cheese and tomato sandwiches. At a nearby table someone rises and leaves the saloon, abandoning half a sandwich. When I hope no one is looking, I reach across, and slip it into my coat pocket. Waste not want not.

The ferry moves out to sea as the darkness closes in. I go on deck for some fresh air, eat my recently acquired sandwich and watch the approaching lights along the French coast. I lean over the side, watching the ship's wake glowing, phosphorescent, the wash of waves. On the French coast, the light gleams and is gone.

When I grew up in South Africa, Paris had seemed an impossible dream. Johannesburg was such a backwater. How could you compare Johannesburg with Paris, the city of lights with the city of gold? Of gold? A dreary city, built at right angles to itself. Mine dumps and dust and decaying mine headgear. Johannesburg, a sordid mining town, whore to the ambition of empire. The Randlords, Rhodes, Barnato, Albue, Robertson. A city dedicated to the hypocrisies of greed; a city virtually abandoned at sunset. Its most famous address, a bland 120 Main Street. Who had heard of Eloff Street? Of Hillbrow? Canyons of grey concrete. Where cinemas, theatres and bars were closed on Sundays. Where life was lived according to strictly enforced codes that ensured that most of the population hardly existed, living anonymous lives in townships securely out of sight. Post-Apartheid Johannesburg is very different. The dead hand of Afrikaner Calvinism has been removed. The emergent black middle-class, so long suppressed in the townships, has moved into the centre of town and is establishing itself in the suburbs. Johannesburg has become a truly African city, vital, vibrant and violent, but never boring. Not then. ... .

But Paris, Montmartre, the writers, artists, musicians, sidewalk cafes. How could the mine dumps compare with the Left Bank? Like most

Staring Memory in the Face

white children in the 1950s, I had little incentive and few opportunities to discover Africa. Kipling, Walter Scott and Jack London were my fare. The closest I got to Africa was Rider Haggard. Gagool, not Modadji the Rain Queen, filled my romantic vision. I was vaguely aware of Spokes Mashyiane and his penny whistle. *King Kong* was all the rage but it was *La Bohème* that rang in my ears. Gauguin and van Gogh filled my overheated imagination.

The bravado of adolescence required that I understand no more than the title. So, Edith Piaf's *Je ne regrette rien* was my theme song. Sartre's *Being and Nothingness* had instant appeal, but whether existence preceded essence or the other way around, I hadn't a clue. I had yet to read Orwell's *Down and Out in Paris and London,* but even when I did, it did not dampen my enthusiasm.

I had fallen under the spell of that most dangerous of adolescent influences, the charismatic teacher, Lynn Cloete who inspired me to risk everything for a life on the stage. He believed that artists, writers, musicians and actors were an elite. But they were an elite that could only find true expression in Europe. Africa had nothing to offer. Culture, true culture was European. Who was Pierneef next to Cezanne? Khumalo beside Rodin? It was an easy creed to sell to a captive impressionable adolescent. The power of great art, by which he meant the Renaissance and the Impressionists, healed the soul. Truth was beauty, beauty truth. That was all you needed to know. And beauty was essentially Michelangelo, Raphael, and Leonardo; the glory that was Greece; Beethoven, Puccini, Bizet. The creative spirit was the wellspring of life. Recognise and nurture talent, and anything was possible. The pursuit of money and material success was for lesser beings without vision, without soul. Convincing me that I could become one of the chosen few was not difficult: I longed to be among the elect.

Paris was the Mecca of art. True believers had to make a pilgrimage at least once in their lifetime. The Place de la Concorde, Sacré Coeur, the Champs-Élysées, the Arc de Triomphe, the Eiffel Tower, Nôtre-Dame, the Left Bank and Montmartre were about to become more than just names.

A certain smile

The Louvre, with its great collections of Impressionist and Renaissance painting, was the altar at which I was determined to take the host. I felt as if my existence was about to take on a new significance. All I needed was to hold fast and I would be able to claim the places I had only read about. I would be able to say: "I have been there. I have seen that. I have walked on that pavement, breathed that air."

I was especially excited at the thought of seeing *The Mona Lisa*. The most famous painting in the world by the greatest genius of the Renaissance. I was entranced by the mysterious eyes that followed you wherever you stood. The enigmatic smile. The romantic landscape. And, of course, the mystery of her identity. The story, as much as anything, fascinated me. As a schoolboy, I had read the first edition of Helen Gardner's *A History of Art* from cover to cover accepting uncritically all her claims for art.

The ferry draws alongside the quay. Hawsers are thrown over the side and gangways run onto the dockside. Foreign voices echo in the shadows. Shunting railway trucks rattle in the night. Apart from Customs, all the buildings are in pitch dark.

I have nothing to declare.

My toggle-bag is searched. Even the Customs man cannot conceal his contempt for my few worldly possessions.

Ashore, I look for road signs pointing the way to Paris. It is 11.30 at night. There is little traffic and few pedestrians, none of whom I assume can speak English. My menu French does not extend to asking directions. There is only one thing for it. Start walking and hope I find a road sign pointing in the right direction. As luck will have it, half an hour later I find myself at a major intersection. PARIS 292km. That's only about 180 miles. Things are looking up. I'm on my way. The houses thin out. Streetlights are few and far between. I can just make out fields beyond the hedgerows. The occasional car appears, and disappears into the night. Mysterious shapes shift in the shadows, lift their heads at my approach, snort, cough and complain. It begins to get cold. A thick fog settles over the countryside. I make my way from one mist shrouded pool of light to the next, hoping I am still going in the right direction.

Staring Memory in the Face

I have been walking blindly down a dark country road for some time when I decide to rest under a hedge at the side of the road. There seems no point to continue blundering about in the dark. It does not take me long to discover how big a gap there is between the romantic descriptions I have read about the joys of sleeping under hedges and the reality. It may be late summer but it is bitterly cold. My toggle bag is a poor pillow, my duffle coat is not a blanket, the ditch is more than damp, the hedge has thorns. There is nothing for it: the only way to keep warm is to keep walking.

The night passes slowly and painfully as I continue from one dimly lit village to the next. Hours pass. I am tired, hungry and thirsty, my feet are sore and the cord from my toggle-bag is cutting into my shoulder. Light begins filtering through the dark. Hesitant dawn. Forms assume shape and become houses still wreathed in sleep. Warm breath rises from barns and sheds. A church door overhung with gargoyles beckons. A cock crows. Dogs bark. Moving shapes emerge from the dark accompanied by bicycle bells and *"Bonjour. Bonjour"* and disappear into the rising mist.

A dim light beckons from an open door at the edge of a village. A bistro is open for early morning trade. I pause at the door. A large woman with voluminous breasts standing behind the counter reassures me: I enter. The locals who have dropped in for their early morning coffee and absinthe pay me no attention. The room is warm with the smell of newly baked bread and fresh coffee. I plunge in, recklessly pronouncing a phrase I had learned years previously when I had surreptitiously listened to the French lesson my classmates were having while I was supposed to be doing extra maths. How I wish I had listened to more.

"Bonjour. Comment allez-vous?"

There is a rapid-fire response against which I have no reserves. I stand helpless and dumb. Exposed. I have exhausted my vocabulary; or nearly. My menu French does not entirely desert me though. With an effort of will I summon up *"cafe et pain et fromage s'il vous plaît."* And then remember, in a flash of inspiration, that the French for sandwich, if the

A certain smile

menu is to be trusted, is *sandwich*. A *le* in front of it won't go amiss. "*Le sandwich*".

She reaches behind her and clutches a loaf to her more than ample bosom, hacks off two slices onto which she slaps, with two swipes of her knife, slabs of butter that melt into the bread. I know what must follow. Instead, she opens a packet of processed cheese and delicately selects a triangle wrapped in silver foil. This is no time to express disappointment. I am too hungry for that. Anyway, my vocabulary will not extend to asking for something different.

As I leave the bistro I flag down a passing car, to my amazement, it stops.

"*Bon jour. J'e suis Anglaise,*" I begin, not having learned my lesson. Bad French apart, I'm shy of admitting I'm a South African. Sharpeville was a recent memory. Apartheid was becoming familiar as a term for oppression. Laughter and amused smiles greet me. It was not until much later that I discovered why. I get in and sit in the back between two pretty girls. Two young Belgian couples are returning from a weekend in Normandy. They are on their way home via Lille. It is a bit out of my way but it is a start. Besides, I am not in a hurry.

It is obvious their weekend has not ended. A hamper of cold chicken and slices of ham, cheese (not in silver foil this time) and bread is passed round followed by a bottle of wine. Wedged between two warm female bodies, a piece of chicken in one hand and a paper cup full of wine in the other, it's a bit of a squash, I know life cannot get any better. By dint of much sign language I explain I am on my way to Paris. As they speak amongst themselves I realise they must be Flemish. Many of the words and phrases are familiar. My Afrikaans is going to be useful after all. Life is full of surprises.

Once communications have been more or less established the atmosphere in the car becomes even more convivial. My Afrikaans is marginally better than my French. They are intrigued to hear a language, not Dutch, close to their own. More wine is pressed on me. "*Baie dankie, dus baie goed wyn. Dit smaak lekker.*" I tell them of how I have come from

Staring Memory in the Face

South Africa to study music in London and of my ambition to see Paris. My fractured Afrikaans seems no obstacle. In fact, my vocabulary seems to expand by the minute as I boast about my talent and the good life in South Africa. Land of perpetual sunshine and unspoiled beaches. At their prompting, I sing: *"Uit die blou van ons se hemel, uit die diepte van ons see ...."*

The wine, the warm bodies on either side of me, the food and thirty-six hours without sleep have their combined effect. I wake as the car comes to a halt. Lille. This is where we have to part. They are going on to Brussels. The girls press a packet of bread, ham and figs on me. We wish each other luck and they promise to see me when I sing at La Scala.

It is a glorious day. The sun shines, birds sing and I have eaten and drunk well. I have no idea where I am, but no matter. All the signs point to Paris. A car stops and I introduce myself, again, as an English woman. *"Bon jour J'e suis Anglaise. Je suis en route pour Paris."* My Belgian friends must have amused themselves with the thought of me making my way through France under the mistaken idea that at least I could identify and introduce myself unambiguously. Fortunately, this driver speaks some English. He smiles. He's on his way to Paris. At this rate I will be there just after lunch.

At least that is what I thought. I'd underestimated how tired I was. It was not long before I fell asleep again. I woke sometime later when the car stopped at a filling station in St Quentin. My driver rummaged in his pockets and turned to me. *"'ave you any money?"* he asked. I pass him a 100 new franc note. One hundred new francs made quite a dent in my cash. Too bad, I thought, as I wrote it off. At least I was going to get to Paris that day. We drove off. At every village en route, I hear my driver ask passers-by about *"Credit Suisse"*. Our route was becoming more and more erratic and I was beginning to doubt we would get to Paris that day. Martel, Guiscard, Tergnier, Soissons, Villiers-Cotterets, Crêpy-en-Valois. Many of the names were familiar, associated in my mind with the battlefields of the First World War. It was an erratic journey. Anyway, I was having a very pleasant trip seeing the sights of northern France.

A certain smile

We are passing through a deep forest of oak, ash, beech and birch when suddenly the trees clear. In front of us, a fairy castle floating in the middle of a lake. It is magical. The dark forest provides a backdrop to a gleaming white château reflected in the lake. A clear sky overhead and banks of hydrangeas. Pink, white and blue.

Eventually, the car stopped in nearby Chantilly. A sign proclaimed: *Credit Suisse*. My companion jumped out and returned a few moments later. He thrust 100 new francs into my hand and drove on without a word.

He dropped me at the Arc de Triomphe. The Champs-Élysées stretches down the hill to the Place de la Concorde. *Tricouleurs*, banners and bunting festoon the avenue. In the distance the Eiffel Tower and the Seine. A summer haze lies over the city. A sea of grey and green roofs. A huge red, white and blue flag hangs within the arch.

Once I have drawn breath, it takes me ten minutes to pluck up courage to cross the Champs-Élysées. There seem to be no rules of the road. The traffic careers around the arch; wailing sirens, demented drivers, hooting, shouting, shaking fists at each other. *Gendarmes* wave their arms and blow whistles to no apparent effect. The traffic appears to do exactly as it likes. Pedestrians have to take their chances.

Coffee at a sidewalk café is an essential rite of passage.

I have an extra 100 new francs I had not counted on. At least I can order coffee without exhausting my menu French. I sit, order coffee without any trouble and look around, trying to appear as urbane as possible. A young American at the next table is reading the international edition of the *New York Times*. He catches me reading the headlines. *South Africa leaves the Commonwealth*. A conversation opener.

"Hi. I hope you don't mind me reading over your shoulder, but I'm South African and I haven't heard the latest news."

"So, you're South African? What do you think of Sharpeville?"

There's nothing like the direct approach. My heart sinks.

It is not often that I meet anyone with any knowledge or understanding of my country. But then, Sharpeville did get world headlines. I have learned, in the few months I've been in England, how difficult it is to guess the political affiliations of people I meet. In South Africa we had to develop early warning systems to avoid treading on delicate political toes. None of them seem to work with the English, let alone Americans who have their own complicated racial history. One of the things I most enjoyed about being in England was that I no longer had to be on my guard. Few people had any interest in what was going on in South Africa, and I was enjoying a holiday not having to think about it. Not that I had been particularly involved in politics. I hadn't. But the political situation was so much a part of every South African's consciousness, there was no escaping it. Everything one did, or thought or said was mediated through a political and racial filter.

Tentatively, I say I think it was a great tragedy. There is no telling. I might be dealing with the Grand Wizard of the Klu Klux Klan. As it turns out, he is a politics student at Harvard and much better informed than I am about the ins and outs of South African politics. In an attempt to change the subject before my ignorance is shown up too glaringly, I ask him if he knows of a cheap hotel. He recommends one near the Gare du Nord. I can afford two nights.

The following morning, I walk down the Boulevard de Sébastopol hardly aware of the city bustle. The blur of traffic, the smells of early morning bread and coffee, people hurrying to work, I am oblivious to them all. At last, I am going to see *The Mona Lisa*. A dream is about to be fulfilled.

I expect to drink at the fountain of beauty and truth. By simply standing in front of *The Mona Lisa* I will be transformed. A new sophisticated me will raise from the ashes of my ignorance and I will understand the world with penetrating wisdom. The truths of art are, after all, universal.

As I turn into the Rue Rivoli I feel a little queasy. Slight nausea, not something I'd eaten. A familiar feeling as if a bucket of ice-cold water has been emptied over me. The sensation is so strong I stop and look up to see if someone has thrown water from a window above. My confidence evaporates. I'm startled by a white face reflected in a café window.

A certain smile

The Louvre looms in front of me, forbidding, intimidating. I sit on a bench in the Jardin des Tuileries and contemplate the façade. Louis XIV. Versailles. Napoleon's tomb. I'm drenched. This is not how it's supposed to be. It's meant to be a culmination, a triumphant fulfilment. Instead, I'm overcome by dread. Hands trembling, drenched, almost gasping for breath. Sculptured images of delirium cling to the gutters. Torrents of ice-cold water soak me from head to foot.

I know I can't enter the building. I'm soaked in sweat. I can't go in. I sit for another ten minutes or so, and then get up and walk away without looking back. I find an empty table in a sidewalk café down a side street and order a beer. The day is hot. The beer is cold. I make it last. Not a cloud in the sky. Boxes of red geraniums hang from every window. Gendarmes blow whistles. People hurry by. As I pause over my beer and reflect on my failure to fulfil my dream, I notice a girl at a nearby table sipping *café au lait*. Her tongue lingers delicately between her lips.

She feels my gaze, looks up and smiles, enigmatically.

~ 21 ~

"Yes, that's him."

A storm moved in from the South Atlantic three days ago, coinciding with this month's spring tide. Chapman's Peak has been swathed in cloud as gusts of rain driven by a dark northwester beat about the house. The Noordhoek beach, stretching for nearly five miles from the foot of Chapman's Peak towards Kommetjie, disappears for vast stretches beneath the surf. I can hear the dull roar of the breakers half a mile away. Rain splatters against the window. Milkwood trees about the house shift restlessly. Nearly sixty years on, I recall a cold Highveld afternoon in June 1962.

Three of us stood in the chapel and faced the Presbyterian minister standing next to the coffin containing my father's body. I stood woodenly, not listening to the drone of well-meant platitudes, staring fixedly at the melodramatic brass gates and purple curtain that would part shortly.

I had seen Tommy twice in the previous six months. The first occasion was sometime after I had returned to South Africa. I had managed to track him down to a squalid little flat somewhere at the bottom of Bree Street in Johannesburg. He had a job as secretary to the Dean of the School of Mines at Wits University. When I phoned him, he invited me to come around and have supper. A couple of evenings later I found myself outside a derelict block of flats trying to identify his name on the post-boxes in the entrance. It was a Friday evening and the last remnants of the rush hour were trickling by. The muggy February air had been washed clean by a late afternoon storm. The last rumbles of thunder still echoed faintly in the distance. The hiss of traffic in the still drenched streets sounded in the hallway. I was not sure of the number he had given me and there were few names on the post-boxes. I knocked on several doors until I found the correct one. Pat came to the door.

She and I had not had a good relationship before I left for England and it was clear from the way she greeted me that she had not changed

"Yes, that's him."

her mind. It was six in the evening and it was quite evident she had already had a lot to drink. Tommy appeared behind her and ushered me in. Would I like a drink? How had my time in England been? At least I could fill the silences telling them about my experiences as a hall porter, farm labourer, barman, factory hand, at the Royal Academy and my decision to return to South Africa to train as a primary school teacher. I had just registered for a three-year diploma at the Johannesburg College of Education.

The evening went as well as could be expected. As I talked my eye wandered over the flat. I could see they had fallen on hard times. The attrition inflicted by days and nights of drunken violence showed on the furniture. The curtains had not been properly hung. The threadbare carpet covering the parquet floor was badly stained. A number of dead light bulbs had not been replaced. We sat in the gathering gloom; the sounds of other lives filtering through the thin walls punctuated by occasional dull thuds from the floor above. He could not have been earning much. Pat did not have a job. They were certainly drinking very heavily.

It was made clear to me that I could not expect, nor did I expect any help from them. I had no income, but I had managed to get, notwithstanding my dismal school record, a bursary for three years that would cover my board and lodging during term time. There was a shortage of male teachers and the training colleges were accepting almost everyone who applied. During the holidays, I would have to fend for myself. Somehow Pat managed to pull a curry together and we got through the evening. I left without making any arrangements to see them again, nor did they suggest any.

About four months later I was called to the phone at Knockando, the men's residence at the College of Education. Tommy wanted to see me. Would I meet him at the Devonshire Pub in Braamfontein at five that afternoon? I found him at the bar hunched over a large brandy. It was evidently not his first. Pat had committed suicide a week earlier he informed me. He was in the depths of depression and could not see the point of carrying on.

Staring Memory in the Face

"It's as though" he said "I keep opening a cupboard door only to discover infinite black emptiness. There is nothing there. An infinity of nothingness. I have an overwhelming longing to enter and close the door behind me."

I made some inadequate comments about depression and that he would get over it in time. My response must have been devastating. He was crying out for help and I was too insensitive or stupid or both to recognise his need. Camus is apposite: *"Absurdity is born of a confrontation between the human cry and the world's unreasoning silence."*[31] It was ever thus. I was his only link with life and I could not help him. I had no words. I could not hear him. I felt detached. Indifferent. Anyhow, I had not liked her. The failure was mine. He talked for a while longer in a similar vein about feeling he would not be able to resist going through the door and, that it might be for the best in the end. A couple of drinks later we parted. I left him sitting at the bar gazing vacantly at his distorted image between bottles of whiskey, brandy and gin ranked in front of a mirror, a half empty glass on the counter in front of him.

A week later I was standing on the lawn at Longwood House where I had gone for the weekend. Joyce came out onto the stoep: "Michael, there is only one way to tell you this. Your father's dead. He committed suicide last night. I've just had a call from the police."

The following day I went back to Johannesburg to identify his body in the morgue. I stood on the pavement outside the yellow brick building, wondering what I was doing there. This time there was no sense of relief, no thought of forcing myself to cry. I was numb, not so much with grief as with emptiness. I was shown into a small room at the end of which was a large curtain-covered window. The curtains were drawn apart and I could see his corpse through the glass laid out beneath a white shroud in the next room. They had removed his false teeth. His sunken jaw was covered with two- or three-day's growth. He resembled someone I had known once a long time ago. Camus again: *"There is but*

---

31. Albert Camus: *The Myth of Sisyphus.*

"Yes, that's him."

one truly serious philosophical problem and that is suicide."[32] This was the fourth suicide I had had to face.

"Yes, that's him," I said and turned away without another glance.

After I left the morgue I went and hid myself away for about a week or so. Unbeknown to me the University decided to take on the financial responsibility for the funeral. I can't remember how it came about, but as far as I knew I had not told anyone about what had happened, though I must have been in touch with someone at the University. In any event, on the afternoon of the funeral I expected no one to be there. This was something I believed I had to see through by myself. As I entered the chapel I discovered Prof Linde, the JCE rector, and one of my lecturers, Monty Sholund, who had decided on hearing what had happened that I should not have to face it alone. Monty realised that a door had opened on an infinity of darkness for me as well, which no well-intentioned platitudes were likely to assuage.

What went wrong? I have no answers, just some vague and inadequate speculation that cannot do justice to the waste that was his life. Was it the War? Certainly, he had been severely traumatised by his experiences and had ended up in a mental ward having shock treatment. But the question must be asked, was the War simply the trigger? Was there something else, something that pre-dated it? From the little I have been able to discover, it would appear that there was a propensity for alcoholism in the family. His brother Jim was also an alcoholic, but had somehow managed to sustain a career in medicine and hold his family together; though at what cost I don't know. But my father's life seems to have lost direction fairly early on. He drifted from one job to another in journalism, never managing to stay on any newspaper for any length of time. Journalism certainly has a reputation for encouraging hard drinking. It may be that he started drinking compulsively then and it was probably exacerbated later by the War.

But what of his relationship, if there was a relationship, with Elizabeth Fenton? Was it a cause or a consequence, or merely a symptom of

---

32. Ibid.

his psychological disintegration? And why did he cut himself off from his family? Was it guilt at having made a mess of his life, or did he hope that if he did so he could start anew in a new country with a clean sheet? His marriage to Flora was a disaster. He never indicated to me what might have gone wrong. Sex may have had something to do with it. When sex is right in a marriage everything else is manageable; when it is wrong it assumes a disproportionate influence, casting a bleak shadow over every aspect of the relationship. As far as she was concerned, alcohol was the reason for the breakdown. She never missed an opportunity to tell me about the evils of drink, blaming all our misfortunes on what it had done to Tommy. But I am inclined to think it was much more complex than that. I doubt if she could provide the kind of support he needed; it's a moot point whether anyone could. I always experienced her as cool and distant, caught up in her own anguish and incapable of responding to the emotional needs of others. On the other hand, he was a highly emotional man, deeply sentimental and easily moved to tears. Nothing's new. Whatever the case, whether it was alcoholism, the trauma of war or some other cluster of factors too obscure to identify now, he was a deeply unhappy man racked by existential despair about the meaningless of life, his lack of personal fulfilment and the pain he had caused those whom he loved and for whom he was responsible.

A poem for my father:

Pilate on the road from Bethal to Ermelo

In this hemisphere of contradictions, when seasons
fall at the wrong time of the year,
symbols of hope and order faintly flicker in the night;
those who care can look up,
for those who don't, or don't dare gaze,
a blaze, a trinity of lights
beside the road, in lands of rasping, rattling mielie stalks and khakibos:
magenta, pink and white.
At the feast of body and blood, and bread and wine
not spring

<blockquote>"Yes, that's him."</blockquote>

but dust and drought and long brown grass heavy with seed,
waiting for the first fires,
not the paraclete;
a field of flowers:
magenta, pink and white.
an accidental present from the past
not emblematic like roses, red or white,
the lilies of Lorraine or poppies sold to remind us –
our aloes with bloodied shields and spears stand yet against the light –
but seed
borne in horse manure to flourish here;
the cosmos: magenta, pink and white.

Life goes on, college, teaching, marriage, children, ambition. Life goes on as it will, as it must. Meaning continues to elude, but the narrative continues.

I gave everything he possessed to the Salvation Army.

~ 22 ~

Becoming a teacher

I owe an enormous debt to the men and women at the Johannesburg College of Education who taught me and oversaw my psychological survival and intellectual awakening during the next three years, until I graduated in 1964. I was not an easy student to have in class. I was at turns arrogant and overbearing, uncooperative, withdrawn and uncommunicative. My fellow students found me very difficult. I was older than most of them. My experience of life was broader, and I was certainly better read and could draw on a vast array of (unacknowledged) sources to undermine and belittle whatever they had to say. I rapidly became an intellectual snob. No small irony that. I often missed lectures, yet none of my teachers was ever unapproachable. It was entirely due to their support that I was sufficiently self-confident to register for the first year of a BA through UNISA in 1964, the final year of my teaching diploma. As a mature student, I qualified for matric exemption. I was not brilliant, but was doggedly determined to take advantage of the opportunity I had not so long ago thought impossible.

Little did I realise it at the time, but I was following in a family tradition. My grandfather had been the Rector of Peterhead Academy a position he held for over 20 years. There is a memorial dedicated to him at the school: *"To him and to men like him a great credit is due in that they secured for the teaching profession more adequate recognition by the public and its place of due importance in the social economy. His profession honoured him and loved him and respected him.... Teaching was not only his profession but it was...his true vocation."* If I'd known, it would have been a daunting shadow under which to live. Even so, his and my life have some curious parallels. He was offered the position of Secretary of Education in Scotland, which he declined; I would, against my better judgement, eventually become a Special Advisor to the Minister of Education on teacher training in Thabo Mbeki's government. My cousin, Duncan, had a distinguished

Becoming a teacher

career as Principal of Aberdeen University. Was my career pre-ordained? Somehow in my DNA?

Until I began my first year at JCE, my reading had been random and indiscriminate. I now had to submit myself to a systematic regimen. This was the era of Practical Criticism and The Great Tradition, I. A. Richards and F. R. Leavis. I was fortunate too in my teachers, particularly Malcolm Armstrong, Jacques van Oortmeesten and Joyce Rapson, personalities that a whole generation of teachers can look back to with affection and gratitude. English teaching in South African would be the poorer without their influence. They subscribed to the Leavisite thesis that only the best works were worthy of study. They made no apologies for their elitism. Students were expected to have a background in all the great works of world literature beginning with the *Epic of Gilgamesh*, the Bible, Homer, Plato, the Greek tragedies, St Augustine and St John of the Cross.

My haphazard reading began to pay off. Van Oort, as he was known, was passionate about Hopkins and Eliot. I had a tutorial with him every Saturday morning for three years in which we ranged over the whole canon of English literature. These tutorials were one of the most important influences on my life. They gave substance to my love of literature and provided me with a vocabulary and standards of excellence. All of which begs the question, what is literature? This question was recently put to my grandson, Jack, all of 12 years old. His reply: art in words. You can't do much better than that.

Monty Sholund kept me focused and psychologically afloat. I owe him much. He had come to my father's funeral and remained on hand to pick up the pieces when necessary. It was he who persuaded me to start my first degree. At the end of 1964 I wrote my final exams for a primary school teaching diploma, a Trinity College licentiate in drama and four first year university subjects. I would never have pulled it off if it hadn't been for the faith Monty, van Oort and Joyce Rapson had in me. They encouraged me to test my fledgling intellectual wings, read my execrable attempts at poetry, and endured my existential angst with a combination of humour, irony and occasional robust debate. I have been lucky in those I have known. They challenged me and paid me the compliment of listening without condescension.

Hamlet: JCE Shakespeare celebrations (1964) Johannesburg

I quickly established myself as one of a small group of eccentric rebellious souls who challenged the institution and the students in it in uncomfortable ways, confronting them on politics, the arts and religion. Ernie Saks, Lawrence Bam, Derek Joubert and Mike Muller have remained firm friends through a lifetime. We saw ourselves as free spirits, not to be constrained by petty bourgeois norms or fascist visions of a racially pure future. Heated arguments, lubricated with cheap red wine, often raged into the small hours. I don't think we were popular, but I know that Monty and Joyce thought enough of us to plead our cause on

Becoming a teacher

a number of occasions when we were in danger of being thrown out. At times like these we would comfort ourselves with the thought that Herman Charles Bosman who exercised a powerful influence on how we thought we should conduct ourselves, had suffered similar treatment at the College thirty years previously. He was finally expelled for painting communist slogans all over the rector's office one night. South African literature is the richer.

The College was not cocooned from what was happening in the rest of South Africa. The Rivonia Trial was in full swing. My future father-in-law Bram Fischer, was leading the Defence team. It was 1964, the papers were full of the Station Bombing. John Harris had been on the Wits staff. Hugh Lewin was picked up and sentenced to seven years imprisonment for sabotage. Nor was he the only one whom I would consider a close friend in the future. Sholto Cross was in solitary confinement, as was Terry Bell who had the misfortunate to be arrested more or less at the same time as Harris.

Christian National Education was denounced as neither Christian, national nor education by Dr Holmes our vice-rector at a mass meeting of the College staff and students in which he showed that it was a deliberate attempt to stamp out critical thinking in our schools and ensure support for Apartheid. His lecture, which was particularly brave given the gathering political climate, struck a particular cord with me as I continued to be sensitive to anything that I thought could compromise and manipulate my integrity as an independent individual. I had struggled too hard to welcome any restrictions on what I was supposed to think and say. The Universities Act, severely limiting the number of black students who could be admitted to the English-speaking universities, was passed in the face of fierce opposition. These issues were discussed in class and it is a credit to our lecturers that they were. We saw ourselves as the last bastion of liberal values in education in the country.

Staring Memory in the Face

It was the Sixties after all, and students around the world were infused with a new radical idealism. The Beatles were in full swing, *Yesterday* was a hit. The Vietnam war was hotting up, and President Johnson signed the *Civil Rights Act* that abolished racial segregation in the States. Athol Fugard had just produced *The Blood Knot*. And Harold Macmillan had made his "*Winds of Change*" speech in Cape Town. A popular slogan was "In 1963 we will be free." As it turned out, the country was turning in on itself and becoming more and more isolated from the rest of the world. South Africa had recently left the Commonwealth. Dark days were ahead. I was expected to have political opinions and to argue them in defence of a broad commitment to liberty and justice. Consciousness is much more complicated than that. We read Rousseau's *Emile*, Bertrand Russell on education, Orwell's essays, Koestler's *Darkness at Noon*, Alan Paton's *Cry the Beloved Country*, all of which were prescribed reading. Nadine Gordimer's short stories and early novels such as *The Lying Days* were beginning to appear. A disintegrating copy of Peter Abrahams's *Tell Freedom* circulated surreptitiously. Nat Nakasa, who was making his name as a journalist on *Drum Magazine*, attended our parties shortly before he left for the States where he tragically committed suicide. Before he left he pressed on to me a well-worn copy of Bloke Modisane's *Blame Me on History* which I kept until it finally fell apart. Blacks and whites were not allowed to drink alcohol together, but Nat and his friends regularly pitched up cadging free drinks and smokes, sprouting revolutionary talk.

We were shocked and horrified that police spies were in our midst. Gerald Ludi was unmasked as a police spy masquerading as a student at Wits, as Toni Bernstein would learn to her cost. Students demonstrated with placards and banners and wild speeches at the main entrance to the university and on the college steps in Hoofd Street to show our defiance and determination to defend academic freedom. The University senate took a stand and published a charter defending its right to teach what it liked to whom it liked regardless of race, colour or creed. But, as is always the case, it was a very small minority that made these issues central to their existence. Marius Schoon was one of them.

Becoming a teacher

I met him one morning in a coffee shop in Hillbrow. The previous night I had borrowed a friend's car and had a minor accident. However, when I borrowed the car I had neglected to mention that I did not have a driver's license. I was in a state of considerable agitation, imagining the police would pick me up. I confessed all this to Marius who listened to me with great sympathy.

"Don't worry," he said, "you can borrow my license. You can give my name and no one will know."

There was a flaw in his suggestion that made me hesitate, and I said I would take up his offer if I needed to. What I did not know, and only discovered in the newspapers a few days later, was that Marius was planning to blow up the Hillbrow police station that night. His attempt was a dismal failure and he was arrested almost immediately and spent several years in jail as a result. Fortunately for me, no attempt was made to follow up on the accident. Had I accepted his offer, it is likely that my career as an opponent of Apartheid would have taken a much more sudden and dramatic turn. As it was, I was much too timid to turn conviction into action, preferring the rhetoric of classroom debate where I could belittle the prejudices of my fellow students without fear of arrest. Blinding Gloucester: *"Out, vile jelly/ Where is thy lustre now?"*[33] was as close as I wanted to be to rebellion. Marius's wife, Jenny and their six-year-old daughter Katryn, were killed by a parcel bomb, when they were living in exile in Angola in 1984. Their killer, Craig Williamson, who had also murdered Ruth First in 1982, was to receive amnesty from the Truth and Reconciliation Commission.

By the time I graduated from JCE at the end of 1964, I had decided to break my contract with the Transvaal Education Department. This would involve me in considerable debt, but it was one I was more than willing to assume. For instead of working off my commitment to the

---

33. Shakespeare: *King Lear* Act 3 Sc. 7.

Staring Memory in the Face

Department I would have to pay back all I owed. I was determined to go ahead as I felt that my debt to Cloete was the greater obligation. Hadn't he provided for me for the last four years of my schooling? Hadn't he awakened my mind to life's possibilities? To books, music and art? And the ambitions I had for a life on the stage? True, I had not managed to make a living in the theatre, but the important thing was I would never have had any idea that such an adventure was possible without him. I owed him everything. The debt had to be repaid. I would do it in the only way I could by working for him simply for my bed and board and a little pocket money.

And so, it was arranged. I duly started the new school year, in 1965, at Longwood teaching Standard Six all their subjects. And, because it was Longwood I was given the freedom to make up my own syllabuses, choose what I wanted to teach and left to get on with it. With no experience but plenty of idealism and enthusiasm I fell to the task. I was never off duty. All my hours outside of the classroom, including most weekends, were filled with coaching sport, mending broken windows and desks, fetching and carrying sports teams, umpiring cricket, refereeing soccer, taking prep at night, providing a role model and counselling youngsters like myself who had washed up on the shores of Longwood, abandoned by their parents. Organising, organising. And, of course, getting on with my UNISA studies.

After about three or four months I began to sense a change in my relationship with Cloete. It began in subtle and insignificant ways. I found I was not being told of certain meetings. Information was being withheld. I was excluded from certain activities I had hitherto taken for granted. At first, I was puzzled, then gradually began feeling I was in some way at fault. Suddenly the school bus was no longer available to take the cricket team to matches as arrangements had already been made and I was not required. I felt more and more isolated. Cloete virtually stopped talking to me.

What was I doing wrong? There was no explanation. No complaint. Nothing was said. Where once I had felt free to drop in of an

Becoming a teacher

evening and discuss the day's events, I now felt constrained. Every time I volunteered for anything I was told I was not needed. I began to feel more and more demoralised. I knew I owed Cloete more than I could ever repay him. I was desperate to do my best, to please, to help in any way I could. But every effort was rejected and rejected in such a way that I was left feeling unwanted, unworthy and humiliated. The following is a record of my feelings at the time.

> *A soft white worm is crawling, spawning*
> *in my brain.*
> *it gave no warning*
> *it came when I was sane.*
> *A loathsome thing*
> *that needs no mate;*
> *that stings with a scarlet sting,*
> *and stinging, fills with hate.*
> *And I am glad, yes glad,*
> *for as it feeds and breeds*
> *it too is going mad*
> *supping on its seeds.*

I resigned at the end of that term. Years later, long after he was dead, his long-suffering wife, Joyce told me that he was intensely threatened by and jealous of all the male teachers he employed. My experience of being frozen out was not unique. What none of us knew was that he had no formal qualifications beyond matric. His posture as an educationalist, as an authority on French culture, literature, life, art and music was a confidence trick. No wonder he was so unpredictable, so authoritarian, and so charismatic. It was all a façade. The tragedy was, he was a visionary; he cared deeply about the children in his care. He inspired them and was rewarded by their largely uncritical admiration. He had to surround himself with acolytes. He could not afford to ever be in a position where he might be seriously challenged.

~ 23 ~

"She's pretty!"

My second teaching post was at Sir Edmund Hillary Primary in Kensington in Johannesburg. I joined the staff in August 1965. I quickly discovered my limitations. Teaching for the Transvaal Education Department was a far cry from the kind of life I had enjoyed at Longwood. I now entered a world where conformity was rewarded. My brand of individualism was definitely not approved of by the Department; its inspectors expected bureaucratic efficiency and ideological neutrality, if not support. The drudge of marking and preparing lessons bored me. Dealing with aggressive working-class parents was worse. My colleagues had no intellectual ambitions or interests. Conversation in the staffroom was limited to preparations for the coming inter-school sports or complaining about some or other child and announcements about new departmental regulations.

I went through the motions of following the Standard Four curriculum, but abandoned it and the official time-table whenever I could, reading the class stories from Greek mythology instead of religious instruction, producing plays and a class newspaper instead of grammar, playing Scrabble instead of spelling, and reading and teaching and performing poetry at every opportunity. Instead of the Great Trek I spent my time on ancient history. Every now and again the ghost of Miss Kane rose before me and I turned reluctantly to highest common factors, lowest common denominators and the times table. One thing I had in common with her was my reluctance to teach Afrikaans, though in my case it was not because I thought it below my dignity, but because I was incompetent. It is an old truism in teaching that one teaches as one was taught. My models had been Miss Kane and Cloete: opposite ends of the spectrum, but in many ways very similar. It took me a long time to break free of their influences and find my own voice. Ironically,

"She's pretty!"

the one thing they had given me was confidence in my authority. For the rest, my teaching style was a reaction to their influences.

Towards the end of the year I met Ruth Collett whom I married five months later in April 1966. She was the most important emotional stabilising force in my life. I had never known, until I met her, anyone who simply loved me for myself. It often puzzled me that she did so. She could have had any number of the eligible young men with much better prospects than I. Like most of those who knew her, I was attracted by her calm self-possession. The agonies of young adulthood seemed to pass her by. She was much admired by her troubled friends at university as a beacon of stability. Nothing seemed to ruffle her. While many of her friends were racked with self-doubt, unspecified guilt and a general sense of doom, she remained self-contained and a source of comfort to her more anguished friends. Her enormous yellow eyes looked on the world with serene confidence. She had unshakeable integrity. She knew who she was and she was happy with the knowledge.

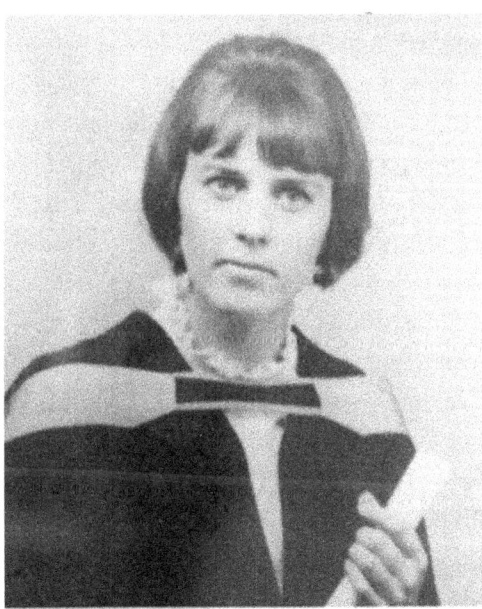

The first Ruth (Graduation 1964).

Staring Memory in the Face

Her parents were horrified. They had had high hopes for their beautiful and talented daughter. I was hardly the doctor or lawyer they were anticipating. A primary school teacher with no family did not bode well. But Ruth was determined to have me no matter what her parents thought. I did not make things any better when I expressed liberal views about black people and challenged fundamentalist views of the Bible.

The Sixties was not a good time for the generation that had survived the Depression and the Great Drought of the Thirties. In many respects, the Collet's were typical of white English-speaking South Africa; resentful beneficiaries of Nationalist Party rule. Ruth was the first in her family to go to university. Practical and literal, they clung to what they imagined was their English heritage; something along the lines of Rhodes, that the English were God's Chosen People.

Fortunately, Ruth could not be swayed.

One afternoon she fetched me from school. The children in my class knew I was going to get married and were agog to know what she was like. One of the girls followed me to the car, took one look at Ruth and jumped into the air, turned around and shouted: "she's pretty!"

We had their approval.

Ruth had a wonderfully spontaneous nature and zest for life. Like many young women growing up on the platteland, she was an excellent rider. As a young girl, shortly before she wrote matric, she and a friend, Lorna Mockford were riding in the bush one hot Saturday morning on the Mockford farm, Redlands, in the Northern Transvaal. The air was electric with the sound of Christmas beetles. They had been in the saddle for several hours and were hot and covered in dust. As they reached the edge of a dam in a remote corner of the farm, she turned and challenged Lorna to join her, strip naked and swim her horse bareback across the dam and then race to the top of a nearby koppie. The heat made a swim very inviting, but the thought of galloping bareback and naked through the bush, the still wet horse beneath her and the blazing sun high in the sky, was the kind of dare she relished for the sheer joy of it. She later told me that, astride their horses at the top of the koppie, they had surveyed

"She's pretty!"

miles and miles of the silent thornbush, away to the blue mountains at Chuniespoort, the Lowveld and Olifants River beyond. Nothing moved. It seemed as if they were the only living creatures in the world but for a bateleur riding the wind above them.

We met at the end of 1965, at the end of my first year of teaching, and just after she had graduated from Wits with a teaching degree in art. She was looking for someone to share the drive to her uncle's farm Inunwa, just outside of Bulawayo where she was going to spend her holidays before getting a teaching post. I was at a loose end and volunteered, intending to hitchhike on to Beira in Mozambique, and then make my way back to Johannesburg in time for the opening of the school term in the new year. In the event, once we arrived at the farm, Inunwa, 50 miles outside Bulawayo and deep in the bush, it had been decided that I would spend Xmas on the farm, rather than leave immediately.

Shortly after Xmas we were sitting under a baobab tree watching our horses dry in the sun after swimming them across the dam when Ruth suddenly said: "I want to bear your children."

I was completely taken by surprise. We hadn't even kissed. Not a romantic thought had passed through my mind, though I must admit to the odd lustful one. I had dismissed any possibility of romance because it had always been assumed that I would move on shortly and that would be the end of our relationship. Three months later *I* had become *we*.

It was an innocent time. We were on the brink of adult responsibilities for which we were only partially equipped. The Hartleys, on whose farm we spent that Xmas, were Seventh Day Adventists. True to form, I found myself engaged in fruitless augments with Ginny, Ruth's cousin. Our worlds were too far apart for there to be any real understanding. I thought she had been cocooned by her religion from facing complexity and ambiguity. Nothing for me was without doubt. Ginny was armoured with certainty. When challenged on the contradictions implicit in the way the family regarded black people and Christ's injunctions to love your neighbour as yourself, or to reject the pursuit of wealth, her response was that one had to be practical. I found her capacity to hold these contradictory views incomprehensible.

But, there were darker and more immediate clouds gathering. None of us could conceive of how our lives would change, nor what the forces were, that would shape our experience and understanding of the world. The Rhodesian war was still in its very early beginnings. Ginny's family reacted to it, when it could no longer be ignored, as did most white Rhodesians with a mixture of incomprehension and bellicosity; no proof against history. They eventually joined the diaspora going south where they found opportunities to prosper, but no sanctuary against the violence they feared.

My own response to the conflict to come in South Africa was destined to lead me into dangerous and treacherous byways, but none as tragic as that which befell Ginny. Her daughter Lindi was killed in an APLA attack on the Heidelberg Tavern in Observatory in Cape Town in December 1993, nearly 30 years later. There is no telling how people will respond to tragedy, but Ginny's capacity to forgive and seek reconciliation with her daughter's killers is the embodiment of her faith and Nelson Mandela's vision. I don't know many people who could have taken that path, but without them humanity doesn't stand much of a chance. Guilt. Expiation. Redemption. There are no guarantees.

Ruth and I were married in April 1965. We hunted for the prettiest church we could find in Johannesburg. We found it. St Luke's in Norwood. Modelled on a Norman English country church it was built of yellow dressed stone and set in a beautiful garden off the street in a leafy suburb.

I had not been baptised much less confirmed in the Anglican Church. Nothing daunted, I presented myself at the vestry door one afternoon and announced to the priest that I was going through a spiritual crisis and wanted to be baptised. The Rev. Tiny Glover (he was a huge genial man, fully six foot six) said I could join confirmation classes and prepare myself to be tested on the *Manual of Instruction of the Catholic Religion*. This was rather more than I had bargained for as I had rather imagined the Church was so desperate to save souls that it took on all

"She's pretty!"

comers, no questions asked. Nonetheless, I set to and started studying the *History of The Anglican Church, The Ends for which the Church Exists,* and *The Faith and Practice of the Church, The Sacraments and Prayers.* Come Wednesday afternoon, I presented myself at the vestry to discuss the mystery of the Holy Trinity, transubstantiation and the problems of faith.

After two weeks, I thought sufficient time had passed for me to broach the subject of my desire to get married. Ah, the subtlety of youth. I have no doubt that Tiny Glover was not taken in for a moment. Even so, the question of my baptism and confirmation into the Church could not be avoided. The unbaptised could not be married according to Anglican ritual and we were dead set on St Luke's. It was arranged that I would present myself the following Wednesday evening.

Ruth, Luke Fitzgerald and I duly turned up at eight o'clock that night. We were completely cynical about what we were doing and why. Luke kept on making limp-wristed jokes about spiritual incest, his voice rising to a hysterical giggle. Ruth was to be my Godmother; Luke who was a self-styled screaming queen, my Godfather. He was particularly interested in whether I would have to strip and climb into the font naked, or would I be dunked like a doughnut? (His phrase) Luke also had much to say, most of it unsavoury, about the apostles, as we drove to the church in a hilarious mood.

∼

We arrived at the church not long after dark; a dim glow from the half open door the only light. It was very beautiful, dark and mysterious. Ruth's enormous eyes seemed even bigger in the gloom. Huge jacaranda trees and lush vegetation smelled dank after the rains. There had been a late afternoon storm and the sky was occasionally lit up by lightening. The distant rumble of thunder could still be heard. In a light hearted and cynical mood the three of us entered the nave where we found Tiny Glover in his vestments waiting for us. The interior was in almost complete darkness with only one small light in a side chapel. We gathered in the gloom round the font where I was asked to renounce the devil and all his works; to believe in God; and, to serve Him; Luke digging me in the ribs all the while. After saying I would, I was asked to approach the font and bend over it.

The Rev. Glover poured water over my head reciting: *"Verily, verily, I say unto thee, except a man be borne of water and of the Spirit, he cannot enter into the kingdom of God."*

As the water trickled down the back of my head and I renounced the devil, I experienced the most extraordinary sensation, as though I was being washed clean throughout my entire being. Was this absolution? For what? My cynicism evaporated. Confused and bewildered I felt I was being saturated by a divine presence that suffused my whole being; an inner illumination. It was quite palpable. Not an external sensation but an inner effusion, a physical consciousness. Not the tingling of the skin which I often experienced when under stress, but an inner sensation of cleanliness from the crown of my head to the soles of my feet. It was completely unexpected. My immediate reaction was surprise, then a feeling of frantic desperation, wanting to hold onto what I experienced as a kind of hyper-consciousness, but knowing at the same time that it would not last. I must be drawn back into the grubbiness and rub of life.

I felt outside that rub of life. Detached. Separated from time, as if I was standing at the entrance to a mystery beyond experience. That sounds melodramatic. I have searched for the right words for years and have never found any that can capture my sense of awe. It was beyond language, and still is. An overwhelming calm welled up and embraced me. For the first and only time in my life I knew what was meant by the peace that passes all understanding. I did not want to touch anything, move or speak but remain suspended forever as I was. I knew I was in another realm. The last thing I wanted was to be drawn back into the cynical banter of the last hour or so. I tried to distance myself in an attempt to hold on to the sensation. It was not to be. I left the church a while later in a very different mood from which I had entered it.

"She's pretty!"

I have often wondered about that experience. Was it residual guilt? A panic attack? Or merely, an over-emotional response to the atmosphere and the occasion? I cannot ascribe it to divine intervention. I find it impossible to believe in a personal god who takes a direct interest in my existence. There has been too much arbitrary and unjust suffering to believe in an interventionist god, especially one who would find my existence significant given the hundreds of millions of people who have existed; given the immensity of time and space. If there were an interventionist god, he would have an awful lot of bookkeeping to do. Belief in a personal god is surely at best wishful thinking, at worst narcissism. 'Believe' is a loosely used word today, almost without meaning. It is pointless to say one does or does not believe in evolution. The only thing relevant is evidence. At the same time, it is impossible to escape subjectivity.

For all that, it is belief that sustains us and gives us meaning and the courage to continue. That is, what can't ultimately be proved or defined. What a paradox. Therein lies the bargain we have made, trading certainty for uncertainty, rational speculation for belief. Belief underpins our emotions; underpins hope. The price we pay is the price of bewildered consciousness that separates us from ourselves.

Perhaps we look at experiences like this from the wrong end, and should start by wondering if what we take to be God revealing himself to us, is not the other way around; we reveal ourselves. But to what? To whom? What is this self that is revealed? If, in fact, it is revealed. The problem is, any god we could conceive of would not be much of a god. To be God he/she/it must be beyond the bounds of human understanding; beyond language, beyond human imagination. Of one thing I can be sure, I have a capacity, no less than anyone else, to attribute significance, if not meaning, to emotional episodes in my life. Whatever I experienced that evening has remained in my memory as a physical sensation that gave me a disconcerting comfort. The imagination has its truths as well. What did Hobbes say about the imagination and memory?

~ 24 ~

Breaking eggs

Neither of us had jobs to begin with, but we soon found teaching posts in Cape Town and started putting our lives together. Our combined salaries did not amount to much, but they were sufficient to make ends meet with a little over to start acquiring the basic necessities. Five months later Ruth fell pregnant. Neither of us had a clue about birth control. The wonder is it took so long. All our plans for the future which had included spending a year overseas once we had saved enough money, had to be changed. One salary was hardly enough for us to survive on, never mind with the addition of a baby. I now realised that I was going to have to complete my degree as quickly as possible. The prospect of having to provide for a family provided the necessary focus. I was driven by a mixture of motives ranging from academic and professional ambition, a need to prove to myself that I could do it and, of course, the need to earn more money.

In between whiles, I became involved with a group of young liberals who were doing drama and poetry readings in District Six, Ottery, Bonteheuwel, and Retreat. The intention was to provide coloured children in matric with the opportunity to experience their matric English syllabus as more than something that had to be endured for an exam. Unbeknown to me, Clive Emdon, then a journalist on *The Cape Times*, who organised these events, had a political agenda that became apparent towards the end of the evening of our first performance. He used the opportunity to present poetry by coloured and black writers not included in the syllabus but which had a powerful social and political message. This was my introduction to art put to work for political purposes. Until then I had naively assumed that art was for art's sake, that it had nothing to do with the grubbiness of everyday existence, especially politics.

Breaking eggs

Clive read a number of poems by coloured and black poets, including Adam Small whose work lifted the scales from my eyes. What it did for the youngsters in the audience I can only surmise:

> *"Die Here het geskommel: Lat die wereld ma' praat pellie los en vas*
> *'n sigaretjie en 'n kannetjie Oem Tas*
> *en dis allright pellie dis allright*
> *ons kannie worrie nie...."* [34]

And,

> *"Diana was 'n wit nooi*
> *Martin was 'n bruin boy/ dey fell in love*
> *dey fell in love/dey fell in love...."* [35]

The audience was suddenly electrified from polite attention into gasping disbelief and then wild enthusiasm. I shyly read my own poetry for the first time in public.

> *Between trains, an exhibition,*
> *le Corbusier, poet of the right angle.*
> *I hurried by two old men dozing in the sun.*
> *'You don't live forever,' said one.*
> *Sweat trickled down my back.*
> *19 lithographs tacked to a wall*
> *like butterflies gathering dust.*
> *Somewhere someone's made love instead of lunch.*
> *You don't live forever.*

The last two lines, at least, were greeted with approval.

The political temperature in the country had been rising. John Harris, convicted and sentenced to death for the station bombing in Johannesburg, had been executed. Bob Dylan's *"We shall overcome"* was on our lips. Rumour had it Harris had gone to the gallows singing it. One afternoon Clive invited us to see a friend off on the mail ship leaving Cape

---

34. Adam Small: 'Die Here het geskommel'.
35. Adam Small: 'Diana was 'n wit nooi'.

Staring Memory in the Face

Town that evening. The sight of a considerable police presence at the docks should have alerted me, but it was only once we were on board I discovered that Clive's friend was John Harris's widow, Anne.

The political climate had changed. It was no longer possible to think about South Africa's politics as an extension of the Boer War with Afrikaner pitched against British imperialism. Bram Fischer, who had successfully evaded the security police for nearly a year, had been caught and sentenced to life imprisonment. There had been a number of sensational trials including Hugh Lewin's who was one of the chief victims of Adrian Leftwitch's betrayal of the anti-Apartheid Resistance Movement (ARM) to the security police. Sholto Cross was held in solitary confinement for nine months from which he tried disastrously and unsuccessfully to escape. Who could tell where the threads in the pattern would emerge? My life was destined to be inextricably and intimately involved with all of them.

Recently, in post-Apartheid, in post-millennium South Africa, there have been several attempts to rehabilitate John Harris, culminating most recently in Jonty Driver's book on Harris. While there can be no disputing what Harris did, his motives must remain a matter of conjecture and debate. There are those who knew him, like Terry Bell who occupied a cell next to Harris, who claims he had no intention of causing any serious loss of life or limb; that he gave the press and the police fair warning of where he had placed the bomb in the station and when it was likely to go off. However, there are others who knew him as well, if not better, who say he was indifferent to the amount of suffering he would cause. He had greater concerns than a few dead or maimed. In fact, the more damage done, the more powerful the message would be to the Apartheid government that the armed struggle had entered a new phase. At this remove it is impossible to say what the truth is, except that what Harris did exemplified Lenin's dictum that one cannot make an omelette without breaking eggs. In the end, one has to make up one's own mind whether the omelette is edible.

Breaking eggs

Well into the future, some eggs, some omelette.

We are sitting on a patch of lawn in a back garden in Brixton, Johannesburg, listening to Kenny tell his story. His left eye is bruised, swollen and bandaged. What he has to say comes out haltingly.

"She stood in front of me and accused me of being an informer. When I denied it… she hit me in the eye with this big ring she was wearing on her finger…again and again…. Each time… in the eye…. She encouraged the others in the football team, including Jerry, to hit me as well…. Thabiso and Pello were there…. They can tell you…. They were also beaten up…. Also, Stompie…. He was beaten so bad he couldn't stand. I think he was unconscious. He was just lying where they dropped him…not even making a sound…covered in blood…. Winnie told them to take him away…. That was the last time I saw him…. Then Thabiso and Pello and me were locked in a room. I decided to escape. I broke a window and we got out that night. …Paul brought us here."

Kenny Kgasi (1989).

Staring Memory in the Face

Kenny, Thabiso and Pello were fairly representative of the innumerable disaffected black youths caught up in the township trauma of Apartheid South Africa in the 1980s. They had cut themselves off from their families on the platteland, left school and drifted into Soweto where they lived a nomadic hand to mouth existence. Some found refuge in Paul Verryn's Methodist manse.

Paul Verryn was one of the very few white religious leaders who lived in Soweto; dedicated to his calling and brave beyond comprehension. Absurdly young, in his mid-twenties when we met him, he faced down the Security Police, gangsters, thugs and in fact anyone he considered a bully of the poor and defenceless. His innocent face belied a tough uncompromising nature. He won the respect of everyone who had any dealings with him. On one occasion, he managed to talk a gang that had broken into his house and held him captive for a weekend, with every intention of killing him, into releasing him unharmed. He is unpretentious and without material ambition, often giving away whatever money, or food, or clothes he possesses. He has no holy cows, and is as critical of our present political leaders as he was of those in the past. He also has an enormous enthusiasm for life and a deeply cynical, often politically incorrect, but wicked sense of humour.

At one time he and Ruth had a regular Detainees Counselling Service meeting that often went on till midnight. They would come home, wake me up and the three of us would go nightclubbing until three in the morning. In those years we seized every opportunity we could to party. There was a desperation in our need to enjoy ourselves, dancing till we were exhausted. And we drank much too much. Ruth would have to begin her therapy sessions at eight, often seven in the morning. I always had first lecture at eight. I often arrived for my first class unshaven and hollow-eyed with a severe hangover. Paul seemed inexhaustible. He, of course, did not drink, which probably made all the difference.

Breaking eggs

Paul Verryn

Winnie Mandela's solution to keeping the many youngsters who turned up on her doorstep was to create a soccer team: Mandela United. As the 'Mother of the Nation' she was a natural rallying point for the youths whose lives had been dislocated by the growing chaos in the country. She provided a focus for their idealism as well as a degree of material support, food and often a roof over their heads. Mandela United soon became more than a football club. It provided her with bodyguards and guards of honour at ceremonial events and funerals, which Winnie used to boost morale and keep the fires of resistance alive in the community. The team was in fact a private militia. It soon assumed, with her collusion, it was a law unto itself, policing the community, maintaining security and dispensing rough justice. After all, they were protecting the Mother of the Nation and were carrying out a vital role in helping to fight Apartheid. Jerry, her driver, the team coach, was in a position to convey her wishes directly to the team. Stories soon began to circulate about a reign of terror.

The end justified the means. Informers had to be rooted out and dealt with. There were rumours that the highest echelons of the ANC in Lusaka and London had been infiltrated. Winnie was under constant police surveillance. She was banished to Brandfort in the Free State, but returned to Soweto after a few years in triumph. Whether it was desperation or other factors were at work, there were rumours of drugs and drink. Her behaviour became more and more erratic and irresponsible, not to say irrational.

There was considerable concern within the ANC about the need to control her, especially after the speech she made in which she said that no matter what the Apartheid regime did black people would always have boxes of matches with which to light the fires of revolution. When I was in the Washington in 1987 at the time of the 'Free the Children' campaign, I was questioned closely by a senior ANC official about her behaviour and the need to rein her in. Nor were these the only signs to raise suspicions.

The signs of megalomania were all there. Her extravagant life style led many to wonder where all the money was coming from. She saw herself as above the law; as literally a law unto herself. And she was ruthless in dealing with real and perceived opposition around her. Spies were everywhere. No means was too drastic to deal with them, including necklacing and murder. She also brooked no rivals. Anyone, in her perception, who looked likely to challenge her popularity in any way suffered the consequences. A case in point was Paul who lived in the Methodist manse in Soweto, where he provided a refuge and safe house to up to a dozen youngsters at any one time. Winnie, working through his

Breaking eggs

housekeeper, spread rumours that he was abusing them sexually, and she ordered that Stompie, Kenny, Thabiso and Pello be brought to her for safekeeping. When they refused to confirm Winnie's accusations against Paul, she turned against them.

I had encountered Stompie Sepi previously though my work with the Detainees Parents Support Committee, and there had been some uneasiness about him. He was not an attractive child. He had been on the streets for a number of years and at twelve years old was experienced in the ways of the world. There was no doubt he possessed enough cunning to survive in a turbulent and violent world. He was often seen hanging about at Khotso House where many organisations like the Black Sash, the DPSC and the churches had offices. Generally, he was not trusted, but there was no evidence he was an *impimpi*, a spy. Rumours fed on rumours. Accusations were made and it was almost impossible for anyone to establish their innocence once they had. Of course, some accusations were based on solid evidence, but there were many cases in which grudges, jealousy and envy were the motive. It was understandable that Stompie should end up in Winnie's house at some stage. He had been hanging around various support groups, running errands, cadging food and occasionally money for some time. Winnie was a natural target. There must have been dozens of similar street kids who passed through her house. Most went back onto the streets; some stayed and were integrated into the soccer team. Flotsam and jetsam.

Kenny's story was a tale of suspicion, betrayal, torture and humiliation, and ultimately complete psychological breakdown. Ruth and I offered to take the three youngsters in and provide them with a safe house, as we had done for Benjy Olifant another youngster eventually murdered by the Special Branch. In the meantime, Stompie's body had been discovered and the press was agog with rumours that Winnie might be implicated in his death. As the trial proceeded, we could see Paul visibly ageing. Kenny tried to keep himself busy by writing, while Thabiso and Pello tried to prepare themselves for their school exams. No one achieved very much. The trial preoccupied all our minds. Our own

Staring Memory in the Face

children, especially Gretel, rose to the occasion and accepted the three new additions to our family with the best of grace. Gretel and Dammon slipped out of school on several occasions and attended the trial when Kenny, Thabiso and Pello were giving evidence to provide sandwiches and moral support.

More and more evidence emerged of the reign of terror the football team exercised in Soweto. In the meantime, we had to cope with the three youngsters every night, going over their evidence, reassuring them, checking details, making sure their stories were consistent. At one stage, Thabiso and Pello were meant to be preparing themselves for a geography exam, part of which involved understanding the moon's influence on tides. We were sitting in the kitchen and with the aid of a couple of oranges and a light over the table, comment from Brendan, Dammon and Gretel and Ruth, I tried to explain the effects of gravitational attraction and the difference between spring and neap tides. Somehow, none of it made sense. The trial and Stompie were at the back of our minds all the time.

Dammon, Brendan and Gretel in happier times.

Breaking eggs

A trial developed within Winnie's trial in which Paul was placed in the impossible position of having to deny that he was sexually abusing the children who stayed in the manse. There was no evidence against him, but the opportunity was used to distract attention from Winnie and to suggest that she had acted out of genuine concern for the welfare of the children. Kenny, Thabiso and Pello could hardly be described as children. Kenny was in his mid-twenties and the other two were 18 or 19 at the time. But that was no matter. Kenny suffered from a massive psychological breakdown during the trial, and never recovered. Winnie's lawyer, George Bizos, distracted attention from the main accusations against her and she got off with a suspended sentence.

On a dark and stormy night in the middle of the trial when George was cross examining Paul in the most lurid and degrading way, as part of his strategy to discredit him, I asked Raymond Sutner, recently released after serving a lengthy sentence under the Suppression of Communism Act who I knew was in touch with the ANC leadership in Lusaka, to send a message to Oliver Tambo explaining what was going on. I hoped we could get him to intervene on Paul's behalf. He was in a terrible state verging on a psychological and physical collapse. But Raymond's commitment to preserving the public face of the Party's integrity and Winnie's image as the "Mother of the Nation" won out. Whether it would have made any difference, who knows? But politics triumphed over humanity. Betrayal is never pretty and never rises above the machinations of expediency

Even so, the evidence against her was so convincing that she never fully recovered her position and prestige and gradually lost her influence within the ANC hierarchy, if not among its supporters, especially those who had been too young to participate in the Struggle or were unaware of the stakes when the negotiations for the transition to democracy took place and now conveniently accuse Mandela and Ramaphosa of being sell-outs.

As for Kenny, we heard from him from time to time for a number of years after the trial in long rambling and largely incoherent letters which showed his progressive mental deterioration. He died in a mental institution in Sweden. Thabiso is still part of our lives and phones every couple of months to tell us about his latest promotion, his family and to wish Ruth happy birthday. He took a number of years to find his feet, but once he got married, settled into a job and started doing a series of courses that gave him a sense of purpose and ambition, he seems to have grown beyond the trauma of those years. He has two children called Paul and Ruth. Pello, who disappeared from our lives, phoned out of the blue recently.

Paul finally confronted Winnie face to face at one of the hearings of the Truth and Reconciliation Commission in 1997. Paul blamed himself for Stompie's death saying: "I see that Mrs Seipei (Stompie's mother) is in the audience. The thing that has been most difficult for me is that I did not remove him from the manse and get him to a place where he could be safe. Had I acted in another way, he could be safe and with us now. I apologise to Mrs Seipei."

Paul then turned to Winnie and looked her straight in the face. "I don't really know Mrs Mandela. We have met only briefly. But my feelings about this have taken me in many directions. I long for reconciliation. I have been profoundly hurt by the things you have accused me of. I have been cut to the quick. I have struggled to learn and find forgiveness. I forgive you even if you do not want it, or do not think I deserve to give it."

Winnie's fall from grace has many of the elements of Greek tragedy. It could be argued, she was a heroic figure held in high esteem, brought low by a fatal flaw in her character. Wherein lies her legacy? The facts are well known. What is in dispute is their interpretation. Whatever the interpretation, it inevitably reveals not only the political alignment but the moral acumen of those involved in the debate. According to Aristotle, character is that which reveals moral purpose; that which shows the kinds of actions one chooses or rejects. Further, it could be argued that Winnie was not brought low by circumstances beyond her control, such as the depravity visited upon her by the Apartheid State, but as Aristotle would have it, by some personal error or weakness.

Breaking eggs

In other words, she was not simply an agentless victim. In fact, the machinations of the security police, ironically, enabled her heroic status. Before history forced itself upon her, she was, like the rest of us, neither eminently good or bad; just an ordinary young woman making her way in a conflicted world. But morality is meaningless without choice. In the face of suffering she had choices and the choices she made led not only to her moral collapse, but had fatal consequences for those upon whom she directed her malevolence.

What makes her fate especially controversial and moving is that we can identify with her. Given similar circumstances, which one of us could say with absolute conviction that we would have resisted our darkest impulses and acted with restraint? If anything, her legacy lies in the fact that she truly can stand for the rest of us. It is a terrible warning, especially for those who enjoy occupying the moral high ground. But, as those responsible for her interrogation at the TRC knew full well, without remorse there can be no redemption.

Recently, Paul was told that the ANC in Lusaka had suspected that Winnie was an informer herself. The Party had been infiltrated at the highest level. There had been too many security leaks and assassinations. Suspicion was rife. So, they had decided not to send anyone to her for safe-keeping, and chose to send those they were trying to protect to Paul instead. Hence her determination, fuelled by jealousy, a sense of betrayal or the need to protect herself, to destroy him.

A tangled web with no order and no end, or an unfinished tapestry still on the loom?

∽

But I have run on many years. On the 1st June 1967, I watched my son Brendan being born. His mother was wheeled into a surgical theatre at Groote Schuur. Arch lights, stainless steel, white tiles, the hum of electrical equipment. Green-robed figures hover, going about their mysterious and appointed tasks, unhurried, unflurried, efficient, waiting for the moment.

Staring Memory in the Face

"Pray for us at the hour of our birth." I stand to one side holding her hand, muttering platitudes to cover my anxiety. She smiles encouragingly. I am pushed to one side. Irrelevant. As the head begins to appear. The earth has suddenly split wide. Life emerges. I remembered another birth beside a river in the midst of war.

Poem for my son

make it out of leather
build it out of wood
weave your clothes from wool
walk in any kind of weather
regardless of your mood
roof your house with thatch
daub the walls with lime

swim in a mountain stream
catch
your salmon in its upward leap
laugh before you sleep.

Somerset West (1967).

~ 25 ~

Hottentots Holland

Although nominally a parallel-medium school with classes for both Afrikaans and English children, Hottentots Holland High was predominantly English. The staff was almost entirely Afrikaans-speaking and committed to Christian National Education. Soon after arriving at the school in 1969, I scandalised them by breaking with protocol and getting Helen Suzman, the solitary member of the Opposition to sponsor a visit to Parliament by my matric class. I should have approached the local MP, but he was a Nationalist. I thought it only fair that my pupils should meet a politician who was not part of the governing party and get another point of view.

I also took an unpopular position on corporal punishment. Mr Vlok had a fearsome reputation for maintaining discipline and had caned all the boys in the school because their hair did not conform to his idea of short back and sides. Schoolboys' hair assumed a significance in the minds of most teachers that heralded the end of order and discipline. Ignore it or lower standards and we would have chaos. During a staff meeting I insisted having my objections to mass caning minuted. It did not make any difference. The next time it happened I phoned *The Sunday Times*. The front page screamed, *"Whole school caned."* The Somerset West community was in an uproar, divided between those who supported traditional methods of discipline, and a vocal minority that threatened court action if their children suffered this kind of punishment again. Staff meetings were held, inspectors arrived at the school and a statement from the Department appeared in the press detailing the conditions under which corporal punishment could be administered. Mass caning was explicitly not allowed. Fortunately, *The Sunday Times* had kept my name out of their report, but there were suspicions.

The staff, with one or two exceptions, did not know how to treat me. I was obviously a dangerous liberal element. On the other hand, the

Staring Memory in the Face

English results had never been better even though I was using teaching methods that could easily get out of hand such as group work and peer tuition. To make things worse, I did not have any discipline problems and never had to resort to corporal punishment. When it was revealed that I had been working with the Drug Squad to break up a syndicate that had infiltrated the school, they were even more confused. Liberals were next to communists, and were believed to be committed to undermining the forces of law and order. Mr van der Merwe, the principal, tried on several occasions to fathom my motives. He prided himself on his ability to speak English. His master's dissertation had been on the poets of the First World War which he felt gave him an intellectual edge in our discussions. Not many Afrikaners had degrees in English literature. He was about ten years older than I and was a rising star in the education department. Our conversations were doomed to go around in fruitless circles.

"You know, Michael," he said affecting an informal mode of address reserved for extra-mural activities (we were watching the school's first rugby team being thoroughly beaten by SACS) "I can't understand why you must always challenge authority. Don't you realise that the people who decide on educational policy are very intelligent and highly qualified? They wouldn't be in those positions if they weren't. They all have doctorates. They have all been in education for a long time and have a lot of experience, far more than you or I, and are very respected. I am amazed you can question them."

"Yes, but that does not mean they have all the answers. Nobody should be beyond criticism. That's how dictatorships are born."

"True, but it must be positive criticism from properly qualified people who are properly informed and have all the facts."

Positive criticism was one of the mantras of the Nationalist supporting intelligentsia. What it boiled down to was making suggestions to ensure the status quo was made acceptable. Anything more serious that attacked fundamental flaws in an argument was unhelpful, destructive and unpatriotic. Van der Merwe and many like him was typical of those

Hottentots Holland

who had embraced the idea of a closed society, with all its guarantees of certainty and security.

"You can't have people, especially children, criticising whatever they like. You'll have chaos."

That word again.

The central tenet of Fundamental Pedagogics, the education theory underpinning Christian National Education, was submission to authority: the textbook, the teacher, the school principal, the inspector, the examiner, the Department and so on right up to God.

"Everything", I said, "is aimed at preserving order to produce passive citizens who accept the government's policies without thinking. Simply drones who keep politicians in power. They're still fighting the Boer War".

This last remark was not helpful and we got side tracked into an arid debate about who was more committed to South Africa, Afrikaners or English-speaking South Africans. In any event, I was told to stop group work with my classes as it could only lead to discipline problems. I replied I would do so when it did. The clouds were now low over the Hottentots Holland mountains. It began to rain. The rugby field was turning into a quagmire.

Sometime later the Education Department issued a directive asking for all school children to contribute to the building of the Taal Monument in Paarl then being erected to celebrate the birth of the Afrikaans language. The decision to build the monument was extremely controversial and was debated at length in the press. The design, far from symbolising the rise of Afrikaans, was said to look like a giant phallus. It was also at this time that Afrikaans was identified as the "language of the oppressor". Black school children were being forced to learn Afrikaans, and do some of their school subjects (maths and science) in that language. This put them at an enormous disadvantage. Not unnaturally, they associated Afrikaans with all the forces of repression that ruled their lives. These tensions were to erupt eventually in 1976 in the Soweto riots which enflamed the country. In the meanwhile, increasing numbers of alienated coloured families in

Staring Memory in the Face

the Western Cape were abandoning Afrikaans as their home language. There had always been tension between Afrikaans and English-speaking people which had been exacerbated by politicians who saw advantage in resurrecting the antagonisms of the Boer War. On the other hand, Afrikaner nationalism had never been stronger and more unassailable. The Nationalist Party had increased its majority in election after election. The opposition had virtually withered away.

Just before the final bell on Friday, I announced in the midst of a plethora of instructions about homework, supporting the rugby team on Saturday and a meeting of the cultural group to be held after school: "Please don't forget to bring your donations for the Taal Monument on Monday."

Monday morning dawned. I sat at my desk waiting for my class to arrive from assembly. The door opened. All twenty-six were present. They entered, led by the head boy and head girl, each one deposited, without comment, a half-cent on my desk. I looked at the pile of coins. Twenty-six half cents, thirteen cents. I could see trouble looming. At the end of the lesson I would have to take all twenty-six half cents to the school secretary, Mrs Ehlers, who was guaranteed to tell the principal and as many of the staff she could of how much and in what denominations I had managed to collect. How was I going to explain this pitiful and insulting amount? There would be an enquiry, of that I was certain, possibly involving the circuit inspector. There had been complaints already that I was filling the pupils' heads with all sorts of communist ideas. This surely would bring things to a head. I sighed and said: "Sit down. Open your books. Act 1 Scene 2." And began to read: *"O, that this too, too solid flesh would melt, Thaw and resolve itself into a dew,..."*[36]

In the middle of the morning Mrs Ehlers's voice came over the intercom: "Sorry to interrupt Mr Rice. Mr van der Merwe would like to see you during break." The class looked at me. I looked at the class.

I knocked at the principal's door.

"Come in. Sit down."

---

36. Shakespeare: *Hamlet*, Act 1 Sc 2.

Hottentots Holland

An ostentatious rustling of papers and signing of documents continued for some minutes. The pile of coins was on the desk in front of him. I settled into my chair and waited, my eyes wandering around the room from the prominently framed set of diplomas and degree certificates above the desk to the bland regulation grey filing cabinet, colour studio photographs of smiling wife and children on top of the trophy cabinet, and finally out of the window at the blue Hottentots Holland mountains rising in the distance. My conscience was clear. I had not attempted to influence my class and had simply passed on the request as instructed, without comment.

"How do you explain this?" interrupting my reverie.

"What?"

"This," pointing at a pile of coins.

"That's the money my class donated this morning. I collected it as you instructed."

"But why all these half cents. What does it mean? What does it mean?"

"I've no idea."

"What do you mean, you've no idea? You must have put them up to it. If you didn't who did?"

"I said nothing to them. If you don't believe me, call them in and ask them."

"Make no mistake I will. This is outrageous. You do realise I will be writing a report to the Department? There could well be repercussions. There are already a number of question marks against your name."

So, now it was clear. All those friendly intellectual chats about educational theory on the side of the rugby field had been documented and could be used as evidence against me.

"If that's what you are going to do, I can't stop you. But I want you to record this conversation honestly. I repeat, I did not say anything directly or indirectly on Friday about how the donations should be made."

"That may be so, but your whole attitude, the way you teach, everything you encourage in class has led up to this."

Staring Memory in the Face

"You can't prove that."

Fortunately, the bell went for the end of break. I returned to my classroom, seething with rage. Of course, he was right. I had communicated, and not all that indirectly either, what I thought of the government, Apartheid and by implication the Taal Monument. There was a strange anomaly, perhaps symptomatic of a deep moral insecurity felt by those in power at that time that expressed itself in legalistic terms. Laws were passed, rules written according to which the processes of governance had to conform. If one played by the rules there was a modicum of protection. There was no incontrovertible evidence that could be brought against me.

However, a few weeks later an inspector arrived from the Department. He watched me teach for two days. He examined my books, my lesson preparation file and records. Everything was up-to-date. Every pupil I taught wrote at least one full essay a week. The marking I got through was prodigious. The evidence was there. I had learned a thing or two from Miss Kane after all. But more important, there was no denying the standard of English in the school had never been higher. For all that, later in the interview with the inspector and van der Merwe, I was warned in no uncertain terms that I had to reform my ways, otherwise there could be unpleasant consequences.

I took the hint and started applying for what I was told would be more suitable positions where my talents and interests could express themselves. Van der Merwe provided me with a glowing testimonial. The best way to get rid of me, he had decided, was to help me find another job as easily as possible. So, I responded to an advert in *The Sunday Times* for a lectureship at the University of the North.

My friends in Cape Town were appalled. I would be supporting Apartheid, helping to prop up one of its most iniquitous institutions and breaking the academic boycott. But my need to get out of school teaching, where I knew I was in a dead end, triumphed over my fledgling political awareness and any scruples I may have had. Anyway, who said I couldn't make a contribution that would counterbalance my ideological apostasy?

~ 26 ~

"Free, white and over twenty-one"

Our move to Pietersburg in January 1972 was a homecoming for Ruth. She had grown up and gone to school there. We bought another house, a house that had been owned in its remote past by the writer Herman Charles Bosman. I thought it a good omen. And, I started teaching at the university.

The University of the North, Turfloop as it was known, had been established as one of the beacons of the efficacy of Grand Apartheid: separate but equal. It was, of course, nothing of the sort. It was nothing but a façade. Most of the white staff, who were in the majority, were little more than washed-up academics who would not have got a job anywhere else. The black staff, with one or two exceptions, were time servers whose academic credentials did not bear examination. A superficial glance revealed doctorates and master's degrees in abundance. The academic quality was another matter. Those universities that supported Nationalist Apartheid policy had a vested interest in manufacturing academic qualifications that did no more than fulfil the most obvious requirements. Apartheid was above all else an exercise in presenting a false front to the world. It was yet another example, of which the twentieth century had far too many, of reality being made to conform to theory. As long as the outward appearance was preserved, the inner reality did not matter. Surface became substance.

There was one other applicant for the lectureship I applied for, Patrick Chabane. I only realised a couple of years later the extent of the injustice of my appointment. Two years after I was appointed Patrick applied again. I attended one of his interviews. It was immediately apparent to me that he knew more about literary theory than I, and was considerably more articulate. Admittedly, English was my mother tongue and I had more background in English literary culture. But the fact was, I was appointed because the interviewing committee was almost exclusively white, Gessler Nkondo was the only black academic in the department. And, as I came to realise later, Patrick had a greater empathy with the students. They trusted him. He was an excellent role model. He understood their particular social, educational and linguistic problems in a way I never could. On his second attempt he was appointed.

I was blithely innocent of the tensions surrounding me and the pitfalls ahead. I was given two main tasks in my first year. First, to design and introduce a system of tutorials, and second, to introduce and teach black African literature. Neither had been attempted before I joined the staff. I set about designing the tutorials immediately, employing all the latest and most progressive teaching methodologies currently to hand. Schedules were drawn up. Worksheets prepared. Instructions on the purpose and conduct of the tutorials were distributed. The students were divided into groups of seven or eight. The time table was worked out. All that remained was for me to launch the first session. I walked into my first class confident in the knowledge that the students had been well prepared for what was expected of them and that they had had adequate time to prepare themselves.

"Good morning ladies and gentlemen. You know what is expected of you. Let's proceed."

Silence. There could hardly have been a more eloquent comment on my pomposity. Well, I thought to myself, they are anxious and shy, but the weakest link will break and the discussion will start when it does. All I have to do is wait. Five minutes later, sure enough, the weakest link broke.

"Well come on, we are all free, white and over twenty-one. What's the matter with you?"

No sooner were the words out of my mouth than I realised what I had said. If only the earth could have opened at my feet and swallowed me whole. This was a period of growing black consciousness and resistance. The university was closed for part of the year because of student boycotts and riots. I could not have made a bigger, more stupid or more insensitive blunder. I stood revealed for what I was. Nine months later when we were reviewing the year the students confessed to me they had nearly

"Free, white and over twenty-one"

dissolved into hysterical giggles. And, what was worse, they had had to suppress their hilarity until I left the class at the end of the period. It says a lot for them that they were mature enough to see the funny side of it.

My first class in African literature was no more auspicious. I had chosen Achebe's *Things Fall Apart* and Ngugi's *The River Between* for my series of lectures. There was immediate resistance from the students. Just before my first lecture on *The River Between* I faced a delegation who wanted to know why they were being passed off with inferior works. Did I think that they would accept less than the best simply because that is how white people always treated them, giving them cast offs? They knew what the best was: Shakespeare, Milton, Jane Austen, George Eliot and Dickens. They would accept nothing else. I went into the lecture not knowing what I was going to say except that my prepared lecture would have to be abandoned. The hall was full. Nearly 200 students had packed it to capacity, and not all of them were registered for English. The word had obviously gone out and they were expecting something. I looked up from my lectern and took a deep breath.

"I have just had a student delegation in my office complaining that I have prescribed second-rate books for you to read."

There was no avoiding it. I had to confront the issue head on. I pointed out the irony of the situation. Here I was, a white man defending African literature to Africans. I was not prepared to listen to racist drivel about white and black literature and which was better or worse. I then went on to say that all literature is born of particular social and historical circumstances and as such it speaks directly to the cultures from which it is born. There was no question of defining what is the greatest literature in the world. We could argue about that all year. What was important was developing our critical faculties so that we could read and appreciate what Africa was producing as much as the so called Great Tradition.

And, to illustrate that Ngugi's text could stand up to as rigorous analysis as Dickens I then proceeded to dissect the first chapter of *The River Between* from as many points of view as I could. I applied all the principles of Practical Criticism, pointing to literary and Biblical allusions, symbolism, employing linguistic analysis, structuralism, Jung and archetypes, in fact everything I could think of. The students sat in absolute silence. I had no way of gauging their reaction So, I plunged on, mining the text for whatever I could find. At the end of the double period, an hour and a half later, I staggered out of the class exhausted. It was noticeable though that when the essays came in a few weeks later they were much better than anything I had received so far. I think we both learned a valuable lesson.

Shortly after I arrived at Turfloop I attended a graduation ceremony that was destined to be one of the turning points in the University's history. Abraham Tiro as head of the SRC gave a speech that was remembered by everyone present. The graduation hall was crammed to capacity. Staff occupied the first two rows and the stage. About a thousand students were crowded into the rest of the hall. Although I did not know it, the word had gone out among the students that something momentous was about to happen. It was a blazing hot afternoon, the temperature well over 35°C.

Graduation was a significant occasion at the best of times in the students' lives. It represented a triumph over years of struggle and sacrifice in the face of enormous difficulties: poverty, appalling education and every effort by the Nationalist government to limit the numbers who eventually made it into higher education. The staff, of whom at least seventy per cent were white, sat in solemn rows clad in their academic finery, sweating profusely.

The white staff were for the most part stoically, and cynically, enduring what they knew they had to in order to preserve the fiction that Apartheid was a moral system dedicated to providing separate but equal facilities and opportunities. Many of them were Potchestroom graduates whom I learned later were idealistically committed to making Apartheid work. They perceived it as the only moral solution to what they saw as an intractable problem: the fact that where there was mixing of the races there was always conflict and exploitation.

One of my colleagues, Anton Roodt, explained that they were motivated by religious conviction. In the Byzantine world of Afrikaner

"Free, white and over twenty-one"

politics and religion many of the staff were members of the minority Herformde Kerk, one of the more fundamental sects within the Dutch Reformed community, and as such conceived of themselves as morally superior to the other supporters of Apartheid who were motivated for merely political and material reasons. It may be significant that W. A. de Klerk who oversaw the transition from Nationalist rule to democracy in 1994, and who shared the Nobel Peace Prize with Nelson Mandela, was a member of the same church.

In fact, a group of lecturers ran an electrical goods business in Pietersburg which had two entrances: one for whites and one for blacks. Most of the staff who could, were involved in some sort of extracurricular business or other. Farming was high on the list because it was a good way to disguise additional income from the Receiver of Revenue. Come harvest time it was extraordinary how many applied for study leave. The fact that Apartheid was demonstrably unequal and could only be imposed by force were facts that tended to be brushed aside as the inevitable and temporary consequences of implementing policy. Once the policy had been completely implemented the world would applaud the outcome for its vision, honesty and fairness.

The black staff had rather more mixed feelings. Graduation was one of the few occasions during the year when they could show off in all their scarlet splendour. They were justly proud of their academic achievements. This was one of the few opportunities they had to show what black people could achieve in the face of white suppression. On the other hand, all of them were bitterly opposed to Apartheid and a number of them, chief of whom was Gessler Nkondo, were actively promoting student political activism: riots, strikes, boycotts, sit-ins and so on. In the short while I had been at the University of the North I had experienced all of them. Steve Biko, the leader of the black consciousness movement had been expelled from the university the previous year. Cyril Ramaphosa destined to be one of the most influential political figures of the future was a student, as was Frank Chikane. The student riots in Soweto in 1976 were still a few years away, but the revolutionary climate was hotting up. In the middle of my first year there, the army had to be called in to restore order to the campus.

Early on, I had established where my sympathies lay. Gessler and I decided to embarrass one of the most conservative white academics on the campus, Professor Engelbrecht, the professor of philosophy. We waited for him to go to the TOILETS WHITE MALE STAFF ONLY. (The permutations on this theme were a study in themselves: the variables being colour, gender, staff, students, visitors. We often wondered if the plumbing continued in like separated states.) When we were sure he was committed at the urinal we went and stood on either side of him in a joint pee. He went puce with rage but there was nothing he could do. Man is never so vulnerable than when he has his fly unbuttoned in the middle of a piss. Our behaviour was childish and provocative, but great fun. There were repercussions. The Maroela Branch of the National Party demanded that I be fired for being a subversive influence.

As soon as Tiro got up to speak, I realised something was wrong. To begin with, I thought he was very nervous and overcome by the occasion. Sweat poured from his face. His whole body was trembling. By the time he had got to the third or fourth sentence of his speech he could hardly hold the paper on which it was written. It soon became apparent why. Although almost incoherent, it was clear he was denouncing Apartheid, the government and the university. My white colleagues on either side were plainly very uncomfortable.

Although much that Tiro said was wild and almost hysterical there was no denying the truth of his main argument which was that the Nationalist government was a tyranny set in place by the white electorate to ensure their enrichment at the expense of the black population. The growing murmur of approval behind us from the rest of the audience left no room for doubt about the effect of his words. I sat there thinking: "he's signing his own death warrant. There's no way they will let him get away with this." And, of course, he was expelled. I did not anticipate his death a few years later when it was reported that he had fallen from a

"Free, white and over twenty-one"

window in John Voster Square during interrogation. Did he fall or was he pushed?

It became more and more obvious to me that the English Department was not serving the best interests of the students. With the exception of the African literature I had introduced there was no accommodating either the students' needs or interests. We had the worst failure rate in the university because we insisted that students could not pass until they could express themselves fluently in clear coherent written English. The head of English, Prof Smuts was interested in the Arthurian legend, and insisted on teaching *Beowulf* which had to be mastered in Old English.

Something had to be done. I managed to persuade him that I should get a postgraduate qualification in applied linguistics. We would then have one person in the department who would be properly qualified to deal with the students' language problems. The best place to get such a degree was Edinburgh University. Much to my amazement he agreed. I applied, was accepted and left for Scotland at the end of August 1974. Ruth and the children were due to join me at the end of the year once I had set up a place to live.

I was euphoric. I was going to do a postgraduate degree at one of the ancient and great universities. I would be returning to the land of my forefathers, not cap in hand but on my own terms determined to prove myself. I was on a journey to reclaim my heritage and identity. As usual, my capacity for fantasy ran away with me. I felt as if I was coming home after years of exile. I could not believe it. In the ten years since I had completed my diploma as a primary school teacher I had become a university lecturer with a master's degree in English and was beginning to publish my first academic articles. My career looked set. I was happily married and had two beautiful children. I was especially looking forward to meeting my Scots family. There was no end to life's possibilities. Success seemed to beckon at every turn. Something must be wrong.

~ 27 ~

The best laid plans … .

Edinburgh. 5th November 1974. 7.30 am. Guy Fawkes Day.

I wake to persistent knocking on the front door. Half asleep I open the door to find a policeman.

Having established my identity, he said; "Please phone this number in South Africa."

I looked uncomprehendingly at the piece of paper he handed me. The number meant nothing to me.

"Are you alright? Would you like me to come in while you phone?" he said.

"No. No, thank you. I'll be fine. Nothing to worry about."

"Alright, I'll be off then."

"Yes. Fine. Thanks."

I closed the door. On the second or third attempt the connection went through.

"Chris Niland here"

"Chris, it's Michael. What's wrong?"

"Ruth's fallen ill. You must come home immediately."

"What's wrong?"

"It looks as if she's got a tumour on the brain."

I don't remember the rest of the conversation, but I do remember the sensation I had of the world crashing about me.

"What do you mean?"

"She's in a bad way, Michael. You must come home."

As the words began to make sense I felt a yawning chasm opening beneath me. All that I had achieved is about to be swallowed up, marriage, family, career. All is lost. I know she is going to die. *"I did not look for Death.*

The best laid plans ... .

/ *He looked for me.*"[37] The words repeat themselves again and again in my brain like a stuck record.

Death seemed to haunt me. Grief is a very selfish, self-centred, cliché-ridden emotion. I was fated.

I was also awash with guilt. Self-pity overwhelmed me.

I got dressed and caught the bus to Princess Street and walked up the hill to the University. Everything seemed alien, as if I was a creature from another world. I could not understand the sights and sounds of early morning bustle around me. The city was going about its normal business. Traffic lights changed from red to green, traffic jams, the throng of pedestrians hurrying to work, shutters on shop windows were being raised. Life was going on, oblivious. All the signs were there. This couldn't be happening. A dull echo reverberated with each thought that came into my mind. And still the full impact of what I felt escaped me. It was as if I was standing on a frozen pond that had begun to crack under my feet. I was in a panic. I could see the shore and people walking safely on the solid paths. The black tree trunks and autumn leaves on the grass. But the ice had still to open. The cold black water beneath had still to engulf me. I struggled for breath and began hyperventilating as I explained to the head of the Applied Linguistics department, Professor Pitt-Corder, that I would have to leave the University that afternoon.

The train journey down to London was a nightmare. It was the milk run and stopped or seemed to stop at every station on the way. The night passed by, a blurred black and white film of deserted platforms bathed in pools of dim electric light, perhaps a solitary cigarette glowing in the dark, rain dribbling down grimy carriage windows, billowing steam, shunting trucks and the dismal sound of the guard's whistle, banging doors and the monotonous drum of metal wheels.

The flight from Heathrow to Jan Smuts was only marginally better. Margaret Gouverneur, a friend in Pretoria, was at the airport to fetch me and took me straight to the hospital. I walked into the darkened ward. A single bed contained a skeletal figure. Green curtains. One side of her

---

37. [Sic] Emily Dickinson: 'Because I could not stop for Death'.

head had been shaved in preparation for the operation the following morning. She looked like a caricature. The prominent bone structure of her cheeks and high forehead were thrown into relief. A deadly pallor cast over her skin. Blue veins on either side of her temples. Huge dark-ringed eyes recognised me. I fell across her body sobbing.

"Now I know you love me," she said. Had there ever been any doubt?

Guilt reveals itself in many ways. The proposition had been unequivocal. She had made it quite clear. We had passed beyond hints and ambiguous suggestion. Beyond the first exploratory kiss. The door is open; the bed turned down. To quell my conscience, I go for a walk, hiding behind a façade of melodrama and cynicism. I have a choice. There is no getting away from it. Either 'yes', or 'no'. Refuse. Refuse. Refuse. Wherever I look. There is no escaping the word. There is no escaping the responsibility. There is no escaping. A decision has been made. Courtesy of the Johannesburg Municipality, Parks and Gardens: rubbish bins at every turn.

Meaning is where it finds you, whether you will or no.

I know then she is going to die. I cannot think of the children, our plans for the future or the life we have created together. Everything begins to implode. And yet, at the same time I refuse to accept it. It is too melodramatic. Things like this do not happen in real life. She will be alright. This is just a setback. She will recover.

The following afternoon after her operation the surgeon told me there was no hope. She had, at the most, six months to live, even with chemotherapy he said. Her cancer was an astrocytoma. As the name suggests, the tumour was shaped like a star whose arms reached into her brain. It had been growing slowly for years and had suddenly reached a critical stage. When the surgeon had opened her skull, he realised it would be impossible to remove it. It was impossible to distinguish between where the cancer ended and healthy tissue began.

"Was there any indication of a personality change in the past few years? Anything out of character?" he asked.

The best laid plans … .

At first, I thought, no. But on reflection there had been a number of incidents that were dramatically out of character. One of the most notable aspects of her character had always been her equanimity. Nothing seemed to upset her. However, when we had first moved to Somerset West on a couple of occasions she had behaved oddly. More recently, there had been flashes of temper that I could not explain, but wrote off as being a release from the pressures of childrearing. Were they significant or not? There was no telling.

My choice was, as he put it, to prolong her life for at the most six months under the most extreme agony, or simply to let nature take its course. In either event she would die, but if I allowed nature to take its course at least her end would be relatively painless and with dignity. There was, I thought at the time, no choice. And have, of course, wondered ever since if I made the right one. I put on a brave face, pretending that all would be well.

Ruth lingered for three and a half months. There was neither past nor future. Only the present which had to be endured. Every day revealed a change. Every day she grew weaker and weaker. To begin with I maintained the fiction that she was going to get well and that we would be going back to Edinburgh as soon as she recovered. But soon it was no longer possible to deny the inevitable. Silence descended. There was nothing more to say. The children continued to go to school every morning and returned to a house waiting for death every afternoon. They were confused and stoical. Ruth's parents and I spent our days going through the motions of daily life. Getting dressed, making beds, preparing meals, supervising homework. Alan, Ruth's father, and I played endless games of chess to pass the time. I could neither read nor write. I felt immobilised. Her mother, Sally and I assumed the responsibilities of nursing her twenty-four hours a day, washing, feeding, massaging, administering drugs while she could still swallow, simply being at her side. We never mentioned what was increasingly obvious. I sometimes wondered how aware Ruth was as she drifted in and out of consciousness.

Staring Memory in the Face

She asked me one afternoon shortly before she lapsed into a coma: "Why doesn't anyone come to visit me anymore? Is it because I'm dying they don't come? Is it because I'm dying?"

She gradually lost the capacity to communicate. But, so had I. I did not have the words or the courage to answer her.

On her thirty-third birthday, the 9th December 1974, she lapsed into a coma from which she emerged periodically for a few hours for the next two and a half months. She could not eat. She could not drink. Bedsores erupted. Sally and I massaged her, changed her, washed her, fed her, watched over her through the remaining days and nights of her life.

One night I woke with a start at about three in the morning to find her sitting on the edge of her bed. Somehow, she had come to consciousness and had found the strength for the first time in weeks to sit up. I leaped out of my bed, we had twin beds so that I would be available at any time, and caught her as she fell. She was nothing but skin and bones, like an Auschwitz victim, but even so surprisingly heavy. This body that I had known so intimately was now inert, an empty shell. In the dark I nearly overbalanced, but righted myself, her dead weight in my arms. I got her back into bed and lay down afraid to sleep lest she should try to get up again. I lay like that till the sun came up, alert for the slightest movement or sound.

And, so it went for the remaining weeks. As she deteriorated, she endured terrible pain. The doctor showed me how to give her morphine injections. The first one I gave her went exactly according to plan. I felt a small sense of triumph. The needle went in and the relief was instantaneous. The second was a disaster. As I plunged in the needle it hit her femur, there was so little flesh on her arm, and the shock of the needle striking the bone ran up my arm. I lost my nerve. I knew I could not do it again. We arranged for her to be transferred to hospital, for it had become clear that Sally and I could not continue nursing her. Both of us were exhausted, physically and emotionally. It would be best if she spent the last few remaining days under professional care. She was moved to a private ward in the Pietersburg General Hospital.

The best laid plans … .

Although she had been in a coma for weeks, I was not convinced that she did not know what was going on around her. The morning before she died I spoke to her saying that she should let go and leave us. She had endured too much pain. She need not be concerned about the children or me. Life would go on. She would remain alive in them.

A nurse came into the ward. The contrast between the figure in the bed and the young girl opposite me, fresh and alive could not have been more marked. She was plump (I thought, "she's like a partridge") and suntanned, a picture of youth and health. Radiant in contrast to Ruth's grey, emaciated body reeking of death.

There was a subtle change. Regular breathing gave way to laboured gasping, rasping choking breath. The nurse reached across the bed and took my hand and placed it on Ruth's temple.

"When the pulse stops", she said, "is when she will be dead."

I held my finger on the faltering pulse, feeling life depart. Little, less, nothing.

She died on the 26th February 1975, just thirty-three years old. Brendan and Dammon were seven and five respectively.

The last act in this drama was at her funeral a few days later. I was amazed by how many people attended it. Well over five hundred. I had planned to read Robert Frost's poem *Stopping by Woods on a Snowy Evening*, but the minister, Lionel Lawson, took one look at me and realised that I would not be able to manage it. Instead, the organist played Bach's *Jesu Joy of Man's Desiring*, the piece played at our wedding.

As Ruth's coffin was carried from the church and was being loaded into the hearse, a lone Mirage jet fighter appeared silently, without warning, just above rooftop height. The crowd emerging from the church was spellbound. As it came overhead it climbed vertically into the sky, its engines thundering at full throttle, did a victory roll and disappeared into the east.

It has taken me more than a life time before I have been able to write this account. Much has happened in the meantime. Life has gone on, as it will, as it must. Our children have grown up and are living out their own lives and having their own children. The best we can hope for is to find our way and to make a little sense of the muddle.

As for the victory roll? Imagination has its truths as well. Who knows? Coincidence or not, it was a powerful moment.

(William Kentridge)

CODA

One evening, six months later:
Dammon: "Do you ever go where Mommy is buried Daddy?"
"No."
"Why not?"
"Well, because… because… she's not buried."
"What happened to her?"
"She was cremated."
Brendan. "What's cremated dad?"

The best laid plans ... .

"Well, (Brendan's face is flushed. He swallows audibly) its sort of ... sort of..., well her body was burnt in a special way."

Brendan, tears rising, struggling to control his grief, face blotched, eyes wide with fear, red with unwept tears: "That's not nice."

Dammon: "What did you do with her?"

"I scattered her ashes."

"What's ashes?"

"Well..., its what's left after a fire."

Brendan: "Where did you scatter them, Dad?"

"Up in the bushveld."

"Why?"

"Because it was one of Mommy's favourite places and I thought she would like that."

Tears streaming down his face: "Whereabouts?"

Determined not to reveal the actual site, but the vision of it is so clear before my eyes: a little koppie, shards of bone scattered by the wind and lizards as they rattle through the ash: "Near the dam."

"How did you get them?"

"In a box."

"What sort of box?"

I lie. "A wooden one." It was grey cardboard, flimsy.

"How big was it?"

"About so big." Indicating a box about a foot long by four inches deep.

"Is that all? It's so small. Is that all that was left? What did you do with it?"

"Buried it. Come sit on my lap."

He did so. His body wracked with grief and sobbed into my shoulder. Dammon, not understanding, clung to my arm, disturbed: "Tell us the story about the giant, Daddy."

"Which giant?"

"The selfish one."

And then followed a recital of Wilde's *The Selfish Giant*, the children correcting me every few sentences.

~ 28 ~

"That's something special"

Seven lean years, seven rattlesnake years followed. I did not cover myself with glory as I struggled to bring up my children, keep my career on track, write a doctoral thesis and resist (not always successfully) the temptations of self-pity. The year that saw the introduction of television to South Africa and the Soweto riots, 1976, had me briefly in Pretoria teaching at a college for in-service teachers. The following year I moved to Johannesburg where I joined the staff of the College of Education.

The stresses and strains of single parenthood kept me focused on simply surviving from one day to the next, not always with success. And there were women. Inevitably, there were women. One malignant, vindictive and manipulative. The others, for the most part kind but incapable of coping with what they were getting into. And, who can blame them?

When I think back, as I write these words and recreate the emotions, events and conversations of a half a lifetime ago, I remember feeling trapped, incapable of seeing a way through. I had no hope of recouping my losses. Edinburgh was a fast fading dream. My career was going nowhere. A destructive, fortunately brief relationship, almost completely ruined my relationship with my children and undermined my self-confidence. I felt doomed.

We know ourselves but slenderly. We, all of us, carry within an idealised but largely unarticulated image of who we believe we are; the core of our being that encapsulates the values and ideals we hold most dear; the bedrock on which the meaning of our lives lies. And, like all ideals, once exposed and tested it reveals its contradictions. There can be few deeper wounds than being forced to confront your own limitations, your own fallibility, your own capacity for betrayal. It is an awful thing to confront your naked self and know there is no going back. What's done is done.

"That's something special"

Apart from anything else, I was angry; angry with Ruth for having died, angry with myself for not coping, angry with the world for confronting me yet again with my inadequacies and weaknesses. So, I took it out on the children, my friends and colleagues and students, and, of course, myself, as I drifted from one depression to the next. I felt borne down by responsibility, trapped in just the sort of life I had been so desperate to escape and which I was determined my children would never suffer. The gutter loomed. Well, if not the gutter, to mix my metaphors, I must batten down the hatches and endure. I became a trial to my friends. So much so, that one afternoon Colleen Taylor challenged me head on.

She and her husband Mike, kept open house in Yeoville. It was one of the few places in Johannesburg where the Left in every shape, form and colour could meet and party the whole weekend away in relative safety. Political activists, academics, jazz musicians, human rights lawyers, journalists, poets, artists, filmmakers, and the occasional member of the Special Branch, all passed through their front door in an endless procession. There was always somebody interesting to talk to and plenty of wine and music. I had known Colleen and Mike for years since my days at Hottentots Holland when Mike and I had been on the staff together. So, naturally, I was keen to re-establish the relationship when I arrived in Johannesburg, especially as they had known Ruth well. They provided me with some sort of continuity. Colleen had a reputation for straight talking.

"Michael," she said, "you've become a bore. Every time we see you, you're depressed. Gloom and doom is written all over you, and frankly it's boring. You used to have such a lust for life. You've lost your sense of humour. Now you spend your time feeling sorry for yourself and you expect everyone else to feel sorry for you too. I'm sick and tired of it. All our friends are sick and tired of it. In fact, we would rather you didn't come round. You're an embarrassment. The moment you enter the house a great black cloud descends. No one knows what to talk about and it's like that until you go. You're wallowing in self-pity. Ruth is dead. There's nothing you can do about it. You must pull yourself together, or we'd rather not see you. You've become spineless. You never smile.

Staring Memory in the Face

You're betraying Ruth's memory. If nothing else, you've got the kids to consider. It's your choice."

This was tough stuff, but there was no denying the truth of what she was saying. I was wallowing. It was my choice. I needed to redirect my energies, rediscover my enthusiasm. Easier said than done. The fact that I was a bore cut me to the quick. My friends had always been especially important to me. That I was failing Brendan and Dammon was a timely reminder of the promise I had made Ruth on her deathbed. Betrayal was a word that echoed ominously.

If I was going to claw my way out of the pit into which I had fallen, I knew I was going to have to do it by myself. I wasn't sure I had the resources. I felt perpetually exhausted. What had happened to my energy? What had happened to my sense of irony? I needed to restore my sense of humour. I needed to see things in proportion again. "Consider the sum total of human suffering," I told myself wryly. I needed to laugh at myself again. I needed to believe in something outside of myself again. There was no denying that unless I made the effort nothing would be achieved.

As I drove away from Colleen's house, I made a conscious decision. I would find the resources. I had done so in the past. I could do so again. Brutal as her onslaught had been, I realised I owed her a lot. She had shocked me into awareness and a sense of my responsibilities. She also made me aware of a bitter bargain I had made, trading my capacity for openness to life's possibilities for victimhood. Without realising it, I had abandoned one of the mainsprings of my life, and what had I got in return? I was alienated from my friends, my colleagues and my children. Colleen had made me swallow a bitter pill. I didn't like what she had to say, but I could not dodge it.

∼

"That's something special"

"That's something special".

I was completely unprepared, when one evening at Easter in 1981, I walked into a friend's living room. She was sitting next to the fire, a glass of wine in one hand. Another Ruth. I'm a creature of habit. She smiled at me quizzically, her pale face framed by the dark chiaroscuro of her hair and the flickering shadows. I had no idea who she was. "That's something special," I thought.

Later in the evening, I discovered she was the daughter of a famous man, (infamous in some circles) Bram Fischer. I felt awed, knowing she moved in a world remote from anything I had ever known and to which I had never had access. My parents had lived squalid little lives ending in squalid little deaths. Her father had dedicated his life to fighting injustice and had died in prison for a noble cause. She was of Afrikaner aristocratic stock. As far as I knew, I had no lineage worth mentioning. My life had been circumscribed by my struggle to survive. Hers, perhaps even more traumatic, had been lived in the world of public affairs and high policy in which powerful men decided the fate of the nation. At least, that was my immediate impression. No matter what unborn feelings I might harbour, there was no possibility she would be interested in me, a widower with two children and no prospects.

Ruth and I did not see each other again for several months until she invited me to a graduation party to celebrate her qualifying as a clinical psychologist. I felt completely out of my depth but excited at being in the company of international journalists, lawyers, political commentators and trade unionists whose names I had encountered only in the media. Everyone appeared urbane and sophisticated. They discussed the affairs of the day with the assurance born of moving in international circles. They were also very outspoken in their opposition to the Nationalist government and frequently quoted this or that politician or general or security policeman with whom they had had dealings. Meetings with the leaders of the ANC in London and Lusaka were mentioned casually in passing. I could hardly refrain from glancing out of the window, wondering when the security police would burst into the room. Life was about to take on a new set of complexities.

Three months later we decided to put our two families together and Brendan, Dammon and I moved into her house in Auckland Park. The first year or two took a lot of adjusting by everyone. The children had to get used to sharing their parents and space with one another. Our friends had to get used to a new set of dynamics. And, we not only had to cope with the complexities of our new relationship as lovers and parents, but were quickly swept into the vortex of the political crises of the Eighties.

Ruth had the added challenges of setting up her practice as a clinical psychologist. She rapidly became the therapist of choice for many in the Left. She was to count among her clients at least two future Cabinet Ministers and, after he was released, Nelson Mandela consulted her briefly about a member of his family. Her reputation was helped by

"That's something special"

her political pedigree and the role she played as one of the founders of the Detainees Counselling Service.

Paul making sure we get it on the right finger (1986).

In the meantime, I was trying to finish my doctoral thesis and publish articles I hoped would establish my reputation in the academic world. My academic ambitions gradually waned as I became disillusioned with what John Fowles describes as the academic midden, scratched over by cackling hens and cocks crowing at each other. I began to realise that I wasn't really cut out to be an academic. Ruth quite rightly calls me a literaturd. I don't have the kind of discipline to be anything else. I have a magpie mind. My interests are too wide ranging, pragmatic not theoretical. Teacher training suited me, not scratching around in some obscure patch which had no practical value. And, there were the complexities and complications, I've already alluded to, as we became more involved in the work of the Detainees Parents Support Committee.

~ 29 ~

Free the children

Denouncing the minister of Law and Order for restricting the United Democratic Front.
(Wits 1988)

The DPSC was one of a host of anti-Apartheid organisations that came into being in response to the government's increasingly stringent security legislation which included a ban on any multi-racial political activity, the definition of which became more and more embracing with

Free the children

the passage of time. The DPSC had a nominal presence at least in nearly every town in the country, where it was used as a cover for anti-Apartheid work from organising food parcels and getting learning materials into the prisons, to gathering intelligence on police brutality, to organising protest meetings and marches. I contributed to a weekly column which appeared in *The Star,* called *Our View,* in which the evils of Apartheid were highlighted with the object of embarrassing the government and its supporters, and hopefully prodding the white conscience. It also pricked the interest of the Special Branch.

In retrospect, it is now possible to see the death throes of Apartheid in similar terms to the demise of communism in the Soviet Union and Eastern Europe. Although to all intents and purposes both systems were deadly enemies, they were alarmingly similar in their objectives and the methods they employed to keep themselves in power. Like all the totalitarian systems of the twentieth century the Apartheid regime rejected the autonomy of the individual in favour of the group; by declension: the Broederbond (the party elite), the Nationalist Party, Afrikanerdom and lastly, if reluctantly, white South Africa. Us and them. Them was effectively more than eighty per cent of the population.

The pluralism essential to democracy was replaced by a kind of monism in which there was no distinction between private and public life. All of what is normally considered private life had to conform to the dictates of state ideology. The most intimate aspects of personal life, were regulated by the Immorality and the Mixed-Marriages Acts, which proscribed intimacy between people of differently defined races. The old bond between church and state was recreated in the state dogma, which found justification in the theology of the Dutch Reformed Church. Significantly, at one stage the State President and the head of the DRC were brothers: John Voster and his brother Koort.

Like all totalitarian states South Africa was virtually a one-party state, with the opposition reduced to one representative in Parliament, Helen Suzman; she who, to the horror of my colleagues of the time, sponsored my matric class at Hottentots Holland when I was being investigated for sedition. The forms of government were observed with an inordinate amount of legislation being passed to legitimise the creation of two essentially unequal systems. In fact, the law existed for the preservation of white privilege at the expense of black impoverishment. The law certainly did not exist to protect those who opposed the regime who suffered arbitrary persecution. Like other totalitarian systems, Apartheid promised a utopia of sorts in which white people, especially Afrikaners, could live racially pure lives. Pseudoscientific theories about race were used to prove black inferiority and justify what were called 'separate freedoms'. The whole edifice, of course, could only be kept in place with the use of force. I had already experienced in practical terms what this meant in my stints at Hottentots Holland and Turfloop.

Ruth's sister Ilse and Bram

Free the children

The DPSC provided advice on how to deal with the security police. It also provided information and political analysis in the press, interviews with foreign journalists, statistics on police torture, executions, banning's and intimidation. We spent much of our energy on counselling people who had friends and relatives who had been arrested and tortured. Naturally, our work attracted the security police's interest and we were often on the receiving end of their attention. They frequently tried to bug our offices in Khotso House in the middle of Johannesburg. The phones were tapped. People were followed, intimidated, arrested and questioned under a variety of "emergency" regulations.

Restriction bred resistance. Organisations mushroomed into existence, were banned, went underground, and changed their identities under a welter of confusing acronyms. Life was an endless round of clandestine meetings in which we tried to keep one jump ahead of the latest tactics to suppress dissent. Anti-Apartheid groups popped up all over the place and many of us had multiple memberships of them. Meetings with different groups often meant meeting the same people again and again in different venues ostensibly to discuss and plan different but the same strategies and tactics. Police agents frequently tried to infiltrate the meetings. We got pretty used to being spied on. Eventually, the DPSC was declared a restricted organisation and prohibited from carrying out any of its humanitarian or political functions. But that was still well into the future.

After the bombing of Khotso House in 1988 by the security police, it was decided to move the DPSC meetings to a safer venue. My office at the College seemed the most convenient. In retrospect it was a naive move. Once a week the Security Police could have parked a car outside the College and observed who came and who left late at night. The lights were on in my office until ten or eleven o'clock. All it needed was a van parked across the road filled with electronic equipment and they could have heard everything that was said at those meetings. Perhaps they did. They had certainly rented a flat across the road from Khotso House and used it as a listening post.

Staring Memory in the Face

I had boxes of sensitive files, statements taken from torture victims, records of police brutality and evidence of political assassinations hidden among my lecture notes and academic files. One raid and we would all have been implicated. Mercifully, it never happened. But perhaps the police decided to let us have enough rope to hang ourselves or at least provide them with on-going information about what we knew. I discovered that my office phone was tapped one afternoon when a friend phoned from Pretoria. At the end of our conversation, I put down the phone and immediately picked it up again to phone someone else. To my amazement I heard my previous conversation being played back to me. We stopped having our meetings in my office after that.

In the meantime, Ruth, Paul Verryn and a few others set up the Detainees Counselling Service for activists who had been tortured in detention. This work gave her and the rest of us in the DPSC unique insights into what was going on in the country and the lengths to which the security forces would go to suppress dissension. It was also highly dangerous work. For like all repressive regimes, the Apartheid government wanted to preserve the fiction that it was acting out of the purest motives in protecting the country and by extension the world from the evils of terrorism and communism. It was a thin veneer. And it became thinner and thinner as the tales of torture and death in detention mounted up.

Ruth was in the forefront of developing counselling techniques to deal with post-traumatic stress. Unfortunately, she did not document any of the many cases she had to deal with. She was always aware that the security police might descend at any minute and detain her and her colleagues. Meetings in safe houses, dealing with traumatised individuals still on the run, helping at the Wilgespruit refugee centre, were not conducive to writing research papers on a topic soon to become very fashionable in the social sciences. Her priority was dealing with traumatised individuals who were in immediate need of whatever help she and the team at the DCS could provide. It was at this point that Benjy Olifant came to live with us.

Free the children

The event that was to bring me unequivocally to the security police's attention was my role in helping to organise the Free the Children Campaign in 1987. We revealed to the world through the United Nations that approximately 20 000 children were then being held in South African prisons where they were denied any form of legal representation and were often tortured.

~

Just before the winter holidays in July 1987, I slipped out of the country to testify at a special hearing in Washington DC. My colleagues at College, with the exception of the vice-Rector Graham Hall, had no idea where I was or what I was doing. He gallantly covered for me while I disappeared for three weeks.

I was one of fifteen South Africans, doctors, lawyers, political activists and the mother of a child who had been detained, who testified at a symposium on South African children in detention. At that time approximately 19 000 children (the numbers fluctuated from day to day and nobody, not even the police had an exact figure) were held in appalling conditions in police cells around the country. Many were tortured. Many disappeared. Some were killed. Our audience was brought together by the Lawyers' Committee for Civil Rights Under Law and included many eminent academics, lawyers, religious leaders and at least two US senators. After describing what exactly detention meant as opposed to being arrested (the latter presumed certain rights guaranteed under law, there were none for those who were detained) and describing conditions in detention, I was asked by the Rev. Coffin if white people in South Africa were aware that children were being detained and tortured.

I replied: "I think they find themselves very much in the position that perhaps the Germans found themselves in the 1930s. They don't want to know. And there is nothing quite so effective as that kind of censure. The newspapers carry quite a lot of stuff regardless of government attempts to stop them, but it is amazing. You can talk to people and they have not actually read the articles. They don't read the headlines. They are not aware of what is going on in their own country because they don't want to be aware."

Much of the white population suffered from wilful ignorance. They were too comfortable, and too fearful to contemplate change. They were in a state of denial, as we would say today. It is in just such circumstances that tyranny flourishes.

At one point in the proceedings, after the most damning evidence had been produced, condemning the South African government's record on human rights, a film crew working for the Bureau of State Security (BOSS) was discovered to have infiltrated the hearing. They were asked to leave. But it was too late. They had their film and all the evidence they needed.

Later that day I had a debriefing session with a senior member of the ANC in exile, Reggie September, who was particularly interested in Winnie Mandela's recent declaration: "Together hand in hand with that stick of matches, with our necklace, we shall liberate the country." As so often happened, she had caught the leadership by surprise. The story of Stompie and Dr Asvat's murders were still to be revealed. The ANC leadership was already worried. Recently, a book attempting to exculpate her on the grounds of her reputation as the Mother of the Nation was published. The author argues that her suffering for and contribution to the liberation cause exonerated her from whatever cruelty or crimes she committed. The facts were not in dispute. Complexities indeed. Some mother. It says a great deal about the moral duplicity of those still willing to venerate her.

Shortly before I arrived in the States, there had been a spate of necklacings; a car tyre soaked in petrol slung about the victim's neck and set alight. Nor had the Nationalist government been slow to exploit them for propaganda purposes. Necklacing was yet one more proof of the savagery lying just beneath the surface, which could/would break out with the slightest relaxation of police vigilance; further justification for extending the state of emergency.

Free the children

Of course, it was much more complex than that. In fact, few incidences could be linked to political motives. The vast majority of cases were the result of vigilante frustration at the break down of law and order in the townships. But it suited the government to paint them all with the same revolutionary brush. The ANC's position was ambivalent. Nor has it ever been resolved. On the one hand, there was the desire to capitalise on what many saw as an opportunity to provoke local uprisings, while there were others who had moral concerns; nor did they want to undermine Winnie status as Mother of the Nation even if they had misgivings about her methods. Of such incidents are political labyrinths made.

Getting out of South Africa proved to be less traumatic than getting back. The negotiations between the ANC and various South African liberal minded groups were taking place at the time in Dakar in Senegal and we hoped the authorities would have their hands too full monitoring them to be bothered with us, notwithstanding their obvious presence in Washington. What we did not reckon on was the attention we would receive in the world media. But perhaps as intimidating, the violent right-wing Afrikanse Weerstand Beweging (AWB) were waiting for the Dakar delegates when they returned to South Africa and they tried to attack them when they landed at Jan Smuts Airport. I arrived a day later, fully expecting to be arrested.

Just before I left London I had a clandestine meeting with Reggie September at which he passed on information and instructions I was meant to convey to the leadership of the United Democratic Front. It was all cloak and dagger sort of stuff with the two of us sitting apart on a bench in Leicester Square talking to one another out of the sides of our mouths without acknowledging each other's presence. My life as an undercover agent was hardly the stuff of le Carré. Fortunately, the situation had calmed down a bit by the time the plane landed and I managed to slip through immigration unnoticed. Or, at least it appeared I hadn't been noticed. Still, my heart was beating fast as I passed through International Arrivals, picking my way through the broken doors and smashed glass the AWB had left in its wake.

Staring Memory in the Face

Not too long after my return from Washington, at the beginning of the new term, one of my students, a burly young man, an ex-policeman, warned me against making anti-government remarks in class, and to be especially careful about my own safety.

"You don't want to fool around with those 'okes'. They'll use every trick in the book. They're not frightened to use violence. I am just warning you for your own sake. I know those guys. They're bloody tough. I've seen what they can do. You could get yourself into serious trouble. I'm serious."

Friendly advice, or intimidation?

One of the more dramatic of these episodes was when Fikile Bam arrived at our house late one night in a terrible state, on the run from the Special Branch. We gave him a bed and the following morning I undertook to get him to Sidney and Felicia Kentridge's house in Houghton, where he felt he would be safe. A mysterious car with two men was parked in Lothbury Avenue near our house all night. The following morning when the rush hour traffic was at its height we put Fikile into Ruth's blue Mazda wedging him on the floor between the driver's seat and the back seat and covered him with a rug. He was a big man and it was a small car. I waited for the lights in Lothbury Avenue to turn green and slipped into the flood of rush hour traffic. As I turned into the main road, I glanced in the rear-view mirror and saw the car we had seen waiting outside our house all night, jump the lights behind us. Because it was rush hour the trip took us all of half an hour. The car following us was never out of sight. I drove up into the Kentridge's drive way with a huge sense of relief, but I still had to get to College for my first lecture at 8.00 o'clock. The Special Branch's car was parked, fortunately, on the opposite side of the road. I engaged the clutch as I slipped down the drive and nipped through the traffic lights in Houghton Drive before the cops realised what I was doing. I was on time for my lecture.

Steve Biko's death at the hands of the security police, Neil Aggett's suicide in detention, David Webster's assassination, and Stompie Seipei and Dr Asvat's murders, the bombing of Khotso House to mention only

Free the children

some of the more publicised events kept us all in a heightened state of tension. After David Webster's murder I was especially concerned, and was aware on many occasions that I was being followed. Why I was never arrested remains a mystery. I am grateful I wasn't, for I'm sure I wouldn't have held up under interrogation any better than those of my friends who were. It wasn't *"kinder speelitjies."* I narrowly avoided what could only be described as a 'honey trap' after being told in no uncertain terms I was under surveillance. Two of our close associates were murdered. Several disappeared never to be seen again, or went to jail. At least one committed suicide.

～

As much as anything, this tale has been about searching for meaning; of tying the disparate odds and ends and events together that make up a life into some sort of coherent and cohesive narrative. I don't want to leave an impression of a life lived as grim endurance. Nevertheless, nothing concentrates the mind like the imminence of death. One, which has provided sustenance for many years took place in Namibia.

Naukluft, July 1991

So much evidence of death:
confused bones, hide, horns and hooves,
clawed throat and cavernous belly;
afternoon shadows.
A soldier's grave dated 1896
Hendrik Witbooi made a stand in these mountains
that cost the Germans dearly.
Yet in the midst of death,
ficus sycarmorous;
roots flowing over rock face, through cracks, engulf boulders,
containing rivers rising in another time scale
to trunk, branch, leaf and cloudless winter sky;
wild olive, acacia kaffre and the ghost tree conifera.
A scarlet breasted shrike flashes a warning in the undergrowth;

Staring Memory in the Face

a sudden snort, stones clatter in the kloof;
signs everywhere: hoof, paw and pug mark.

And Harry, pack on back,
after a life time spent on Table Mountain, Cedarberg,
Hottentots Holland, Sneeuberg, Swartberg, Winterberg
wherever there was climbing to be done,
trees to rest beneath, and birds to be wondered at,
pausing for breath,
takes in the last light
quartz mountains opposite, pink, mauve, umber and dun,
canyon below, purple, magenta and black.

We found him minutes later, face down beside the track.
In another world, another time
we would have dug a hole on that mountainside
And raised a cairn;
no words
just stone on stone
the sky, the sun and wind.

But shrouded in his sleeping bag
we bound him to a makeshift stretcher and carried him.
I feel his still warm leg press against my arm
as I stumble in the gathering dusk,
struggling to find my way
along the zebra track, dividing, dwindling in the dark
like some desert stream seeping into sand,
through dry water course, over granite
gneiss and shale
to shelter, safe from baboon, jackal and leopard.

A weavers' nest in a bent tree
Hums, settling for the night.
We turn out all our little luxuries
and make our last supper with Harry.
Hip flasks meant to last for days are drained dry;

Free the children

'A little touch of Harry[38] in the night.'
A gentle joke between friends repeated, as such jokes are,
between friends;
bound together by the present, recounting the past.

No, it wasn't a terrible experience
in the Namibian desert.
Food and wine and friends and solid stone walls
against the wind exploding in the kloof,
overhead a hundred million stars.
None of us slept,
save one.

There were lighter moments too. I remember one night, my son Brendan guiding a future cabinet minister through the storm-water drain opposite our house that fed the (to be) mythologised Lombardy poplar, and helping her broad backside over a fence into the Johannesburg Country Club, recreational refuge for the city's capitalist élite, where she was able to mingle unobtrusively and evade the Special Branch.

---

38. Harry Cleminshaw who died on that trip, was our leader on many hiking trips in the mountains.

~ 30 ~

"Guess who's coming to dinner?"

It was thus that the next few years passed until Nelson Mandela's release from prison in 1989 and life began to settle into what was presumed to be normal. The first democratic elections came and went, as did the Truth and Reconciliation Commission. Ruth reminded me recently that we no longer have to look over our shoulders to see if we're being followed. A good thought, that.

I settled into a new career, having taken early retirement at the end of 1992. Our children, Brendan, Dammon and Gretel grew into adulthood with all its attendant aches and pains, and began to establish their separate lives. Over the succeeding years Ruth and I have felt guilty about not having done enough for or with them, but imperfect as our parenting was, we did the best we could in the circumstances. It's small comfort, but there can be few parents who think they could not have done better by their children. One undoubted comfort is, that as I write, they and our grandchildren are all close at hand and we are in regular contact. Life has its little pleasures, one of which is my grandson Jack's definition (aged 12 in Grade 6) of literature: "*Art in words*". You can't do much better than that. Ruth is an indefatigable organiser of family celebrations. This, she claims, is part of her Afrikaner heritage. She relishes her role as Ouma.

The highlight for us in those early days after Mandela's release was his insistence on having supper with us, that is with Ruth and Ilse and their spouses. It was a huge honour. He hadn't been out of jail for more than a month or two, and he sent at least three messages saying he would not be put off. A date was arranged. We were thrown into a frenzy. Ruth and Ilse panicking, convinced their cooking wouldn't be good enough. I pointed out that he had just spent 27 years in jail and probably wasn't all that particular. Did he drink? If so what? Wine? Whiskey? It turned out to be sherry. None of us drank sherry and had no idea what to get.

"Guess who's coming to dinner?"

In the end he drank, perhaps, half a glass of the most expensive I could find. Security had to be assured, and for the first time members of the Secret Service were welcomed in our house. Mandela was of course graciousness itself. Especially in the way he continuously muddled Ruth and Ilse. Much of the evening was spent reminiscing about the Rivonia Trial and the debts he owed Bram for saving him from the hangman's noose, and for revealing to him that not all whites were racial bigots.

Ruth and Mandela

Predictably, the ANC was elected with an overwhelming majority, which has steadily eroded as one broken promise has followed another, and the revolution, like all those before it, has started to devour its own. Disappointment, denial and disillusion aren't in it. The new leadership

Staring Memory in the Face

for all its commitment to dialectical materialism, the ineluctable progress of history and planned transformative economies has been proved to know little history and less economics. Ideology has ruled the day, aided and abetted by corruption at every level. Never let facts get in the way of theory. It's been a bitter pill for those who devoted and sacrificed their lives to liberating the country from Apartheid to see virtually everything they fought for betrayed. A new racial bigotry has come to dominate the headlines. Education and health services have all but collapsed. except for those who can afford private schools and hospitals. The alleviation of poverty has been sacrificed to patronage, while the economy has been ravaged by corruption, incompetence and greed.

It was ever thus.

But the world has moved on, even if South Africa is still mired in its past; still fighting battles that should have been over years ago. The pursuit of power and the competition for popular esteem do not bring out the best in us. A few years ago, I worked for a couple of weeks with someone who had been Kofi Anan's Chief of Party at the United Nations. The United Nations, he told me had a list of the ten most serious challenges facing humanity. Seven of them were what he called 'rogue' viruses. Our present predicament seems to have born him out: Covid-19 may be the first of these in the 21st century, but there will be others as long as we continue to exploit and pollute the planet.

Our situation is unprecedented. None of the political and bureaucratic systems devised since the Enlightenment, and none since the dominance of computers and the Internet, was developed to cope with the stresses they are currently having to deal with. A combination of over population, globalisation, (which makes international travel as easy as catching a bus and thus the spread of disease), climate change, the pollution of the oceans, and the accelerated extinction of animals, plants and insects could quite conceivably combine with a 'rogue' virus to create a perfect storm with devastating consequences.

In comparison, humanity's obsessions with perpetual growth, wealth, power and position will look paltry and stupid. If we don't learn

"Guess who's coming to dinner?"

to control self-indulgence and greed, the consequences will control us. The problems facing humanity are not technical. They are human. What Catholics call 'original sin'. In other words, and less metaphorically, human fallibility. No one is exempt. *"And, so it goes"*[39].

The individual search for meaning is about to become more complicated as life becomes more uncertain and we have to face up to challenges never before encountered. Winter is coming, as the popular TV series would have it. Let's hope Shelley was right: *"If Winter comes, can Spring be far behind?"*[40]

~

Finding a fitting end to a story is as difficult as finding a beginning: getting your readers hooked, keeping the line taut and leaving them feeling they haven't wasted their time. Nor have the problems of telling this tale diminished as it has unfolded. What is relevant, what not? What to include, what to leave out? And, there has always been the problem of memory and imagination, to say nothing of fantasy and myth-making.

It is time to reflect. This tale began with childhood memories, birth and death set in a time of war. I'm ending it at a comparable time. What has it all meant? The unexamined life, said Socrates, is not worth living. He meant, I think, that it is in striving to know and understand ourselves that our lives have any meaning or value. The writing of this tale has been an attempt to get a glimmer of understanding. I have had a privileged, interesting and at times an exciting life. I have lived through an extraordinary epoch of history. A world war, the demise of an empire, social upheaval, a revolution, the emergence of the Internet and Artificial Intelligence, the dominance of technology, a pandemic and the planet threatened by a mass extinction and climate change. There have been times of desperate personal darkness when I have found myself in a labyrinth with many dead ends and false turns, and almost lost my way.

---

39. Kurt Vonnegut: *Slaughter House Five*.
40. Percy Bysshe Shelley: 'Ode to the West Wind'.

Staring Memory in the Face

Even so, now and then I believe, I've had a glimpse of something. The meaning beyond meaning. Some might say a mirage. Certainly, one did appear briefly, in a victory roll.

There have been moments, such as one afternoon when a bus loaded with school kids stopped next to me as I was about to get into my car at Wits. The teacher in charge jumped out, ran across the road calling my name. I had no idea who she was. She insisted on introducing all 67 children in her charge to me. She was supervising a school outing. It turned out I had taught her twelve years previously at Turfloop. And, there have been others. There is no telling where the ripples will end. I'm still in touch with some of those I taught at Hottentots Holland in the late Sixties and early Seventies.

At various times I thought the stage, an academic career, publishing, education research, political activism might hold a clue. There was even one dark and stormy night when I thought there might be something in religion after all. They've all had their moments, but no answers. I can't do much better than the advice my friend Bam gave his granddaughter just before he died: *"Keep adjectives and adverbs to a minimum, and always remain true to yourself."* I have tried to keep the adjectives and adverbs under control and let the tale tell itself. As for always being true to myself, I hope the gods will be generous as they survey the evidence. I would add a third injunction, though. Try to leave the tiny portion of the world you inhabit a better place than when you found it.

It's no small irony that my swan song as an educationalist is *'It Begins at Birth'*, an internet based interactive course on emergent literacy and emergent mathematics for Early Childhood Development teachers and carers.

If nothing else, I have always known that my destiny is in my own hands. Even in the darkest times I have never been able to avoid facing that truth. We are our choices. If we don't manage our circumstances, as I said earlier, they will manage us. Choices are always there whether we will them or no; whether they are contradictory or not. We are not simply victims in an arbitrary universe. There is no doubt I have made

"Guess who's coming to dinner?"

some bad decisions. Experiencing the consequences of bad judgement and struggling to admit them does not necessarily lead to good judgement, but it at least provides one with options.

The freedom to make wrong choices is perhaps the greatest of all freedoms. For, it is only in the act of choosing between good, less good, bad, less bad options that we can assert our moral autonomy; that we have the possibility of insight and growth. Being wrong is sometimes more important than being right.

It's a messy and uncertain business.

So, as I sit at my computer and type away, I ask myself: what was it that made it possible for me to fulfil, (not just survive) in fact, more than fulfil those dreams all those years ago? Good management? Hardly. Good DNA? Who knows? Simple-minded optimism? I'm no Polly-Anna. Luck? Life, as I said earlier, is a bit of a leap in the dark, but never under estimate luck. I have been more than fortunate in my friends.

Celebrating our joint 80th birthday (2019).

Staring Memory in the Face

The fulfilment of our life together, Ruth and I believe, is founded on our enduring passion for one another, supported by the wide range of intellectual, political and social interests we have in common, our sense of humour, books, music, art, and as much as everything else, our love of the bushveld and hiking in the mountains.

Although we live in the perpetual present of which we are only partially aware, the past and future dominate our consciousness. Now, in my eighties, (the Age of Diminishing Returns) I'm conscious the future is at hand. I'm still healthy and vigorous; my mind still clear. I continue to believe, even in the face of implacable reason, there is meaning, not given or imposed, but which we can shape from within, no matter how haphazardly, no matter how blindly, out of the raw material of our experiences and memories and feelings as we struggle to take charge of our lives. What next? Meaning is where it finds you, whether you will or no.

A sense of humour helps. Send in the clowns.

> *I pray – for fashion's word is out*
> *And prayer comes round again –*
> *That I may seem though I die old,*
> *A foolish, passionate man.*[41]

---

41. W.B. Yeats: 'A Prayer for Old Age'.

www.ingramcontent.com/pod-product-compliance
Lightning Source LLC
Chambersburg PA
CBHW081952110426

42744CB00031B/1858